To my Mother and Father this book is lovingly inscribed

Patchwork

A Story of "The Plain People"

Anna Balmer Myers

Patchwork: A Story of "The Plain People"

Copyright © 2012 by Indo-European Publishing

All rights reserved.

The present edition is a reproduction of 1920 publication of this work, produced in the current edition with completely new, easy to read format by Indo-European Publishing.

For an authentic reading experience, the Spelling, punctuation, and capitalization have been retained from the original text.

ISBN: 978-1-60444-733-0

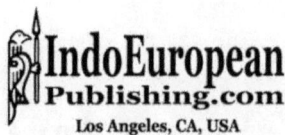

IndoEuropean
Publishing.com
Los Angeles, CA, USA

CHAPTER I
CALICO PATCHWORK

The gorgeous sunshine of a perfect June morning invited to the great outdoors. Exquisite perfume from myriad blossoms tempted lovers of nature to get away from cramped, man-made buildings, out under the blue roof of heaven, and revel in the lavish splendor of the day.

This call of the Junetide came loudly and insistently to a little girl as she sat in the sitting-room of a prosperous farmhouse in Lancaster County, Pennsylvania, and sewed gaily-colored pieces of red and green calico into patchwork.

"Ach, my!" she sighed, with all the dreariness which a ten-year-old is capable of feeling, "why must I patch when it's so nice out? I just ain't goin' to sew no more to-day!"

She rose, folded her work and laid it in her plaited rush sewing-basket. Then she stood for a moment, irresolute, and listened to the sounds issuing from the next room. She could hear her Aunt Maria bustle about the big kitchen.

"Ach, I ain't afraid!"

The child opened the door and entered the kitchen, where the odor of boiling strawberry preserves proclaimed the cause of the aunt's activity.

Maria Metz was, at fifty, robust and comely, with black hair very slightly streaked with gray, cheeks that retained traces of the rosy coloring of her girlhood, and flashing black eyes meeting squarely the looks of all with whom she came in contact. She was a member of the Church of the Brethren and wore the quaint garb adopted by the women of that sect. Her dress of black calico was perfectly plain. The tight waist was half concealed by a long,

1

pointed cape which fell over her shoulders and touched the waistline back and front, where a full apron of blue and white checked gingham was tied securely. Her dark hair was parted and smoothly drawn under a cap of white lawn. She was a picturesque figure but totally unconscious of it, for the section of Pennsylvania in which she lived has been for generations the home of a multitude of women similarly garbed—members of the plain sects, as the Mennonites, Amish, Brethren in Christ, and Church of the Brethren, are commonly called in the communities in which they flourish.

As the child appeared in the doorway her aunt turned.

"So," the woman said pleasantly, "you worked vonderful quick to-day once, Phœbe. Why, you got your patches done soon—did you make little stitches like I told you?"

"I ain't got 'em done!" The child stood erect, a defiant little figure, her blue eyes grown dark with the moment's tenseness. "I ain't goin' to sew no more when it's so nice out! I want to be out in the yard, that's what I want. I just hate this here patchin' to-day, that's what I do!"

Maria Metz carefully wiped the strawberry juice from her fingers, then she stood before the little girl like a veritable tower of amazement and strength.

"Phœbe," she said after a moment's struggle to control her wrath, "you ain't big enough nor old enough yet to tell me what you ain't goin' to do! How many patches did you make?"

"Three."

"And you know I said you shall make four every day still so you get the quilt done this summer yet and ready to quilt. You go and finish them."

"I don't want to." Phœbe shook her head stubbornly. "I want to play out in the yard."

"When you're done with the patches, not before! You know you must learn to sew. Why, Phœbe," the woman changed her tactics, "you used to like to sew still. When you was just five years old you cried for goods and needle and I pinned the patches on the little sewing-bird that belonged to Granny Metz still and screwed the bird on the table and you sewed that nice! And now you don't want to do no more patches—how will you ever get your big chest full of nice quilts if you don't patch?"

But the child was too thoroughly possessed with the desire to be outdoors to be won by any pleading or praise. She pulled savagely at the two long braids which hung over her shoulders and cried, "I don't want no quilts! I don't want no chests! I don't like red and green quilts, anyhow—never, never! I wish my pop would come in; he wouldn't make me sew patches, he"—she began to sob—"I wish, I just wish I had a mom! She wouldn't make me sew calico when—when I want to play."

Something in the utter unhappiness of the little girl, together with the words of yearning for the dead mother, filled the woman with a strange tenderness. Though she never allowed sentiment to sway her from doing what she considered her duty she did yield to its influence and spoke gently to the agitated child.

"I wish, too, your mom was here yet, Phœbe. But I guess if she was she'd want you to learn to sew. Ach, it's just that you like to be out, out all the time that makes you so contrary, I guess. You're like your pop, if you can just be out! Mebbe when you're old as I once and had your back near broke often as I had with hoein' and weedin' and plantin' in the garden you'll be glad when you can set in the house and sew. Ach, now, stop your cryin' and go finish your patchin' and when you're done I'll leave you go in to Greenwald for me to the store and to Granny Hogendobler."

"Oh"—the child lifted her tear-stained face—"and dare I really go to Greenwald when I'm done?"

"Yes. I need some sugar yet and you dare order it. And you can get me some thread and then stop at Granny Hogendobler's and ask her to come out to-morrow and help with the strawberry jelly. I got so much to make and it comes good to Granny if she gets away for a little change."

"Then I'll patch quick!" Phœbe said. The world was a good place again for the child as she went back to the sitting-room and resumed her sewing.

She was so eager to finish the unpleasant task that she forgot one of Aunt Maria's rules, as inexorable as the law of the Medes and Persians—the door between the kitchen and the sitting-room must be closed.

"Here, Phœbe," the woman called sharply, "make that door shut! Abody'd think you was born in a sawmill! The strawberry smell gets all over the house."

Phœbe turned alertly and closed the door. Then she soliloquized, "I don't see why there has to be doors on the inside of houses. I like to smell the good things all over the house, but then it's Aunt Maria's boss, not me."

Maria Metz shook her head as she returned to her berries. "If it don't beat all and if I won't have my hands full yet with that girl 'fore she's growed up! That stubborn she is, like her pop—ach, like all of us Metz's, I guess. Anyhow, it ain't easy raising somebody else's child. If only her mom would have lived, and so young she was to die, too."

3

Her thoughts went back to the time when her brother Jacob brought to the old Metz farmhouse his gentle, sweet-faced bride. Then the joint persuasions of Jacob and his wife induced Maria Metz to continue her residence in the old homestead. She relieved the bride of all the brunt of manual labor of the farm and in her capable way proved a worthy sister to the new mistress of the old Metz place. When, several years later, the gentle wife died and left Jacob the legacy of a helpless babe, it was Maria Metz who took up the task of mothering the motherless child. If she bungled at times in the performance of the mother's unfinished task it was not from lack of love, for she loved the fair little Phœbe with a passion that was almost abnormal, a passion which burned the more fiercely because there was seldom any outlet in demonstrative affection.

As soon as the child was old enough Aunt Maria began to teach her the doctrines of the plain church and to warn her against the evils of vanity, frivolity and all forms of worldliness.

Maria Metz was richly endowed with that admirable love of industry which is characteristic of the Pennsylvania Dutch. In accordance with her acceptance of the command, "Six days shalt thou labor," she swept, scrubbed, and toiled from early morning to evening with Herculean persistence. The farmhouse was spotless from cellar to attic, the wooden walks and porches scrubbed clean and smooth. Flower beds, vegetable gardens and lawns were kept neat and without weeds. Aunt Maria was, as she expressed it, "not afraid of work." Naturally she considered it her duty to teach little Phœbe to be industrious, to sew neatly, to help with light tasks about the house and gardens.

Like many other good foster-mothers Maria Metz tried conscientiously to care for the child's spiritual and physical well-being, but in spite of her best endeavors there were times when she despaired of the tremendous task she had undertaken. Phœbe's spirit tingled with the divine, poetic appreciation of all things beautiful. A vivid imagination carried the child into realms where the stolid aunt could not follow, realms of whose existence the older woman never dreamed.

But what troubled Maria Metz most was the child's frank avowal of vanity. Every new dress was a source of intense joy to Phœbe. Every new ribbon for her hair, no matter how narrow and dull of color, sent her face smiling. The golden hair, which sprang into long curls as Aunt Maria combed it, was invariably braided into two thick, tight braids, but there were always little wisps that curled about the ears and forehead. These wisps were at once the woman's despair and the child's freely expressed delight. However, through all the rigid discipline the little girl retained her natural

4

buoyancy of childhood, the spontaneous interestedness, the cheerfulness and animation, which were a part of her goodly heritage.

That June morning the world was changed suddenly from a dismal vale of patchwork to a glorious garden of delight. She was still a child and the promised walk to Greenwald changed the entire world for her.

She paused once in her sewing to look about the sitting-room. "Ach, I vonder now why this room is so ugly to me to-day. I guess it's because it's so pretty out. Why, mostly always I think this is a vonderful nice room."

The sitting-room of the Metz farm was attractive in its old-fashioned furnishing. It was large and well lighted. The gray rag carpet—woven from rags sewed by Aunt Maria and Phœbe—was decorated with wide stripes of green. Upon the carpet were spread numerous rugs, some made of braided rags coiled into large circles, others were hooked rugs gaily ornamented with birds and flowers and graceful scroll designs. The low-backed chairs were painted dull green and each bore upon the four inch panel of its back a hand-painted floral design. On the haircloth sofa were several crazy-work cushions. Two deep rocking-chairs matched the antique low-backed chairs. A spindle-legged cherry table bore an old vase filled with pink and red straw flowers. The large square table, covered with a red and green cloth, held a glass lamp, the old Metz Bible, several hymn-books and the papers read in that home,—a weekly religious paper, the weekly town paper, and a well-known farm journal. A low walnut organ which Phœbe's mother brought to the farm and a tall walnut grandfather clock, the most cherished heirloom of the Metz family, occupied places of honor in the room. Not a single article of modern design could be found in the entire room, yet it was an interesting and habitable place. Most of the Metz furniture had stood in the old homestead for several generations and so long as any piece served its purpose and continued to look respectable Aunt Maria would have considered it gross extravagance, even a sacrilege, to discard it for one of newer design. She was satisfied with her house, her brother Jacob was well pleased with the way she kept it—it never occurred to her that Phœbe might ever desire new things, and least of all did she dream that the girl sometimes spent an interesting hour refurnishing, in imagination, the same old sitting-room.

"Yes," Phœbe was saying to herself, "sometimes this room is vonderful to me. Only I wished the organ was a piano, like the one Mary Warner got to play on. But, ach, I must hurry once and make this patch done. Funny thing patchin' is, cuttin' up big pieces of good calico in little ones and then sewin' them up in big ones again! I don't like it"—she spoke very softly for she knew her aunt disapproved of the habit of talking to one's self—"I don't like patchin' and I for certain don't like red and green quilts! I got one on my bed now and it hurts my eyes still in the morning when I get awake. I'd like a pretty blue and white one for my bed. Mebbe Aunt Maria will leave me make one when I get this one sewed. But now my patch is done and I dare to go to Greenwald. That's a vonderful nice walk."

A moment later she stood again in the big kitchen.

"See," she said, "now I got them all done. And little stitches, too, so nobody won't catch their toes in 'em when they sleep, like you used to tell me still when I first begun to sew."

The woman smiled. "Now you're a good girl, Phœbe. Put your patches away nice and you dare go to Greenwald."

"Where all shall I go?"

"Go first to Granny Hogendobler; that's right on the way to the store. You ask her to come out to-morrow morning early if she wants to help with the berries."

"Dare I stay a little?"

"If you want. But don't you go bringin' any more slips of flowers to plant or any seeds. The flower beds are that full now abody can hardly get in to weed 'em still."

"All right, I won't. But I think it's nice to have lots and lots of flowers. When I have a garden once I'll have it full——"

"Talk of that some other day," said her aunt. "Get ready now for town once. You go to the store and ask 'em to send out twenty pounds of granulated sugar. Jonas, one of the clerks, comes out this way still when he goes home and he can just as good fetch it along on his home road. Your pop is too busy to hitch up and go in for it and I have no time neither to-day and I want it early in the morning, and what I have is almost all. And then you can buy three spools of white thread number fifty. And when you're done you dare look around a little in the store if you don't touch nothing. On the home road you better stop in the post-office and ask if there's anything. Nobody was in yesterday."

"All right—and—Aunt Maria, dare I wear my hat?"

"Ach, no. Abody don't wear Sunday clothes on a Wednesday just to go to Greenwald to the store. Only when you go to Lancaster and on a Sunday you wear your hat. You're dressed good enough; just get your sunbonnet, for it's sunny on the road."

Phœbe took a small ruffled sunbonnet of blue checked gingham from a hook behind the kitchen door and pressed it lightly on her head.

6

"Ach, bonnets are vonderful hot things!" she exclaimed. "A nice parasol like Mary Warner's got would be lots nicer. Where's the money?" she asked as she saw a shadow of displeasure on her aunt's face.

"Here it is, enough for the sugar and the thread. Don't lose the pocketbook, and be sure to count the change so they don't make no mistake."

"Yes."

"And don't touch things in the store."

"No." The child walked to the door, impatient to be off.

"And be careful crossin' over the streets. If a horse comes, or a bicycle, wait till it's past, or an automobile——"

"Ach, yes, I'll be careful," Phœbe answered.

A moment later she went down the boardwalk that led through the yard to the little green gate at the country road. There she paused and looked back at the farm with its old-fashioned house, her birthplace and home.

The Metz homestead, erected in the days of home-grown flax and spinning-wheels, was plain and unpretentious. Built of gray, rough-hewn quarry stone it hid like a demure Quakeress behind tall evergreen trees whose branches touched and interlaced in so many places that the traveler on the country road caught but mere glimpses of the big gray house.

The old home stood facing the road that led northward to the little town of Greenwald. Southward the road curved and wound itself about a steep hill, sent its branches right and left to numerous farms while it, still twisting and turning, went on to the nearest city, Lancaster, ten miles distant.

The Metz farm was just outside the southern limits of the town of Greenwald. The spacious red barn stood on the very bank of Chicques Creek, the boundary line.

"It's awful pretty here to-day," Phœbe said aloud as she looked from the house with its sheltering trees to the flower garden with its roses, larkspur and other old-fashioned flowers, then to the background of undulating fields and hills. "It's just vonderful pretty here to-day. But, ach, I guess it's pretty most anywheres on a day like this—but not in the house. Ugh, that patchin'! I want to forget it."

As she closed the gate and entered the country road she caught sight of a familiar figure just ahead.

"Hello," she called. "Wait once, David! Is that you?"

"No, it ain't me, it's my shadow!" came the answer as a boy, several years older than Phœbe, turned and waited for her.

"Ach, David Eby," she giggled, "you're just like Aunt Maria

7

says still you are—always cuttin' up and talkin' so abody don't know if you mean it or what. Goin' in to town, too, once?"

"Um-uh. Say, Phœbe, you want a rose to pin on?" he asked, turning to her with a pink damask rose.

"Why, be sure I do! I just like them roses vonderful much. We got 'em too, big bushes of 'em, but Aunt Maria won't let me pull none off. Where'd you get yourn?"

"We got lots. Mom lets me pull off all I want. You pin it on and be decorated for Greenwald. Where all you going, Phœbe?"

"And I say thanks, too, David, for the rose," she said as she pinned the rose to her dress. "Um, it smells good! Where am I goin'?" she remembered his question. "Why, to the store and to Granny Hogendobler and the post-office——"

"Jimminy Crickets!" The boy stood still. "That's where I'm to go! Me and mom both forgot about it. Mom wants a money order and said I'm to get it the first time I go to town and here I am without the money. It's home up the hill again for me."

"Ach, David, don't you know that it's vonderful bad luck to go back for something when you got started once?"

The boy laughed. "It is bad luck to have to climb that hill again. But mom'll say what I ain't got in my head I got to have in my feet. They're big enough to hold a lot, too, Phœbe, ain't they?"

She giggled, then laughed merrily. "Ach," she said, "you say funny things. You just make me laugh all the time. But it's mean, now, that you are so dumb to forget and have to go back. I thought I'd have nice company all the ways in, but mebbe I'll see you in Greenwald."

"Mebbe. Goo'bye," said the boy and turned to the hill again.

Phœbe stood a moment and looked after him. "My," she said to herself, "but David Eby is a vonderful nice boy!" Then she started down the road, a quaint, interesting little figure in her brown chambray dress with its full, gathered skirt and its short, plain waist. But the face that looked out from the blue sunbonnet was even more interesting. The blue eyes, golden hair and fair coloring of the cheeks held promise of an abiding beauty, but more than mere beauty was bounded by the ruffled sunbonnet. There was an eagerness of expression, an alert understanding in the deep eyes, a tender fluttering of the long lashes, an ever varying animation in the child face, as though she were standing on tiptoe to catch all the sunshine and glory of the great, beautiful world about her.

Phœbe went decorously down the road, across the wooden bridge over the Chicques, then she began to skip. Her full skirt fluttered in the light wind, her sunbonnet slipped back from her head and flapped as she hopped along the half mile stretch of country road bordered by green fields and meadows.

"There's no houses here so I dare skip," she panted gleefully. "Aunt Maria don't think it looks nice for girls to skip, but I like to do it. I could just skip and skip and skip——"

She stopped suddenly. In a meadow to her right a tangle of bulrushes edged a small pond and, perched on a swaying reed, a red-winged blackbird was calling his clear, "Conqueree, conqueree."

"Oh, you pretty thing!" Phœbe cried as she leaned on the fence and watched the bird. "You're just the prettiest thing with them red and yellow spots on your wings. And you ain't afraid of me, not a bit. I guess mebbe you know you got wings and I ain't. Such pretty wings you got, too, and the rest of you is all black as coal. Mebbe God made you black all over like a crow and then got sorry for you and put some pretty spots on your wings. I wonder now"—her face sobered—"I just wonder now why Aunt Maria says still that it's bad to fix up pretty with curls and things like that and to wear fancy dresses. Why, many of the birds are vonderful fine in gay feathers and the flowers are fancy and the butterflies—ach, mebbe when I'm big I'll understand it better, or mebbe I'll dress up pretty then too."

With that cheering thought she turned again to the road and resumed her walk, but the skipping mood had fled. She pulled her sunbonnet to its proper place and walked briskly along, still enjoying thoroughly, though less exuberantly, the beauty of the June morning.

The scent of pink clover mingled with the odor of grasses and the delicate perfume of sweetbrier. Wood sorrel nestled in the grassy corners near the crude rail fences, daisies and spiked toad-flax grew lavishly among the weeds of the roadside. In the meadows tall milkweed swayed its clusters of pink and lavender, marsh-marigolds dotted the grass with discs of pure gold, and Queen Anne's lace lifted its parasols of exquisite loveliness. Phœbe reveled in it all; her cheeks were glowing as she left the beauty of the country behind her and came at last to the little town of Greenwald.

CHAPTER II
OLD AARON'S FLAG

Greenwald is an old town but it is a delightfully interesting one. It does not wear its antiquity as an excuse for sinking into mouldering uselessness. It presents, rather, a strange mingling of the quaint, romantic and historic with the beautiful, progressive and modern. Though it clings reverently to honored traditions it is ever mindful of the fact that the welfare of its inhabitants is dependent upon reasonable progress in its religious, educational and industrial life.

The charming stamp of its antiquity is revealed in its great old trees; its wide Market Square from which narrower streets branch to the east, west, north and south; its numerous houses of the plain, substantial type of several generations ago; its occasional little, low houses which have withstood the march of modern building and stand squarely beside houses of more elaborate and later design; but chiefly in its old-fashioned gardens. All the old-time flowers are favorites there and refuse to be displaced by any newcomer. Sweet alyssum and candytuft spread carpets of bloom along the neat garden walks, hollyhocks and dahlias look boldly out to the streets, while the old-fashioned sweet-scented roses grow on great bushes which have been undisturbed for three or more generations.

To Phœbe Metz, Greenwald, with its two thousand inhabitants, its several churches, post-office and numerous stores, seemed a veritable city. She delighted in walking on its brick sidewalks, looking at its different houses and entering its stores. How many attractions these stores held for the little country girl! There was the big one on the Square which had in one of its windows a great lemon tree on which grew real lemons. Another store had a large Santa Claus in its window every Christmas—not that Phœbe Metz had ever been taught to believe in that patron saint of the children—oh, no! Maria Metz would have considered it foolish, even sinful, to lie to a child about any mythical Santa Claus coming down the chimney Christmas Eve! Nevertheless, the smiling, rotund face of the red-habited Santa in the store window seemed so real and so emanative of cheer that Phœbe delighted in him each year and felt sure there must be a Santa Claus somewhere in the world, even though Aunt Maria knew nothing about him.

Most little towns can boast of one or more persons like Granny Hogendobler, well-nigh community owned, certainly community appropriated. Did any one need a helper in garden or kitchen or sewing room, Granny Hogendobler was glad to serve. Did a housewife remember that a rose geranium leaf imparts to apple jelly a delicious flavor, Granny Hogendobler was able and willing to furnish the leaf. Did a lover of flowers covet a new phlox or dahlia or other old-fashioned flower, Granny Hogendobler was ready to give of her stock. Should a young wife desire a recipe for crullers, shoo-fly pie, or other delectable dish, Granny had a wealth of reliable recipes at her tongue's end. This admirable desire to serve found ample opportunities for exercise in the constant demands from her friends and neighbors. But Granny's greatest joy lay in the fond ministrations for her husband, Old Aaron, as the town people called him, half pityingly, half accusingly. For some said Old Aaron was plain shiftless, had always been so, would remain so forever, so long as he had Granny to do for him. Others averred that the Confederate bullets that had shattered his leg into splinters and necessitated its amputation must have gone astray and struck his liver—leastways, that was the kindest explanation they could give for his laziness.

Granny stoutly refuted all these charges—gossip travels in circles in small towns and sooner or later reaches those most concerned—"Aaron lazy! I-to-goodness no! Why, he's old and what for should he go out and work every day, I wonder. He helps me with the garden and so, and when I go out to help somebody for a day or two he gets his own meals and tends the chickens still. Some people thought a few years ago that he might get work in the foundry, but I said I want him at home with me. He gets a pension and we can live good on what we have without him slaving his last years away, and him with one leg lost at Gettysburg!" she ended proudly.

So Old Aaron continued to live his life as pleased his mate and himself. He pottered about the house and garden and spent long hours musing under the grape arbor. But there was one day in every year when Old Aaron came into his own. Every Memorial Day he dressed in his venerated blue uniform and carried the flag down the dusty streets of Greenwald, out to the dustier road to a spot a mile from the heart of the town, where, on a sunny hilltop, some of his comrades rested in the Silent City.

Only the infirm and the ill of the town failed to run to look as the little procession passed down the street. There were boys in khaki, the town band playing its best, volunteer firemen clad in vivid red shirts, a low, hand-drawn wagon filled with flowers, an old cannon, also hand-drawn, whose shots over the graves of the dead veterans would thrill as they thrilled every May thirtieth—all received attention and admiration from the watchers of the procession. But the real honors of the day were accorded the "thin blue line of heroes," and Old Aaron was one of these. To Granny Hogendobler, who walked with the crowd of cheering children and adults and kept step on the sidewalk with the step of the marchers on the street, it was evident that the standard bearer was growing old. The steep climb near the cemetery entrance left him breathless and flushed and each year Granny thought, "It's getting too much for him to carry that flag." But each returning year she would have spurned as earnestly as he any suggestion that another one be chosen to carry that flag. And so every three hundred and sixty-fifth day the lean straight figure of Old Aaron marched directly under the fluttering folds of Old Glory and the soldier became a subject worthy of veneration, then with customary nonchalance the little town forgot him again or spoke of him as Old Aaron, a little lazy, a little shiftless, a little childish, and Granny Hogendobler became the more important figure of that household.

Granny was fifteen years younger than her husband and was undeniably rotund of hips and face, the former rotundity increased by her full skirts, the latter accentuated by her style of wearing her hair combed back into a tight knot near the top of her head and held in place by a huge black back-comb.

From this style of hair dressing it is evident that Granny was not a member of any plain sect. She was, as she said, "An Evangelical, one of the old kind yet. I can say Amen to the preacher's sermon and stand up in prayer-meeting and tell how the Lord has blessed me."

There were some who doubted the rich blessing of which Granny spoke. "I wouldn't think the Lord blessed me so much," whispered one, "if I had a man like Old Aaron, though I guess he's good enough to her. And that boy of theirs never comes home; he must have a funny streak in him too." "But think of this," one would answer, "how the Lord keeps her cheerful, kind and faithful through all her troubles."

Granny's was a wonderful garden. She and Old Aaron lived in a little gray cube of a house that had its front face set straight to the edge of Charlotte Street. However, the north side of the cube looked into a great green yard where tall spruce trees, overrun with trumpet vines and woodbine, shaded long beds of flowers that love semi-shady places. The rear of the house overlooked an old-fashioned garden enclosed with a white-washed picket fence. Always were there flowers at Granny's house. In the cold days of winter blooming masses of geraniums, primroses and gloxinias crowded against the little square panes of the windows and looked defiantly out at the snow; while all the old favorites grew in the garden, from the first March snowdrop to the late November chrysanthemum. In June, therefore, the garden was a "Lovesome spot" indeed.

12

"It vonders me now if Granny's home," thought Phœbe as she opened the wooden gate and entered the yard.

"Here I am," called Granny. "Back in the garden. I-to-goodness, Phœbe, did you come once! I just said yesterday to Aaron that I didn't see none of you folks for long, and here you come! You haven't seen the flowers for a while."

"Oh!" Phœbe breathed an ecstatic little word of delight. "Oh, your garden is just vonderful pretty!"

"Ain't," agreed Granny. "Aaron and me's been working pretty hard in it these weeks. There he is, out in the potato patch; see him?"

Phœbe stood on tiptoe and looked where Granny's finger pointed to the extreme end of the long vegetable garden, where the white head of Old Aaron was bending over his hoeing.

"He's hoeing the potatoes," Granny explained. "He don't see you. But he'll soon be done and come in."

"What were you doin'?" asked the child.

"Weeding the flag."

"Weedin' the flag—what do you mean?" Phœbe's eyes lighted with eagerness. "I guess you mean mendin' the flag, Granny." She looked toward the porch as if in search of Old Glory.

"I said weeding the flag," the woman insisted. "It's an idea of Aaron's and I guess I'll tell you about it, seeing your eyes are open so wide. See the poppies, that long stretch of them in the middle of the garden?"

"Um-uh," nodded Phœbe.

"Well, that patch at the back is all red poppies, the buds just coming on them nice and big. Then right in front of them is another patch of white poppies; the buds are thick on them, too. And right in front of them—you see what's there!"

"Larkspur, blue larkspur!" cried Phœbe. "Oh, I see—it's red, white and blue! You'll have it all summer in your garden!"

"Yes. When it blooms it'll be a grand sight. I said to Aaron that we'll have all the children of Greenwald in looking at his flag and he said he hopes so, for they couldn't look at anything better than the colors of Old Glory. Aaron's crazy about the flag."

"'Cause he fought for it, mebbe."

"Yes, I guess. His father died for it at Gettysburg, the same place where Aaron lost his leg. . . . The only thing is, the larkspur's getting ahead of the poppies—seems like the larkspur couldn't wait"—her voice continued low—"I always love to see the larkspur come."

"I too," said the child. "I like to pull out the little slippers from the middle of the flowers and fit 'em into each other and

13

make circles with 'em. I made a lot last summer and pressed 'em in a book, but Aunt Maria made me stop."

"That's just what Nason used to do. I have some pressed in the big Bible yet that he made when he was a little boy." She spoke half-absently, as though momentarily forgetful of the child's presence.

"Who's Nason?" asked Phœbe.

Granny started. "I-to-goodness, Phœbe, I forgot! You don't know him, never heard of him, I guess. He's our boy. We had a little girl, too, but she died."

"Did the boy die too, Granny?"

"No, ach no! You wouldn't understand. He's living in the city. He writes to me often but he don't come home. He and his pop fell out about the flag once when Nason was young and foolish and they're both too stubborn to forget it."

"But he'll come back some day and live with you, of course, won't he?" Phœbe comforted her.

"Yes—some day they'll see things different. But now don't you bother that head of yourn with such things. You forget all about Nason. Come now, sit on the bench a little under the arbor."

"Just a little. I must go to the store yet."

"You have lots to do."

"Yes. And I almost forgot what I come for. Aunt Maria wants you should come out to our place to-morrow early and help with the strawberries if you can."

"I'll come. I like to come to your place. Your Aunt Maria is so straight out, nothing false about her. I like her. But now I bet you're thinking of how many berries you can eat," she added as she noted the child's abstracted look.

"No—I was thinkin'—I was just thinkin' what a funny name Nason is, like you tried to say Nathan and got your tongue twisted."

"It's a real name, but you must forget all about it."

"If I can. Sometimes Aunt Maria tells me to forget things, like wantin' curls and fancy things and pretty dresses but I don't see how I can forget when I remember, do you?"

"It's hard," Granny said, a deeper meaning in her words than the child could comprehend. "It's the hardest thing in the world to forget what you want to forget. But here comes Aaron——"

"Well, well, if here ain't Phœbe Metz with her eyes shining and a pink rose pinned to her waist and matching the roses in her cheeks!" the old soldier said as he joined the two under the arbor. "Whew! Mebbe it ain't hot hoeing potatoes!"

"You're all heated up, Aaron," said Granny. His fifteen years seniority warranted a solicitous watchfulness over him, she thought. "Now you get cooled off a little and I'll make some lemonade. It'll taste good to me and Phœbe, too."

"All right, Ma," Aaron sighed in relaxation. "You know how to touch the spot. Did you tell Phœbe about the flag?"

"Yes."

"Oh, I think it's fine!" cried the child. "I can't wait till all the flowers bloom. I want to see it."

"You'll see it," promised the man. "And you bring all the boys and girls in too."

"And then will you tell us about the war and the Battle of Gettysburg? David Eby says he heard you once tell about it. I think it was at some school celebration. And he says it was grand, just like being there yourself."

"A little safer," laughed the old soldier. "But, yes, when the poppies bloom you bring the children in and I'll tell you about the war and the flag."

"I'll remember. I love to hear about the war. Old Johnny Schlegelmilch from way up the country comes to our place still to sell brooms, and once last summer he came and it began to thunder and storm and pop said he shall stay till it's over and then he told me all about the war. He said our flag's the prettiest in the whole world."

"So it is," solemnly affirmed Old Aaron.

"I wonder if anybody it belongs to could help liking it," said the child, remembering Granny's words.

"Well," the veteran answered slowly, "I knew a young fellow once, a nice fellow he seemed, too, and his father a soldier who fought for the flag. Well, the father was always talking about the flag and what it means and how every man should be ready to fight for it. And one day the boy said that he would never fight for it and be shot to pieces, that the old flag made him sick, and one soldier in the family was enough."

"Oh!" Phœbe opened her eyes wide in surprise and horror.

"And the father told the boy," the old man went on in a fixed voice as though the veriest details of the story were vividly before him, "that if he would not take back those words he never wanted to see him again. It was better to have no son, than such a son, a coward who hated the flag."

Here Granny appeared with the lemonade and the story was abruptly ended. Phœbe refrained from questioning the man about the story but as she sat under the arbor and afterwards, as she started up the street of the little town, she wondered over and over

15

how a boy could be the son of a soldier and hate the flag, and whether the story Old Aaron told her was the story of himself and Nason.

CHAPTER III
LITTLE DUTCHIE

"Aunt Maria said I dare look around a little," thought Phœbe as she neared the big store on the Square. Her heart beat more quickly as she turned the knob of the heavy door—little things still thrilled her, going to the store in Greenwald was an event!

The clerk's courteous, "What can I do for you?" bewildered her for an instant but she swallowed hard and said, "Why, we want twenty pounds of granulated sugar; ourn is almost all and Aunt Maria wants to make some strawberry jelly to-morrow. She said for Jonas to fetch it along on his home road."

"All right. Out to Jacob Metz?"

"Yes, he's my pop."

"I see. Anything else?"

"Three spools white thread, number fifty."

"Anything else?"

She shook her head as she handed him the money. "No, that's all for to-day. But Aunt Maria said I dare look around a little if I don't touch things."

"Look all you want," said the clerk and turned away, smiling.

Phœbe began a slow tramp about the big store. There was the same glass case filled with jewelry. The rings and pins rested on satin that had faded long since, the jewelry itself was tarnished but it held Phœbe's interest with its meagre glistening. One little ring with a tiny turquoise aroused her desire but she realized that she was longing for the impossible, so she moved away from the coveted treasures and paused before the ribbons. Some of those same ribbons had been in the tall revolving case ever since she could remember going to that store. The pale sea-green and the crushed-strawberry were faded horribly, yet she looked at them with longing. "Suppose," she thought, "I dared pick out any ribbon I want for a sash—guess I'd take that funny pink one, or mebbe that nice blue one. But I kinda think I'd rather have a set of dishes or a doll. But then I got that rag doll at home and that pretty one that pop got for me in Lancaster and that Aunt Maria won't leave me play with. That's funny now, that she says still I daren't play with it for I might break it, that I shall keep it till I'm big. But when I'm big I won't want a doll, and then I vonder what! What will I do with it then?"

She stood a long time before a table crowded with a motley gathering of toys, dolls and books. With so much coveted treasure before her it was hard to remember Aunt Maria's injunction to refrain from touching.

"Well, anyhow," she decided finally, "I won't need any of these things to play with now, for I'm going to be out in the garden and the yard with the flowers and birds. So I guess my old rag doll will be plenty for playin' with. But I mustn't look too long else Aunt Maria won't leave me come in soon again. I'll walk down the other side of the store now yet and then I must go."

She passed slowly along, her keen eyes noticing the varied assortment of articles displayed for sale. A long line of red handkerchiefs was fastened to a cord high above one counter. Long shelves were stacked high with ginghams, calicoes and finer dress materials. There were gaudy rugs and blankets tacked to the walls near the ceiling. Counters were filled with glassware, china and crockery; other counters were laden with umbrellas, hats, shoes——

"Ach," she sighed as she went out to the street, "I think this goin' to Greenwald to the store is vonderful nice! It's most as much fun as goin' in to Lancaster, only there I go in a trolley and I see black niggers"—she spoke the word with a little shiver, for Greenwald had no negro residents—"and once in there me and Aunt Maria saw a Chinaman with a long plait like a girl's hangin' down his back!"

After asking for the mail at the post-office she turned homeward, feeling like singing from sheer happiness. Then she looked down at her pink damask rose—it was withered.

"I'm goin' home now so I guess I won't be decorated no more." She unpinned the flower, clasped its short stem in her hand and raised the blossom to her face.

"Um-m-m!" She drew deep breaths of the rose's perfume. "Um-m!"

"Does it smell good?"

Phœbe turned her head at the voice and looked into the face of a young woman who sat on the porch of a near-by house.

"Does it smell good?" The question came again, accompanied by a broad smile.

Quickly the hand holding the flower dropped to the child's side, her eyes were cast down to the brick pavement and she went hurriedly down the street. But not so hurriedly that she failed to hear the words, "Little Dutchie" and a merry laugh from the young woman.

"She—she laughed at me!" Phœbe murmured to herself under the blue sunbonnet. "I don't know who she is, but that was at Mollie Stern's house that she sat—that lady that laughed at me. She called me a Dutchie!"

The child stabbed a fist into one eye and then into the other to fight back the tears. She felt sure that the appellation of Dutchie was not complimentary. Hadn't she heard the boys at school tease each other by calling, "Dutchie, Dutchie, sauer kraut!" But no one had ever called her that before! Her heart ached as she went down the street of the little town. She had planned to look at all the gardens of the main street as she walked home but the glory of the June day was spoiled for her. She did not care to look at any gardens. The laughing words, "Does it smell good?" rang in her ears. The name, "Little Dutchie," sent her heart throbbing.

After the first hurt a feeling of wrath rose in her. "Anyhow," she thought, "it's no disgrace to be a Dutchie! Nobody needn't laugh at me for that. But I just hate that lady that laughed at me! I hate everybody that pokes fun at me. And I ain't goin' to always be a Dutchie. You see once if I don't be something else when I grow up!"

"Hello, Phœbe," a cheery voice rang out, followed by a deeper exclamation, "Phœbe!" as she came to the last intersection of streets in the town and turned to enter the country road.

She turned a sober little face to the speakers, David Eby and his cousin, Phares Eby.

"Hello," she answered listlessly.

"What's wrong?" asked the older boy as they joined her.

Both were plainly country boys accustomed to hard farm work, but their tanned faces were frank and honest under broad straw hats. Each bore marked family resemblances in their big frames, dark eyes and well-shaped heads, but there was a distinct line drawn between their personalities. Phares Eby at sixteen was grave, studious and dignified; his cousin, David, two years younger, was a cheery, laughing, sociable boy, fond of boyish sports, delighting in teasing his schoolmates and enjoying their retaliation, preferring a tramp through the woods to the best book ever written.

The boys lived on adjacent farms and had long been the nearest neighbors of the Metz family; thus they had become Phœbe's playmates. Then, too, the Eby families were members of the Church of the Brethren, the mothers of the boys were old friends of Maria Metz, and a deep friendship existed among them

18

all. Phœbe and the two boys attended the same little country school and had become frankly fond of each other.

"What's wrong?" asked Phares again as Phœbe hung her head and remained silent.

"Ach," laughed David, "somebody's broke her dolly."

"Nobody ain't not broke my dolly, David Eby!" she said crossly. "I wouldn't cry for that!"

"What's wrong then?—come on, Phœbe." He pushed the sunbonnet back and patted her roguishly on the head. But she drew away from him.

"Don't you touch me," she cried. "I'm a Dutchie!"

"What?"

She tossed her head and became silent again.

"Come on, tell me," coaxed David. "I want to know what's wrong. Why, if you don't tell me I'll be so worried I won't be able to eat any dinner, and I'm so hungry now I could eat nails."

The girl laughed suddenly in spite of herself—"Ach, David, you're awful simple! Abody has to laugh at you. I was mad, for when I was in Greenwald I was smellin' a rose, that pink rose you gave me, and some lady on Mollie Stern's porch laughed at me and called me a Little Dutchie! Now wouldn't you got mad for that?"

But David threw back his head and laughed. "And you were ready to cry at that?" he said. "Why, I'm a Dutchie, so is Phares, so's most of the people round here. Ain't so, Phares?"

"Yes, guess so," the older boy assented, his eyes still upon Phœbe. "D'ye know," he said, addressing her, "when you were cross a few minutes ago your eyes were almost black. You shouldn't get so angry still, Phœbe."

"I don't care," she retorted quickly, "I don't care if my eyes was purple!"

"But you should care," persisted the boy gravely. "I don't like you so angry."

"Ach," she flashed an indignant look at him—"Phares Eby, you're by far too bossy! I like David best; he don't boss me all the time like you do!"

David laughed but Phares appeared hurt.

Phœbe was quick to note it. "Now I hurt you like that lady hurt me, ain't, Phares?" she said contritely. "But I didn't mean to hurt you, Phares, honest."

"But you like me best," said David gaily. "You can't take that back, remember."

She gave him a scornful look. Then she remembered the flag in the Hogendobler garden and became happy and eager again as she said, "Oh, Phares, David, I know the best secret!"

"Can't keep it, I bet!" challenged David.

"Can't I?" she retorted saucily. "Now for that I won't tell you till you get good and anxious. But then it's not really a secret." The flag of growing flowers was too glorious a thing to keep; she compromised—"I'll tell you, because it's not a real secret." And she proceeded to unfold with earnest gesticulations the story about the flowers of red and white and blue and the invitation for all who cared to come and see the colors of Old Glory growing in the garden of Old Aaron and Granny, and of the added pleasure of hearing Old Aaron tell his thrilling story of the battle of Gettysburg.

"I won't want to hear about any battle," said Phares. "I think war is horrible, awful, wicked."

"Mebbe so," said the girl, "but the poor men who fight in wars ain't always awful, horrible, wicked. You needn't turn your nose up at the old soldiers. Folks call Old Aaron lazy, I heard 'em a'ready, lots of times, but I bet some of them wouldn't have fought like he did and left a leg at Gettysburg and—ach, I think Old Aaron is just vonderful grand!" she ended in an impulsive burst of eloquence.

"Hooray!" shouted David. "So do I! When he carries the flag out the pike every Decoration Day he's somebody, all right."

"Ain't now!" agreed Phœbe.

"Been in the stores?" David asked her, feeling that a change of subject might be wise.

"Yes."

"See anything pretty?"

"Ach, yes. A lots of things. I saw the prettiest finger ring with a blue stone in. I wish I had it."

"What would Aunt Maria say to that?" wondered David.

"Ach, she'd say that so long as my finger ain't broke I don't need a band on it. But I looked at the ring at any rate and wished I had it."

"You dare never wear gold rings," Phares told her.

"Not now," she returned, "but some day when I'm older mebbe I'll wear a lot of 'em if I want."

The words set the boys thinking. Each wondered what manner of woman their little playmate would become.

"I bet she'll be a good-looking one," thought David. "She'd look swell dressed up fine like some of the people I see in town."

"Of course she'll turn plain some day like her aunt," thought the other boy. "She'll look nice in the plain dress and the white cap."

Phœbe, ignorant of the visions her innocent words had

20

called to the hearts of her comrades, chattered on until they reached the little green gate of the Metz farm.

"Now you two must climb the hill yet. I'm glad I'm home. I'm hungry."

"And me," the boys answered, and with good-byes were off on the winding road up the hill.

As Phœbe turned the corner of the big gray house she came face to face with her father.

"So here you are, Phœbe," he said, smiling at sight of her. "Your Aunt Maria sent me out to look if you were coming. It's time to eat. Been to the store, ain't?"

"Yes, pop. I went alone."

"So? Why, you're getting a big girl, now you can go to Greenwald alone."

"Ach," she laughed. "Why, it's just straight road."

They crossed the porch and entered the kitchen hand-in-hand, the sunbonneted little girl and the big farmer. Jacob Metz was also a member of the Church of the Brethren and bore the distinctive mark: hair parted in the middle and combed straight back over his ears and cut so that the edge of it almost touched his collar. A heavy black beard concealed his chin, mild brown eyes gleamed beneath a pair of heavy black brows. Only in the wide, high forehead and the resolute mouth could be seen any resemblance between him and the fair child by his side.

When they entered the kitchen Maria Metz turned from the stove, where she had been stirring the contents of a big iron pan.

"So you got back safe, after all, Phœbe," she said with a sigh of relief. "I was afraid mebbe something happened to you, with so many streets to go across and so many teams all the time and the automobiles."

"Ach, I look both ways still before I start over. Granny Hogendobler said she'll get out early."

"So. What did she have to say?"

"Ach, lots. She showed me her flowers. Ain't it too bad, now, that her little girl died and her boy went away?"

"Well, she spoiled that boy. He grew up to be not much account if he stays away just because he and his pop had words once."

"But he'll come back some day. Granny knows he will." The child echoed the old mother's confidence.

"Not much chance of that," said Aunt Maria with her usual decisiveness. "When a man goes off like that he mostly always stays off. He writes to her she says and I guess she's just as good off with that as if he come home to live. She's lived this long without him."

"But," argued Phœbe, the maternal in her over-sweeping all else, "he's her boy and she wants him back!"

"Ach," the aunt said impatiently, "you talk too much. Were you at the store?"

"Yes. I got the thread and ordered the sugar and counted the change and there was nothing in the post-office for us."

"Did you enjoy your trip to town?" asked the father.

"Yes—but——"

"But what?" demanded Aunt Maria. "Did you break anything in the store now?"

"No. I just got mad. It was this way"—and she told the story of her pink rose.

Maria Metz frowned. "David Eby should leave his mom's roses on the stalks where they belong. Anyhow, I guess you did look funny if you poked your nose in it like you do still here."

"But she had no business to laugh at me, had she, pop?"

"You're too touchy," he said kindly. "But did you say the lady was on Mollie Stern's porch?"

"Yes."

"Then I guess it was her cousin from Philadelphia, the one that was elected to teach the school on the hill for next winter."

"Oh, pop, not our school?"

"Yes. Anyhow, her cousin was elected yesterday to teach your school. It seems she wanted to teach in the country and Mollie's pop is friends with a lot of our directors and they voted her in."

"I ain't goin' to school then!" Phœbe almost sobbed. "I don't like her, I don't want to go to her school; she laughed at me."

"Come, come," the father laid his hands on her head and spoke gently yet in a tone that she respected. "You mustn't get worked up over it. She's a nice young lady, and it will be something new to have a teacher from Philadelphia. Anyhow, it's a long ways yet till school begins."

"I'm glad it is."

"Come," interrupted the aunt, "help now to dish up. It's time to eat once. We're Pennsylvania Dutch, so what's the use gettin' cross when we're called that?"

"Yes," Phœbe's father said, smiling, "I'm a Dutchie too, but I'm a big Dutchie."

Phœbe smiled, but all through the meal and during the days that followed she thought often of the rose. Her heart was bitter toward the new teacher and she resolved never, never to like her!

CHAPTER IV
THE NEW TEACHER

The first Monday in September was the opening day of the rural school on the hill. Phœbe woke that morning before daylight. At four she heard her Aunt Maria tramp about in heavy shoes. It was Monday and wash-day and to Maria Metz the two words were so closely linked that nothing less than serious illness or death could part them.

"Ach, my," Phœbe sighed as she turned again under her red and green quilt, "this is the first day of school! Wish Aunt Maria'd forget to call me till it's too late to go."

At five-thirty she heard her father go down-stairs and soon after that came her aunt's loud call, "Phœbe, it's time to get up. Get up now and get down for I have breakfast made."

"Yes," came the dreary answer.

"Now don't you go asleep again."

"No, I'm awake. Shall I dress right aways for school?"

"No. Put on your old brown gingham once."

Phœbe made a wry face. "Ugh, that ugly brown gingham! What for did anybody ever buy brown when there are such pretty colors in the stores?"

A moment later she pushed back the gay quilt and sat on the edge of the bed. The first gleams of day-break sent bright streaks of light into her room as she sat on the high walnut bed and swung her bare feet back and forth.

"It's the first time I wasn't glad for school," she soliloquized softly. "I used to could hardly wait still, and I'd be glad this time if we didn't have that teacher from Phildelphy. Miss Virginia Lee her name is, and she's pretty like the name, but I don't like her! Guess she's that stuck up, comin' from the city, that she'll laugh all the time at us country people. I don't like people that poke fun at me, you bet I don't! I vonder now, mebbe I am funny to look at, that she laughed at me. But if I was I think somebody would 'a' told me long ago. I don't see what for she laughed so at me."

She sprang from the bed and ran to the window, pulled the cord of the green shade and sent it rattling to the top. Then she stood on tiptoe before the mirror in the walnut bureau, but the glass was hung too high for a satisfactory scrutiny of her features. She pushed a cane-seated chair before the bureau, knelt upon it and brought her face close to the glass.

"Um," she surveyed herself soberly. "Well, now, mebbe if my hair was combed I'd look better."

She pulled the tousled braids, opened them and shook her head until the golden hair hung about her face in all its glory.

"Why"—she gasped at the sudden change she had wrought, then laughed aloud from sheer childish happiness in her own miracle—"Why," she said gladly, "I ain't near so funny lookin' with my hair opened and down instead of pulled back in two tight plaits! But I wish Aunt Maria'd leave me have curls. I'd have a lot, and long ones, longer'n Mary Warner's."

"Phœbe!" Aunt Maria's voice startled the little girl. "What in the world are you doing lookin' in that glass so? And your knees on a cane-bottom chair! You know better than that. What for are you lookin' at yourself like that? You ought to be ashamed to be so vain."

Phœbe left the chair and looked at her aunt.

"Why," she said in an amazed voice, "I wasn't being vain! I was just lookin' to see if I am funny lookin' that it made Miss Lee laugh at me. And I found out that I'm much nicer to look at with my hair open than in plaits. You say still I mustn't have curls, but can't you see how much nicer I look this way——"

"Ach," interrupted her aunt, "don't talk so dumb! I guess you ain't any funnier lookin' than other people, and if you was it wouldn't matter long as you're a good girl."

"But I wouldn't be a good girl if I looked like some people I saw a'ready. If I had such big ears and crooked nose and big mouth——"

"Phœbe, you talk vonderful! Where do you get such nonsense put in your head?"

"I just think it and then I say it. But was that bad? I didn't mean it for bad."

She looked so like a cherub of absolute innocency with her deep blue eyes opened wide in wonder, her golden hair tumbled about her face and streaming over the shoulders of her white muslin nightgown, that Aunt Maria, though she had never heard of Reynolds' cherubs, was moved by the adorable picture.

"I know, Phœbe," she said kindly, "that you want to be a good girl. But you say such funny things still that I vonder sometimes if I'm raisin' you the right way. Come, hurry, now get dressed. Your pop's goin' way over to the field near Snavely's and you want to give him good-bye before he goes to work."

"I'll hurry, Aunt Maria, honest I will," the child promised and began to dress.

A little while later when she appeared in the big kitchen her father and Aunt Maria were already eating breakfast. With her hair drawn back into one uneven braid and a rusty brown dress upon her she seemed little like the adorable figure of the looking-glass, but her father's face lighted as he looked at her.

"So, Phœbe," he said, a teasing twinkle in his eyes, "I see you get up early to go to school."

"But I ain't glad to go." She refused to smile at his words.

"Ach, yes," he coaxed, "you be a good girl and like your new teacher. She's nice. I guess you'll like her when you know her once."

"Mebbe so," was the unpromising answer as she slipped the straps of a blue checked apron over her shoulders, buttoned it in the back and took her place at the table.

Breakfast at the Metz farm was no light meal. Between the early morning meal and the twelve o'clock dinner much hard work was generally accomplished and Maria Metz felt that a substantial foundation was necessary. Accordingly, she carried to the big, square cherry table in the kitchen an array of well-filled dishes. There was always a glass dish of stewed prunes or seasonable fresh fruit; a plate piled high with thick slices of home-made bread; several dishes of spreadings, as the jellies, preserves or apple-butter of that community are called. There was a generous square of home-made butter, a platter of home-cured ham or sausage, a dish of fried or creamed potatoes, a smaller dish of pickles or beets, and occasionally a dome of glistening cup cheese. The meal would have been considered incomplete without a liberal supply of cake or cookies, coffee in huge cups and yellow cream in an old-fashioned blue pitcher.

That morning Aunt Maria had prepared an extra treat, a platter of golden slices of fried mush.

The two older people partook heartily of the food before them but the child ate listlessly. Her aunt soon exclaimed, "Now, Phœbe, you must eat or you'll get hungry till recess. You know this is the first day of school and you can't run for a cookie if you get hungry. You ain't eatin'; you feel bad?"

"No, but I ain't hungry."

"Come now," urged her father, as he poured a liberal helping of molasses on his sixth piece of mush, "you must eat. You surely don't feel that bad about going to school!"

"Ach, pop," she burst out, "I don't hate the school part, the learnin' in books; that part is easy. But I don't like the teacher, and I guess she laughed at my tight braids. Mebbe if I dared wear curls—— Oh, pop, daren't I have curls? I'd like to show her that I

25

look nice that way. Say I dare, then I won't be so funny lookin' no more!"

Jacob Metz looked at his offspring—what did the child mean? Why, he thought she was right sweet and surely her aunt kept her clean and tidy. But before he could answer his sister spoke authoritatively.

"Jacob, I wish you'd tell her once that she daren't have curls! She just plagues me all the time for 'em. Her hair was made to be kept back and not hangin' all over."

"Why then," Phœbe asked soberly, "did God make my hair curly if I daren't have curls?" She spoke with a sense of knowing that she had propounded an unanswerable question.

"That part don't matter," evaded Aunt Maria. "You ask your pop once how he wants you to have your hair fixed."

The child looked up expectantly but she read the answer in her father's face.

"I like your hair back in plaits, Phœbe. You look nice that way."

"Ach," her nose wrinkled in disgust, "not so very, I guess. Mary Warner has curls, always she has curls!"

"Come," said the father as he rose from his chair, "you be a good girl now to-day. I'm going now."

"All right, pop. I'll tell you to-night how I like the teacher."

After the breakfast dishes were washed and the other morning tasks accomplished Phœbe brought her comb and ribbons to her aunt and sat patiently on a spindle-legged kitchen chair while the woman carefully parted the long light hair and formed it into two braids, each tied at the end with a narrow brown ribbon.

"Now," Aunt Maria said as she unbuttoned the despised brown dress, "you dare put on your blue chambray dress if you take care and not get it dirty right aways."

"Oh, I'm glad for that. I like that dress best of all I have. It's not so long in the body or tight or long in the skirt like my other dresses. And blue is a prettier color than brown. I'll hurry now and get dressed."

She ran up the wide stairs, her hands skimming lightly the white hand-rail, and entered the little room known as the clothes-room, where the best clothes of the family were hung on heavy hooks fastened along the entire length of the four walls. She soon found the blue chambray dress. It was extremely simple. The plain gathered skirt was fastened to the full waist by a wide belt of the chambray. But the dress bore one distinctive feature. Instead of the usual narrow band around the neck it was adorned with a wide round collar which lay over the shoulders. Phœbe knew that the collar was vastly becoming and the knowledge always had a soothing effect upon her.

When the call of the school bell floated down the hill to the gray farmhouse Phœbe picked up her school bag and her tin lunch kettle and started off, outwardly in happier mood yet loath to go to the old schoolhouse for the first session of school.

From the Metz farm the road to the school began to ascend. Gradually it curved up-hill, then suddenly stretched out in a long, steep climb until, upon the summit of the hill, it curved sharply to the west to a wide clearing. It was to this clearing the little country schoolhouse with its wide porch and snug bell-tower called the children back to their studies.

Goldenrod and asters grew along the road, dogwood branches hung their scarlet berries over the edge of the woods, but Phœbe would have scorned to gather any of the flowers she loved and carry them to the new teacher. "I ain't bringing her any flowers," she soliloquized.

She trudged soberly ahead. As she reached the summit of the hill several children called to her. From three roads came other children, most of them carrying baskets or kettles filled with the noon lunch. All were eager for the opening of school, anxious to "see the new teacher once."

From the farm nearest the schoolhouse Phares Eby had come for his last year in the rural school. From the little cottage on the adjoining farm David Eby came whistling down the road.

"Hello, Phœbe," he called as he drew near to her. "Glad for school?"

"I ain't!" She flung the words at him. "You know good enough I ain't."

"Ha, ha," he laughed, "don't be cranky, Phœbe. Here comes Phares and he'll tell you that your eyes are black when you're cross. Won't you, Phares?"

"I——" began the sober youth, but Phœbe rudely interrupted.

"I don't care. I don't like the new teacher."

"You must like everybody," said Phares.

"Well, I just guess I won't! There's Mary Warner with her white dress and her black curls with a pink bow on them—you don't think I'm likin' her when she's got what I want and daren't have? Come on, it's time to go in," she added as Phares would have remonstrated with her for her frank avowal of jealousy. "Let's go in and see what the teacher's got on."

"Gee," whistled David, "girls are always thinking of clothes."

27

Phœbe gave him a disdainful look, but he laughed and walked by her side, up the three steps, across the porch and into the schoolhouse.

The red brick schoolhouse on the hill was a typical country school of Lancaster County. It had one large room with four rows of double desks and seats facing the teacher's desk and a long blackboard with its border of A B C. A stove stood in one of the corners in the front of the room. In the rear numerous hooks in the wall waited for the children's wraps and a low bench stood ready to receive their lunch baskets and kettles. Each detail of the little schoolhouse was reproduced in scores of other rural schools of that community. And yet, somehow, many of the older children felt on that first Monday a hope that their school would be different that year, that the teacher from Philadelphia would change many of the old ways and teach them, what Youth most desires, new ways, new manners, new things. It is only as the years bring wisdom that men and women appreciate the old things of life, as well as the new.

The new teacher became at once the predominating spirit of that little group. The interest of all the children, from the shy little beginners in the Primer class to the tall ones in the A class, was centered about her.

Miss Lee stood by her desk as Phœbe and the two boys entered. It was still that delightful period, before-school, when laughter could be released and voices raised without a fear of "keep quiet." The children moved to the teacher's desk as though drawn by magnetic force. Mary Warner, her dark curls hanging over her shoulders, appeared already acquainted with her. Several tiny beginners stood near the desk, a few older scholars were bravely offering their services to fetch water from Eby's "whenever it's all or you want some fresh," or else stay and clap the erasers clean.

When the second tug at the bell-rope gave the final call for the opening of school there was an air of gladness in the room. The new teacher possessed enough of the elusive "something" the country children felt belonged to a teacher from a big city like Philadelphia. The way she conducted the opening exercises, led the singing, and then proceeded with the business of arranging classes and assigning lessons served to intensify the first feelings of satisfaction. When recess came the children ran outdoors, ostensibly to play, but rather to gather into little groups and discuss the merits of the new teacher. The general verdict was, "She's all right."

"Ain't she all right?" David Eby asked Phœbe as they stood in the brown grasses near the school porch.

"Ach, don't ask me that so often!"

"But honest now, Phœbe, don't you like her?"

"I don't know."

"When will you know?"

"I don't know," came the tantalizing answer.

"Ach, sometimes, Phœbe, you make me mad! You act dumb just like the other girls sometimes."

"Then keep away from me if you don't like me," she retorted.

"Sassbox!" said the boy and walked away from her.

The little tilt with David did not improve the girl's humor. She entered the schoolroom with a sulky look on her face, her blue eyes dark and stormy. Accordingly, when Mary Warner shook her enviable curls and leaned forward to whisper ecstatically, "Phœbe, don't you just love the new teacher?" Phœbe replied very decidedly, "I do not! I don't like her at all!"

For a moment Mary held her breath, then a surprised "Oh!" came from her lips and she raised her hand and waved it frantically to attract the teacher's attention.

"What is it, Mary?"

"Why, Miss Lee, Phœbe Metz says she don't like you at all!"

"Did she ask you to tell me?" A faint flush crept into the face of the teacher.

"No—but——"

"Then that will do, Mary."

But Phœbe Metz did not dismiss the matter so easily. She turned in her seat and gave one of Mary's obnoxious curls a vigorous yank.

"Tattle-tale!" she hurled out madly. "Big tattle-tale!"

"Yank 'em again," whispered David, seated a few seats behind the girls, but Phares called out a soft, "Phœbe, stop that."

It all occurred in a moment—the yank, the outcry of Mary, the whispers of the two boys and the subsequent pause in the matter of teaching and the centering of every child's attention upon the exciting incident and wondering what Miss Lee would do with the disturbers of the peace.

"Phœbe," the teacher's voice was controlled and forceful, "you may fold your hands. You do not seem to know what to do with them."

Phœbe folded her hands and bowed her head in shame. She hadn't meant to create a disturbance. What would her father say when he knew she was scolded the first day of school!

The teacher's voice went on, "Mary Warner, you may come to me at noon. I want to tell you a few things about tale-bearing. Phœbe may remain after the others leave this afternoon."

"Kept in!" thought Phœbe disconsolately. She was going to be kept in the first day! Never before had such punishment been meted out to her! The disgrace almost overwhelmed her.

"Now I won't ever, ever, ever like her!" she thought as she bent her head to hide the tears.

The remainder of the day was like a blurred page to her. She was glad when the other children picked up their books and empty baskets and kettles and started homeward.

"Cheer up," whispered David as he passed out, but she was too miserable to smile or answer.

"Come on, David," urged Phares when the two cousins reached outdoors and the younger one seemed reluctant to go home. "Don't stay here to pet Phœbe when she comes out."

"Ach, the poor kid"—David was all sympathy and tenderness.

"Let her get punished. Pulling Mary's hair like that!"

"Well, Mary tattled. I was wishing Phœbe'd yank that darned kid's hair half off."

"Mary just told the truth. You think everything Phœbe does is right and you help her along in her temper. She needs to be punished sometimes."

"Ach, you make me tired, standing up for a tattle-tale! Anyhow, you go on home. I'm goin' to hang round a while and see if Miss Lee does anything mean."

Phares went on alone and the other boy stole to a window and crouched to the ground.

Inside the room Phœbe waited tremblingly for the teacher to speak. It seemed ages before Miss Lee walked down the aisle and stood by the low desk.

Phœbe raised her head—the look in the dark eyes of the teacher filled her with a sudden reversion of feeling. How could she go on hating any one so beautiful!

"Phœbe, I'm sorry—I'm so sorry there has been any trouble the first day and that you have been the cause of it."

"I—ach, Miss Lee," the child blurted out half-sobbingly, "Mary, she tattled on me."

"That was wrong, of course. I made her understand that at noon. But don't you think that pulling her hair and creating a disturbance was equally wrong?"

"I guess so, mebbe. But I didn't mean to make no fuss. I—I—

why, I just get so mad still! I hadn't ought to pull her hair, for that hurts vonderful much."

"Then you might tell her to-morrow how sorry you are about it."

"Yes." Phœbe looked up at the lovely face of the teacher. She felt that some explanation of Mary's tale was necessary. "Why, now," she stammered, "you know—you know that Mary said I said I don't like you?"

"Yes."

"Why, this summer once, early in June it was"—the child hung her head and spoke almost inaudibly—"you laughed at me and called me a Little Dutchie!" She looked up bravely then and spoke faster, "And for that, it's just for that I don't like you like all the others do a'ready."

"Laughed at you!" Miss Lee was perplexed. "You must be mistaken."

But Phœbe shook her head resolutely and told the story of the pink rose. Miss Lee listened at first with an incredulous smile upon her face, then with dawning remembrance.

"You dear child!" she cried as Phœbe ended her quaint recital. "So you are the little girl of the sunbonnet and the rose! I thought this morning I had seen you before. But you don't understand! I didn't laugh at you in the way you think. Why, I laughed at you just as we laugh at a dear little baby, because we love it and because it is so dear and sweet. And Dutchie was just a pet name. Can't you understand? You were so quaint and interesting in your sunbonnet and with the pink rose pressed to your face. Can't you understand?"

Phœbe smiled radiantly, her face beaming with happiness.

"Ach, ain't that simple now of me, Miss Lee?" she said in her old-fashioned manner. "I was so dumb and thought you was makin' fun of me, and just for that all summer I was wishin' school would not start ever. And I was sayin' all the time I ain't goin' to like you. But now I do like you," she added softly.

"I am glad we understand each other, Phœbe."

Miss Lee was genuinely interested in the child, attracted by the charming personality of the country girl. Of the thirty children of that school she felt that Phœbe Metz, in spite of her old-fashioned dress and older-fashioned ways, was the preëminent figure. It would be a delight to teach a child whose face could light with so much animation.

"Now, Phœbe," she said, "since we understand each other and have become friends, gather your books and hurry home. Your mother may be anxious about you."

"Not my mother," Phœbe replied soberly. "I ain't got no mom. It's my Aunt Maria and my pop takes care of me. My mom's dead long a'ready. But I'm goin' now," she ended brightly before Miss Lee could answer. "And the road's all down-hill so it won't take me long."

So she gathered her books and kettle, said good-bye to Miss Lee and hurried from the schoolhouse. When she was fairly on the road she broke into her habit of soliloquy: "Ach, if she ain't the nicest lady! So pretty she is and so kind! She was vonderful kind after what I done. The teacher we had last year, now, he would 'a' slapped my hands with a ruler, he was awful for rulers! But she just looked at me and I was so sorry for bein' bad that I could 'a' cried. And when she touched my hands—her hands is soft like the milkweed silk we find still in the fall—I just had to like her. I like her now and I'm goin' to be a good girl for her and when I grow up I wish I'd be just like her, just esactly like her."

David Eby waited until he was certain no harm was coming to Phœbe. He heard her say, "Now I do like you" and knew that the matter was being settled satisfactorily. Relieved, yet ashamed of his eavesdropping, he ran down the road toward his home.

"That teacher's all right," he thought. "But Jimminy, girls is funny things!"

He went on, whistling, but stopped suddenly as he turned a curve in the road and saw Phares sitting on the grass in the shelter of a clump of bushes.

The older boy rose. "David," he said sternly, "you're spoiling Phœbe Metz with your petting and fooling around her. What for need you pity her when she gets kept in for being bad? She was bad!"

"She was not bad!" David defended staunchly. "That Mary Warner makes me sick. Phœbe's got some sense, anyhow, and she's not bad. There's nothing bad in her."

"Um," said Phares tauntingly, "mebbe you like her already and next you'll want her for your girl. You give her pink roses and you stay to lick the teacher for her if——"

But the sentence was never finished. At the first words David's eyes flashed, his hands doubled into hard fists and, as his cousin paid no heed to the warning, he struck out suddenly, then partially restraining his rage, he unclenched his right hand and gave Phares a smarting slap upon the mouth.

"I'll learn you," he growled, "to meddle in my business! You mind your own, d'ye hear?"

"Why"—Phares knew no words to answer the insult—"why, David," he stammered, wiping his smarting lips.

But his silence added fuel to the other's wrath.

"You butt in too much, that's what!" said David. "It's just like Phœbe says, you boss too much. I ain't going to take it no more from you."

"I—now—mebbe I do," admitted Phares.

At the words David's anger cooled. He laid a hand on the older boy's arm, as older men might have gripped hands in reconciliation. "Come on, Phares," he said in natural, friendly tones. "I hadn't ought to hit you. Let's forget all about it. You and me mustn't fight over Phœbe."

"That's so," agreed Phares, but both were thoughtful and silent as they went down the lane.

CHAPTER V
THE HEART OF A CHILD

Phœbe's aspiration to become like her teacher did not lessen as the days went on. Her profound admiration for Miss Lee developed into intense devotion, a devotion whose depth she carefully guarded from discovery.

To her father's interested questioning she answered a mere, "Why, I like her, for all, pop. She didn't laugh to make fun at me. I think she's nice." But secretly the little girl thought of her new teacher in the most extravagant superlatives. Her heart was experiencing its first "hero" worship; the poetic, imaginative soul of the child was attracted by the magnetic personality of Miss Lee. The teacher's smiles, mannerisms, dress, and above all, her English, were objects worthy of emulation, thought the child. At times Phœbe despaired of ever becoming like Miss Lee, then again she felt certain she had within her possibilities to become like the enviable, wonderful Virginia Lee. But she breathed to none her ambitions and hopes except at night as she knelt by her high old-fashioned bed and bent her head to say the prayer Aunt Maria had taught her in babyhood. Then to the prayer, "Now I lay me down to sleep," she added an original petition, "And please let me get like my teacher, Miss Lee. Amen."

"Aunt Maria, church is on the hill Sunday, ain't it?" she asked one day after several weeks of school.

"Yes. And I hope it's nice, for we make ready for a lot of company always when we have church here."

"Why," the child asked eagerly, "dare I ask Miss Lee to come here for dinner too that Sunday? Mary Warner's mom had her for dinner last Sunday."

"Ach, yes, I don't care. You ask her. Mebbe she ain't been in a plain church yet and would like to go with us and then come home for dinner here. You ask her once."

Phœbe trembled a bit as she invited the teacher to the gray farmhouse. "Miss Lee—why—we have church here on the hill this Sunday and Aunt Maria thought perhaps you'd like to come out and go with us and then come to our house for dinner. We always have a lot of people for dinner."

"I'd love to, Phœbe, thank you," answered Miss Lee.

The plain sects of that community were all novel to her. She was eager to attend a service in the meeting-house on the hill and especially eager to meet Phœbe's people and study the unusual child in the intimate circle of home.

"Tell your aunt I shall be very glad to go to the service with you," she said as Phœbe stood speechless with joy. "Will you go?"

"Ach, yes, I go always," with a surprised widening of the blue eyes.

"And your aunt, too?"

"Why be sure, yes! Abody don't stay home from church when it's so near. That would look like we don't want company. There's church on the hill only every six weeks and the other Sundays it's at other churches. Then we drive to those other churches and people what live near ask us to come to their house for dinner, and we go. Then when it's here on the hill we must ask people that live far off to come to us for dinner. That way everybody has a place to go. It makes it nice to go away and to have company still. We always have a lot when church is here. Aunt Maria cooks so good."

She spoke the last words innocently and looked up with an expression of wonder as she heard Miss Lee laugh gaily—now what was funny? Surely Miss Lee laughed when there was nothing at all to laugh about!

"What time does your service begin?" asked the teacher. "What time do you leave the house?"

"It takes in at nine o'clock——"

Miss Lee smothered an ejaculation of surprise.

"But we leave the house a little after half-past eight. Then we can go easy up the hill and have time to walk around on the graveyard a little and get in church early and watch the people come in."

"I'll stop for you and go with you, Phœbe."

Sunday morning at the Metz farm was no time for

34

prolonged slumber. With the first crowing of roosters Aunt Maria rose. After the early breakfast there were numerous tasks to be performed before the departure for the meeting-house. There was the milking to be done and the cans of milk placed in the cool spring-house; the chickens and cattle to be fed; each room of the big house to be dusted; vegetables to be prepared for a hasty boiling after the return from the service; preserves and canned fruits to be brought from the cellar, placed into glass dishes and set in readiness.

At eight-fifteen Phœbe was ready. She wore her favorite blue chambray dress and delighted in the fact that Sunday always brought her the privilege of wearing her hat. The little sailor hat with its narrow ribbon and little bow was certainly not the hat she would have chosen if she might have had that pleasure, but it was the only hat she owned, so was not to be despised. She felt grateful that Aunt Maria allowed her to wear a hat. Many little girls, some smaller than she, came to church every Sunday wearing silk bonnets like their elders!—she felt grateful for her hat—any hat!

Tugging at the elastic under her chin, then smoothing her handkerchief and placing it in her sleeve—she had seen Miss Lee dispose of a handkerchief in that way—she walked to the little green gate and watched the road leading from Greenwald.

Her heart leaped when she saw the teacher come down the long road. She opened the gate to go to meet her, then suddenly stood still. Miss Lee as she appeared in the schoolroom, in white linen dress or trim serge skirt and tailored waist, was attractive enough to cause Phœbe's heart to flutter with admiration a dozen times a day; but Miss Lee in Sunday morning church attire was so irresistibly sweet that the vision sent the little girl's heart pounding and caused a strange shyness to possess her. The semi-tailored dress of dark blue taffeta, the sheer white collar, the small black hat with its white wings, the silver coin purse in the gloved hand— no detail escaped the keen eyes of the child. She looked down at her cotton dress—it had seemed so pretty just a moment ago. But, of course, such dresses and gloves and hats were for grown-ups! "But just you wait," she thought, "when I grow up I'll look like that, too, see if I don't!"

Miss Lee, smiling, never knew the depths she stirred in the heart of the little girl.

"Am I late, Phœbe?"

"Ach, no. Just on time. Pop, he went a'ready, though. He goes early still to open the meeting-house. We'll go right away, as soon as Aunt Maria locks up. But what for did you bring a pocketbook?"

"For the offering."

"Offering?"

"The church offering, Phœbe. Surely you know what that is if you go to church every Sunday. Don't you have collection plates or baskets passed about in your church for everybody to put their offerings on them?"

"Why, no, we don't have that in our church! What for do they do that in any church?"

"To pay the preachers' salaries and——"

"Goodness," Phœbe laughed, "it would take a vonderful lot to pay all the preachers that preach at our church. Sometimes three or four preach at one meeting. They have to work week-days and get their money just like other men do. Men come around to the house sometimes for money for the poor, and when the meeting-house needs a new roof or something like that, everybody helps to pay for it, but we don't take no collections in church, like you say. That's a funny way——"

The appearance of Maria Metz prevented further discussion of church collections. With a large, fringed shawl pinned over her plain gray dress and a stiff black silk bonnet tied under her chin, she was ready for church. She was putting the big iron key of the kitchen door into a deep pocket of her full skirt as she came down the walk.

"That way, now we're ready," she said affably. "I guess you're Phœbe's teacher, ain't? I see you go past still."

"Yes. I am very glad to meet you, Miss Metz. It is very kind of you to invite me to go with you."

"Ach, that's nothing. You're welcome enough. We always have much company when church is on the hill. This is a nice day, so I guess church will be full. I hope so, anyway, for I got ready for company for dinner. But how do you like Greenwald?"

"Very well, indeed. It is beautiful here."

"Ain't! But I guess it's different from Phildelphy. I was there once, in the Centennial, and it was so full everywheres. I like the country best. Can't anything beat this now, can it?"

They reached the summit of the hill and paused.

"No," said Miss Lee, "this is hard to beat. I love the view from this hill."

"Ain't now"—Aunt Maria smiled in approval—"this here is about the nicest spot around Greenwald. There's the town so plain you could almost count the houses, only the trees get in the road. And there's the reservoir with the white fence around, and the farms and the pretty country around them—it's a pretty place."

36

"I like this hill," said Phœbe. "When I grow up I'm goin' to have a farm on this hill, when I'm married, I mean."

"That's too far off yet, Phœbe," said her aunt. "You must eat bread and butter yet a while before you think of such things."

"Anyhow, I changed my mind. I'm not goin' to live in the country when I grow up; I'm going to be a fine lady and live in the city."

"Phœbe, stop that dumb talk, now!" reproved her aunt sternly. "You turn round and walk up the hill. We'll go on now, Miss Lee. Mebbe you'd like to go on the graveyard a little?"

"I don't mind."

"Then come." Aunt Maria led the way, past the low brick meeting-house, through the gateway into the old burial ground. They wandered among the marble slabs and read the inscriptions, some half obliterated by years of mountain storms, others freshly carved.

"The epitaphs are interesting," said Miss Lee.

"What's them?" asked Phœbe.

"The verses on the tombstones. Here is one"—she read the inscription on the base of a narrow gray stone—"'After life's fitful fever she sleeps well.'"

"Ach," Aunt Maria said tartly, "I guess her man knowed why he put that on. That poor woman had three husbands and eleven children, so I guess she had fitful fever enough."

Phœbe laughed loud as she saw the smile on the face of her teacher, but next moment she sobered under the chiding of Aunt Maria. "Phœbe, now you keep quiet! Abody don't laugh and act so on a graveyard!"

"Ugh," the child said a moment later, "Miss Lee, just read this one. It always gives me shivers when I read it still.

"'Remember, man, as you pass by,
What you are now that once was I.
What I am now that you will be;
Prepare for death and follow me.'"

"That is rather startling," said Miss Lee.

Phœbe smiled and asked, "Don't you think this is a pretty graveyard?"

"Yes. How well cared for the graves are. Not a weed on most of them."

"Well," Aunt Maria explained, "the people who have dead here mostly take care of the graves. We come up every two weeks or so and sometimes we bring a hoe and fix our graves up nice and even. But some people are too lazy to keep the graves clean. I hoed some pig-ears out a few graves last week; I was ashamed of 'em, even if the graves didn't belong to us."

In the corner near the road the aunt stopped before a plain gray boulder.

"Phœbe's mom," she said, pointing to the inscription.

"PHŒBE
beloved wife of
Jacob Metz
aged twenty-two years
and one month.
Souls of the righteous
are in the hand of God."

"I'm glad," said the child as they stood by her mother's grave, "that they put that last on, for when I come here still I like to know that my mom ain't under all this dirt but that she's up in the Good Place like it says there."

Miss Lee clasped the little hand in hers—what words were adequate to express her feeling for the motherless child!

"Come on," Maria Metz said crisply, "or we'll be late." But Miss Lee read in the brusqueness a strong feeling of sorrow for the child.

Silently the three walked through the green aisles of the old graveyard, Aunt Maria leading the way, alone; Phœbe's hand still in the hand of her teacher.

To Miss Lee, whose hours of public worship had hitherto been spent in an Episcopal church in Philadelphia, the extreme plainness of the meeting-house on the hill brought a sense of acute wonderment. The contrast was so marked. There, in the city, was the large, high-vaulted church whose in-streaming light was softened by exquisite stained windows and revealed each detail of construction and color harmoniously consistent. Here, in the country, was the square, low-ceilinged meeting-house through whose open windows the glaring light relentlessly intensified the whiteness of the walls and revealed more plainly each flaw and knot in the unpainted pine benches. Yet the meeting-house on the hill was strangely, strongly representative of the frank, honest, unpretentious people who worshipped there, and after the first wave of surprise a feeling of interest and reverence held her.

It was a unique sight for the city girl. The rows of white-capped women were separated from the rows of bearded men by a low partition built midway down the body of the church. Each sex entered the meeting-house through a different door and sat in its apportioned half of the building. On each side of the room rows of black hooks were set into the walls. On these hooks the sisters hung their bonnets and the shawls and the brethren placed their hats and overcoats during the service.

The preachers, varying in number from two to six, sat before a long table in the front part of the meeting-house. When the duty of preaching devolved upon one of them he simply rose from his seat and delivered his message.

As Aunt Maria and her two followers took their seats on a bench near the front of the church a preacher rose.

"Let us join in singing—has any one a choice?"

Miss Lee started as a woman's voice answered, "Number one hundred forty-seven." However, her surprise merged into other emotions as the old hymn rose in the low-ceilinged room. There was no accompaniment of any musical instrument, just a harmonious blending of the deep-toned voices of the brethren with the sweet voices of the sisters. The music swelled in full, deliberate rhythm, its calm earnestness bearing witness to the fact that every word of the hymn was uttered in a spirit of worship.

Maria Metz sang very softly, but Phœbe's young voice rose clearly in the familiar words, "Jesus, Lover of my soul."

Miss Lee listened a moment to the sweet voice of the child by her side, then she, too, joined in the singing—feeling the words, as she had never before felt them, to be the true expression of millions of mortals who have sung, are singing, and shall continue to sing them.

When the hymn was ended another preacher arose and opened the service with a few remarks, then asked all to kneel in prayer.

Every one—men, women, children—turned and knelt upon the bare floor while the preacher's voice rose in a simple prayer. As the Amen fell from his lips Miss Lee started to rise, but Phœbe laid a restraining hand upon her and whispered, "There's yet one."

For a moment there was silence in the meeting-house. Then the voice of another preacher rose in the universal prayer, "Our Father, which art in heaven." Every extemporaneous prayer in the Church of the Brethren is complemented by the model prayer the Master taught His disciples.

There was another hymn, reading of the Scriptures, and then the sermon proper was preached.

Aunt Maria nodded approvingly as the preacher read, "Whose adorning let it not be that outward adorning of plaiting the hair, and of wearing of gold, or of putting on of apparel; but let it be the hidden man of the heart, in that which is not corruptible, even the ornament of a meek and quiet spirit, which is in the sight of God of great price."

"You listen good now to what the preacher says," the woman whispered to Phœbe.

The child looked Up solemnly at her aunt, about her at the many white-capped women, then up at Miss Lee's pretty hat with its white Mercury wings—she was endeavoring to justify the pleasure and beauty her aunt pronounced vanity. Was Miss Lee really wicked when she wore clothes like that? Surely, no! After a few moments the child sighed, folded her hands and looked steadfastly at the tall bearded man who was preaching.

The clergy among these plain sects receive no remuneration for their preaching. With them the mercenary and the pecuniary are ever distinct from the religious. Six days in the week the preacher follows the plow or works at some other worthy occupation; upon the seventh day he preaches the Gospel. There is, therefore, no elaborate preparation for the sermon; the preacher has abundant faith in the old admonition, "Take no thought how or what ye shall speak, for it shall be given you in that same hour what ye shall speak, for it is not ye that speak but the spirit of the Father that speaketh in you." Thus it is that, while the sermons usually lack the blandishments of fine rhetoric and the rhythmic ease arising from oratorical ability, they seldom fail in deep sincerity and directness of appeal.

The one who delivered the message that September morning told of the joy of those who have overcome the desire for the vanities of the world, extolled the virtue of a simple life, till Miss Lee felt convinced that there must be something real in a religion that could hold its followers to so simple, wholesome a life.

She looked about, at the serried rows of white-capped women—how gentle and calm they appeared in their white caps and plain dresses; she looked across the partition at the lines of men—how strong and honest their faces were; and the children—she had never before seen so many children at a church service—would they all, in time, wear the garb of their people and enter the church of their parents? The child at her side—vivacious, untiring, responsive Phœbe—would she, too, wear the plain dress some day and live the quiet life of her people?

The eagerness of the child's face as Miss Lee looked at her denoted intense interest in the sermon, but none could know the real cause of that eagerness.

"I won't, I just won't dress plain!" she was thinking. "Anyway, not till I'm old like Aunt Maria. I want to look like Miss Lee when I grow up. And that preacher just said that it ain't good to plait the hair, I mean he read it out the Bible. Mebbe now

Aunt Maria will leave me have curls. I hope she heard him say that."

She sighed in relief as the sermon was concluded and the next preacher rose and added a few remarks. When the third man rose to add his few remarks Phœbe looked up at Miss Lee and whispered, "Guess he's the last one once!"

Miss Lee smiled. The service was rather long, but it was drawing to a close. There was another prayer, another hymn and the service ended.

Immediately the white-capped women rose and began to bestow upon each other the holy kiss; upon the opposite side of the church the brethren greeted each other in like fashion. Everywhere there were greetings and profferings of dinner invitations.

Maria Metz and her brother did not fail in their duty. In a few minutes they had invited a goodly number to make the gray farmhouse their stopping-place. Then Aunt Maria hurried home, eager to prepare for her guests. Soon the Metz barnyard was filled with carriages and automobiles and the gray house resounded with happy voices. Some of the women helped Maria in the kitchen, others wandered about in the old-fashioned garden, where dahlias, sweet alyssum, marigolds, ladies' breastpin and snapdragons still bloomed in the bright September sunshine.

Miss Lee, guided by Phœbe, examined every nook of the big garden, peered into the deserted wren-house and listened to the child's story of the six baby wrens reared in the box that summer. Finally Phœbe suggested sitting on a bench half screened by rose-bushes and honeysuckle. There, in that green spot, Miss Lee tactfully coaxed the child to unfold her charming personality, all serenely unconscious of the fact that inside the gray house the white-capped women were discussing the new teacher as they prepared the dinner.

"She seems vonderful nice and common," volunteered Aunt Maria. "Not stuck up, for a Phildelphy lady."

"Well, why should she be stuck up?" argued one. "Ain't she just Mollie Stern's cousin? Course, Mollie's nice, but nothing tony."

"Anyhow, the children all like her," spoke up another woman. "My Enos learns good this year."

"I guess she's all right," said another, "but Amande, my sister, says that she's after her Lizzie all the time for the way she talks. The teacher tells her all the time not to talk so funny, not to get her t's and d's and her v's and w's mixed. Goodness knows, them letters is near enough alike to get them mixed sometimes. I mix them myself. Manda don't want her Lizzie made high-toned, for then nothing will be good enough for her any more."

41

"Ach, I guess Miss Lee won't do that," said Aunt Maria. "I know I'm glad the teacher ain't the kind to put on airs. When I heard they put in a teacher from Phildelphy I was afraid she'd be the kind to teach the children a lot of dumb notions and that Phœbe would be spoiled—— Here, Sister Minnich, is the holder for that pan. I guess the ham is fried enough. Yes, ain't the chicken smells good! I roasted it yesterday, so it needs just a good heating to-day."

"Shall I take the sweet potatoes off, Maria?"

"Yes, they're brown enough, and the coffee's about done, and plenty of it, too."

"And it smells good, too," chorused several women.

"It's just twenty-eight cent coffee; I get it in Greenwald. I guess the things can be put out now. Call the men, Susan."

In quick order the long table in the dining-room—used only upon occasions like this—was filled with smoking, savory dishes, the men called from the porches and yard and everybody, except the two women who helped Aunt Maria to serve, seated about the board. All heads were bowed while one of the brethren said a long grace and then the feast began.

True to the standards set by the majority of the Pennsylvania Dutch, the meal was fit for the finest. There was no attempt to serve it according to the rules of the latest book of etiquette. All the food was placed upon the table and each one helped herself and himself and passed the dish to the nearest neighbor. Occasionally the services of the three women were required to bring in water, bread or coffee, or to replenish the dishes and platters. Everybody was in good humor, especially when one of the brethren suddenly found himself with a platter of chicken in one hand and a pitcher of gravy in the other.

"Hold on, here!" he said laughingly, "it's coming both ways. I can't manage it."

"Now, Isaac," chided one of the women, "you went and started the gravy the wrong way around. And here, Elam, start that apple-butter round once. Maria always has such good apple-butter."

Miss Lee's ready adaptability proved a valuable asset that day. Everybody was so cordial and friendly that, although she was the only woman without the white cap, there was no shadow of any holier-than-thou spirit. She was accepted as a friend; as a lady from Philadelphia she became invested with a charm and interest which the frank country people did not try to conceal. They spoke freely to her of her work in the school, inquired about the children

42

and listened with interest as she answered their questions about her home city.

When the dinner was ended heads were bowed again and thanks rendered to God for the blessings received. Then the men went outdoors, where the beehives, poultry houses, barns and orchards of the farm afforded several hours of inspection and discussion.

Indoors some of the women began to wash dishes while Aunt Maria and her helpers ate their belated dinner; others went to the sitting-room and entertained themselves by rocking and talking or looking at the pictures in the big red plush album which lay upon a small table.

Later, when everything was once more in order in the big kitchen, Maria stood in the doorway of the sitting-room.

"Now," she said, "I guess we better go up-stairs and see the rugs before the men come in. Susan said she wants to see my new rugs once when she comes. So come on, everybody that wants to."

"You come," Phœbe invited Miss Lee. "I'll show you some of the things in my chest."

Maria led the way to the spare-room on the second floor, a large square room furnished in old-fashioned country style: a rag carpet, rag rugs, heavy black walnut bureau and wash-stand, the latter with an antique bowl and pitcher of pink and white, and a splasher of white linen outlined in turkey red cotton. A framed cross-stitch sampler hung on the wall; four cane-seated chairs and a great wooden chest completed the furnishing of the room.

The chest became the centre of attraction as Aunt Maria opened it and began to show the hooked rugs she had made.

Phœbe waited until her teacher had seen and admired several, then she tugged at the silk sleeve ever so gently and whispered, "D'ye want to see some of the things I made?"

Miss Lee smiled and nodded and the two stole away to the child's room.

Phœbe closed the door.

"This is my room and this is my Hope Chest," she said proudly.

Among many of the Pennsylvania Dutch the Hope Chest has long been considered an important part of a girl's belongings. During her early childhood a large chest is secured and the stocking of it becomes a pleasant duty. Into it are laid the girl's discarded infant clothes; patchwork quilts and comfortables pieced by herself or by some fond grandmother or mother or aunt; homespun sheets and towels that have been handed down from other generations; ginghams, linens and minor household articles that might be useful in her own home. When the girl leaves the old nest for one of her own building the Hope Chest goes with her as a valuable portion of her dowry.

"Hope Chest," echoed Miss Lee. "Do you have a Hope Chest?"

"Ach, yes, long already! Aunt Maria says it's for when I grow up and get married and live in my own home, but I—why, I don't know at all yet if I want to get married. When I say that to her she says still that I can be glad I have the chest anyhow, for old maids need covers and aprons and things too."

"You dear child," Miss Lee said, laughing, "you do say the funniest things!"

"But"—Phœbe raised her flushed face—"you ain't laughing at me to make fun?"

"Oh, Phœbe, I love you too much for that. It's just that you are different."

"Ach, but I'm glad! And that's why I want to show you my things."

She opened the lid of her chest and brought out a quilt, then another, and another.

"This is all mine. And I finished another one this summer that Aunt Maria is going to quilt this fall yet. Then I'll have nine already. Ain't—isn't that a lot?"

"Yes, indeed," laughed the teacher. "Just nine more than I have."

"Why"—Phœbe stared in surprise—"don't you have quilts in your Hope Chest?"

"I haven't even the Hope Chest."

"No Hope Chest! Now, that's funny! I thought every girl that could have a chest for the money had a Hope Chest!"

"I never heard of a Hope Chest before I came to Greenwald."

"Now don't it beat all!" The child was very serious. "We ain't at all like other people, I believe. I wonder why we are so different from you people. Oh, I know we talk different from you, and mostly look different from you and I guess we do things a lot different from you—do you think, Miss Lee, oh, do you think that I could ever get like you?"

"Yes——" Miss Lee showed hesitancy.

"For sure?" Phœbe asked, quick to note the slight delay in the answer.

"Yes, I am sure you could, dear. You can learn to dress, speak and act as people do in the great cities—but are you sure that you want to do so?"

"Want to! Why, I want to so bad that it hurts! I don't want to

44

just go to country school and Greenwald High School and then live on a farm all the rest of my life and never get anywhere but to the store in Greenwald, to Lancaster several times a year, and to church every Sunday. I want to do some things other people in the other parts of the country do, that's what I want. I'd like best of all to be a great singer and to look and dress and talk like you. I can sing good, pop says I can."

"I have noticed you have a sweet voice."

"Ain't!" The child's voice rang with gladness. "I'm so glad I have. And David, he's glad too, for he says that he thinks it's a gift from God to have a voice that can sing as nice as the birds. David and Phares are just like my brothers. David's mom is awful nice. I like her"—she whispered—"I like her almost better than my Aunt Maria because she's so—ach, you know what I mean! She's so much like my own mom would be. I like David better than Phares, too, because Phares bosses me too much and he is wonderful strict and thinks everything is bad or foolish. He preaches a lot. He says it's bad to be a big singer and sing for the people and get money for it, in oprays, he means—is it?"

Miss Lee was startled by the ambition of the child before her and amazed at the determination revealed in her young pupil. Before she could answer wisely Phœbe went on:

"Now David says still I could be a big opray singer some day mebbe, and he don't think it's bad. I think still that singin' is about like havin' curls—if God don't want you to use your singin' and your curls what did He give 'em to you for?"

Much to the teacher's relief she was spared the difficulty of answering the child. The aunt was bringing the visitors to Phœbe's room.

"Come in and see my things," Phœbe invited cordially, as though curls and operatic careers had never troubled her. In the excitement of displaying her quilts she apparently forgot the vital problems she had so lately discussed. But Miss Lee made a mental comment as she stood apart and watched the child among the white-capped women, "That little girl will do things before she settles into the simple, monotonous life these women lead."

CHAPTER VI
THE PRIMA DONNA OF THE ATTIC

"Aunt Maria, dare I go without sewing just this one Saturday?"

It was Saturday afternoon in early October. All the week-end work of the farmhouse was done: the walks and porches scrubbed, the entire house cleaned, the shelves in the cellar filled with pies and cakes. Maria Metz stood by the wooden frame in which she had sewed Phœbe's latest quilt and chalked lines and half-moons upon the calico, preliminary to the actual work of quilting.

Phœbe's face was eloquent as her aunt turned and looked down.

"Why?" asked the woman calmly.

"Ach, because it's my birthday, eleven I am to-day. And pop's going to bring me new hair-ribbons from Greenwald, pretty blue ones, I asked him to bring, and nice and wide"—she opened her hands in imaginary picturing of the width of the new ribbons—"but most of all," she hastened to add as she saw an expression of displeasure on her aunt's face, "I'd like to have a party all to myself. I thought that so long as you're going to have women in to help you quilt, and that is like a party, only you don't call it so, why I could have a party for me alone. I'd like to play all afternoon instead of sewing first like I do still. Dare I, I mean may I?"—in conscientious endeavor to speak as Miss Lee was trying to teach her.

Maria Metz smiled at the little girl's idea of a party, and after a moment's hesitation replied, "Ach, yes well, Phœbe, I don't care."

"In the garret, oh, dare I go in the garret and play?" she asked excitedly.

"Yes, I guess. If you put everything away nice when you are done playin'."

"I will."

She started off gleefully.

"And be careful of the steps. I'm always afraid you'll fall down when you go up there, the steps are so narrow."

"Ach, I won't fall. I'll be careful. I'll play a while and then shall I help to quilt?" she offered magnanimously in return for the privilege of playing in the garret.

"No, I don't need you. But you can quilt nice, too. The last time you took littler stitches than Lizzie from the Home, but she don't see so good. But you needn't help to-day, for so many can't get round the frame good. Phares's mom and David's mom and Lyddy and Granny Hogendobler and Susan are comin', and that's enough for one quilt. You go play."

In a moment Phœbe was off, up the broad stairs to the second floor. There she paused for breath—"Oh, it's like going to a castle somewhere in a strange country, goin' to the garret! I'm always a little scared at first, goin' to the garret."

With a laugh she turned into a small room, opened a latched door, closed it securely behind her, and stood upon the lower step of the attic stairs. She looked about a moment. Above her were the stained rafters of the attic, where a dim light invested it with a strange, half fearful interest.

"Ach, now, don't be a baby," she admonished herself. "Go right up the stairs. You're a queen—no, I know!—You're a primer donner going up the platform steps to sing!"

With that helpful delusion she started bravely up the stairs and never paused until she reached the top step. She ran to a small window and threw it wide open so that the October sunshine could stream in and make the place less ghostly.

"Now it's fine up here," she cried. "And I dare—I may—talk to myself all I want. Aunt Maria says it's simple to talk to yourself, but goodness, when abody has no other boys or girls to talk to half the time like I don't, what else can abody do but talk to your own self? Anyhow, I'm up here now and dare talk out loud all I want. I'll hunt first for robbers."

She ran about the big attic, peered behind every old trunk and box, even inside an old yellow cupboard, though she knew it was filled with old school-books and older hymn-books.

"Not a robber here, less he's back under the eaves."

She crept into the low nook under the slanting roof but found nothing more exciting than a spider. "Huh, it's no fun hunting for robbers. Guess I'll spin a while."

With quick variability she drew a low stool near an old spinning-wheel, placed her foot on the slender treadle and twisted the golden flax in imitation of the way Aunt Maria had once taught her.

"I'll weave a new dress for myself—oh, goody!" she cried, springing from the stool. "Now I know what I'll do! I'll dress up in the old clothes in that old trunk! That'll be the very best party I can have."

She skipped to a far corner of the attic, where a long, leather-covered trunk stood among some boxes. In a moment the clasps were unfastened, the lid raised, a protecting cloth lifted from the top and the contents of the trunk exposed.

The child, kneeling before the trunk, clasped her hands and uttered an ecstatic, "Oh, I'll be a primer donner now! I remember there used to be a wonderful fine dress in here somewhere."

With childish feverishness, yet with tenderness and

47

reverence for the relics of a long dead past, she lifted the old garments from the trunk.

"The baby clothes my mom wore—my mother, Miss Lee always says, and I like that name better, too. My, but they're little! Such tweeny, weeny sleeves! I wonder how a baby ever got into anything so tiny. I bet she was cunning—Miss Lee says babies are cunning. And here's the dress and cap and a pair of white woolen stockings I wore. Aunt Maria told me so the last time we cleaned house and I helped to carry all these things down-stairs and hang them out in the air so they don't spoil here in the trunk all locked up tight. I wish I could see how I looked when I wore these things. I wonder if I was a nice baby—but, ach, all babies are nice. I could squeeze every one I see, only when they're not clean I'd want to wash 'em first. And here's my mom—mother's wedding dress, a gray silk one. Ain't it too bad, now, it's going in holes! And this satin jacket Aunt Maria said my grandpap wore at his wedding; it has a silver buckle at the neck in front. And next comes the dress I like. It was my mother's mother's, and it's awful old. But I think it's fine, with the little pink rosebuds and the lace shawl round the neck and the long skirt. That's the dress I must wear now to play I'm a primer donner."

She held out the old-fashioned pink-sprigged muslin, yellowed with age, yet possessing the charm of old, well-preserved garments. The short, puffed sleeves, lace fichu and full, puffed skirt proclaimed it of a bygone generation.

"It's pretty," the child exulted as she shook out the soft folds. "Guess I can slip it on over my other dress, it's plenty big. It must button in the front, for that's the way the lace shawl goes. Um—it's long"—she looked down as she fastened the last little button. "Oh, I know! I'll tuck it up in the front and leave the long back for a trail! How's that, I wonder."

She unearthed an old mirror, hung it on a nail in the wall and surveyed herself in the glass.

"Um, I don't look so bad—but my hair ain't right. I don't know how primer donners wear their hair, but I know they don't wear it in two plaits like mine."

She pulled the narrow brown ribbons from her braids, opened the braids and shook her head vigorously until her curls tumbled about her head and over her shoulders. Then she knotted the two ribbons together and bound them across her hair in a fillet, tying them in a bow under her flowing curls.

"Now, I guess it's as good as I can fix it. I wish Miss Lee could see me now. I wish most of all my mom—mother could see me. Mebbe she'd say, 'Precious child,' like they say in stories, and

48

then I'd say back, 'Mother dear, mother dear'"—she lingered over the words—"'Mother dear.' But mebbe she is saying that to me right now, seeing it's my birthday. I'll make believe so, anyhow."

She was silent for a moment, a puzzled expression on her face.

"I just don't see," she spoke aloud suddenly, "I don't see why I shouldn't make believe I have a mother, just adopt one like people do children sometimes. Aunt Maria says it's a risk to adopt some one's child, but I don't see that it would be a risk to adopt a mother. Let me see now—of all the women I know, who do I want to adopt? Not Mary Warner's mom—she's stylish and wears nice dresses, but I don't think I'd like her to keep. Not Granny Hogendobler, though she's nice and I like her a lot, a whole lot, and I wish her Nason would come back, but I don't see how I could take her for my mother; she's too old and she don't wear a white cap and my mother did, so I must take one that does. I don't want Phares's mom, either. Now, David's mom I like—yes, I like her. Most everybody calls her Aunty Bab and I'm just goin' to ask her if I dare call her Mother Bab! Mother Bab—I like that vonderful much! And I like her. When we go over to her house she's so nice and talks to me kind and the last time I was there she kissed me and said what pretty hair I got. Yes, I want David's mom for mine. I guess he won't care. He always gives me apples and chestnuts and things and he shows me birds' nests and I think he'll leave me have his mom, so long as he can have her too. I'll ask him once when I see him. I wonder who's goin' on the road to Greenwald."

She gathered up her long skirt and stepped grandly across the bare floor of the attic. As she stood by the window a boyish whistle floated up to her. She leaned over the narrow sill and peered through the evergreen trees at the road.

"That's David now, I bet! Sounds like his whistle. Oo-oo, David," she called as the boy came swinging down the road.

"Hello, Phœbe. Where you at?"

He turned in at the gate and looked around.

"Whew," he whistled as he glanced up and saw her at the little window of the attic. "What you doing up there?"

"Playin' primer donner. I just look something grand. Wait, I'll come down."

"Sure, come on down and let me see you. I'm going to hang around a while. Mom's here quilting, ain't she?"

"Sh!" Phœbe raised a warning finger, then placed her hands to her mouth to shut the sound of her voice from the people in the gray house. "You sneak round to the kitchen door, to the back one, so they can't hear you, and I'll come down. Aunt Maria mightn't like my hair and dress, and I don't want to make her cross on my birthday. Be careful, don't make no noise."

"Ha," laughed the boy. "Bet you're sneaking things, you little rascal."

Phœbe lifted her finger, shook her head, then smiled and turned from the window. She tiptoed down the dark attic stairs, then down the narrow back stairs to the kitchen and slipped quietly to the little porch at the very rear of the house.

"Gee whiz!" exclaimed David. "You're a swell in that dress!"

"Ain't I—I mean am I—ach, David, it's hard sometimes to talk like Miss Lee says we should."

"Where'd you get the dress, Phœbe?"

"Up in the garret. Aunt Maria said I dare go up and play 'cause it's my birthday."

"Hold on, that's just what I came for, to pull your ears."

"No you don't," she said crossly. "No you don't, David Eby, pull my ears." She clapped a hand upon each ear.

"Then I'll pull a curl," he said and suited the action to the word. He took one of the long light curls and pulled it gently, yet with a brusque show of savagery and strength—"One, two, three, four, five, six, seven, eight, nine, ten, eleven, and one to make you grow. Now who says I can't celebrate your birthday!"

"You're mean, awful mean, David Eby!" She tossed her head in anger. But a moment later she relented as she saw him smile. "Ach," she said in friendly tone, "I don't care if you pull my curls. It didn't hurt anyhow. You can't do it again for a whole year. But don't you think I look like a primer donner, David?"

"Oh, say it right! How can you expect to ever be what you can't pronounce? It's pri-ma-don-na."

"Pri-ma-don-na," she repeated, shaking her curls at every syllable. "Do I look like a prima donna?"

"Yes, all but your face."

"My face—why"—she faltered—"what's wrong with my face? Ain't it pretty enough to be a prima donna?"

"Funny kid," he laughed. "Your face is good enough for a prima donna, but to be a real prima donna you must fix it up with cold cream, paint and powder."

"Powder!" she echoed in amazement. "Not the kind you put in guns?"

"Gee, no! It's white stuff—looks like flour; mebbe it is flour fixed up with perfume. Mary Warner had some at school last week and showed some of the girls at recess how to put it on. I was behind a tree and saw them but they didn't see me."

"I thought some of the girls looked pale—so that was what

50

made them look so white! But how do you know all about fixing up to be a prima donna? Where did you learn?" She looked at him admiringly, justly appreciating his superior knowledge.

"Oh, when I had the mumps last winter I used to read the papers every day, clean through. There was a column called the 'Hints to Beauty' column, and sometimes I read it just for fun, it was so funny. It told about fixing up the face and mentioned a famous singer and some other people who always looked beautiful because they knew how to fix their faces to keep looking young. But I wouldn't like to see any one I like fix their faces like it said, for all that stuff——"

"But do you think all prima donnas put such things on their faces?" she interrupted him.

"Guess so."

"What was it, Davie?"

"Cold cream, paint, powder—here, where are you going?" he asked as she started for the door.

"I'll be out in a minute; you wait here for me."

"Cold cream, paint, powder," she repeated as she closed the door and left David outside. "Cream's all in the cellar." She took a pewter tablespoon from a drawer, opened a latched door in the kitchen and went noiselessly down the steps to the cellar. There she lifted the lid from a large earthen jar, dipped a spoonful of thick cream from the jar, and began to rub it on her cheeks.

"That's cold cream, anyhow," she said to herself. "It certainly is cold. Ach, I don't like the feel of it on my face; it's too sticky and wet." But she rubbed valiantly until the spoonful was used and her face glowed.

"Now paint, red paint—I don't dare use the kind you put on houses, for that's too hard to get off; let's see—I guess red-beet juice will do."

She stooped to the cool, earthen floor, lifted the cover from a crock of pickled beets, dipped the spoon into the juice and began to rub the colored liquid upon her glowing cheeks.

"If I only had a looking-glass, then I could see just where to put it on. But I don't dare to carry the juice up the steps, for if I spilled some just after Aunt Maria has them scrubbed for Sunday she'd be cross."

She applied the red juice by guesswork, with the inevitable result that her ears, chin, and nose were stained as deeply as her cheeks.

"Now the powder, then I'm through."

She tiptoed up to the kitchen again, took a handful of flour from the bin and rubbed it upon her face.

51

"Ugh, um," she sputtered, as some of the flour flew into her eyes and nostrils. "I guess that was too thick!" Then she knelt on a chair and looked into the small mirror that hung in the kitchen. She exclaimed in horror and disappointment at the vision that met her gaze.

"Why, I don't like that! I look awful! I'll rub off some of the flour. I have blotches all over my face. Do all prima donnas look this way, I wonder. But David knows, I guess. I'll ask him if I did it right."

She grabbed one end of the kitchen towel and disposed of some of the superfluous flour, then, still doubtful of her appearance, opened the door to the porch where the boy waited for her.

"Do I look——" she began, but David burst into hilarious laughter.

"Oh, oh," he held his sides and laughed. "Oh, your face——"

"Don't you laugh at me, David Eby! Don't you dare laugh!"

She was deeply hurt at his unseemly behavior, but the deluge was only beginning! The sound of David's laughter and Phœbe's raised voice reached the front room where the quilting party was in progress.

"Sounds like somebody on the back porch," said Aunt Maria. "Guess I better go and see. With so many tramps around always abody can't be too careful."

The sight that met Maria Metz's eyes as she opened the back door left her speechless. Phœbe turned and the two looked at each other in silence for a few long moments.

"Don't scold her," David said, sobered by the sudden appearance of the woman and frightened for Phœbe—Aunt Maria could be stern, he knew. "Don't scold her. I told her to do it."

"You did not, David; don't you tell lies for me! You just told me how to do it and I went and done it myself. I'm playing prima donna, Aunt Maria," she explained, though she knew it was a futile attempt at justification. "I'm playing I'm a big singer, so I had to fix up in this dress and put my hair down this way and fix my face."

"Great singer—march in here!" The woman had fully regained her voice. "It's a bad girl you are! To think of your making such a monkey of yourself when I leave you go up in the garret to play! This ends playing in the garret. Next Saturday you sew! Ach, yes, you just come in," she commanded, for Phœbe hung back as they entered the house. "You come right in here and let all the women see how nice you play when I leave you go up in the garret instead of make you sew. This here's the tramp I found," she

52

announced as she led her into the room where the women sat around the quilting frame and quilted.

"What!" several of them exclaimed as they turned from their sewing and looked at the child. Granny Hogendobler and David Eby's mother, however, smiled.

"What's on your face?" asked one woman sternly.

Phœbe hung her head, abashed.

"That's how nice she plays when I leave her go up on the garret and have a nice time instead of making her sew like she always has to Saturdays," Aunt Maria said in sharp tones which told the child all too plainly of the displeasure she had caused.

"I didn't mean," Phœbe looked up contritely, "I didn't mean to be bad and make you cross. I was just playing I was a big singer and I put cold cream and paint and powder on my face——"

"Cream!"

"Paint!"

"Powder!"

The shrill staccato words of the women set the child trembling.

"But—but," she faltered, "it'll all wash off." She gave a convincing nod of her head and rubbed a hand ruefully across the grotesquely decorated cheek. "It's just cream and red-beet juice and flour."

"Did I ever!" exclaimed the mother of Phares Eby.

"I-to-goodness!" laughed Granny Hogendobler.

"Vanity, vanity, all is vanity," quoted one of the other women.

"Come here, Phœbe," said the mother of David Eby, and that woman, a thin, alert little person with tender, kindly eyes, drew the unhappy little girl to her. "You poor, precious child," she said, "it's a shame for us all to sit here and look at you as if we wanted to eat you. You've just been playing, haven't you?" She turned to the other women. "Why, Maria, Susan, I remember just as well as if it were only yesterday how we used to rub our cheeks with rough mullein leaves to make them red for Love Feast, don't you remember?"

Aunt Maria's cheeks grew pink. "Ach, Barbara, mebbe we did that when we were young and foolish, but we didn't act like this."

"Not much different, I guess," said Phœbe's champion with a smile. "Only we forget it now. Phœbe is just like we were once and she'll get over it like we did. Let her play; she'll soon be too old to want to play or to know how. She ain't a bad child, just full of life and likes to do things other people don't think of doing."

"She, surely does," said Aunt Maria curtly, ill pleased by the woman's words. "Where that child gets all her notions from I'd like to know. It's something new every day."

"She'll be all right when she gets older," said David's mother.

"Be sure, yes," agreed Granny Hogendobler; "it don't do to be too strict."

"Mebbe so," said the other women, with various shades of understanding in their words.

Phœbe looked gratefully into the face of Granny Hogendobler, then she turned to David's mother and spoke to her as though there were no others present in the room.

"You know, don't you, how little girls like to play? You called me precious child just like she would——"

"She would," repeated Aunt Maria. "What do you mean?"

"I mean my mother," she explained and turned again to her champion. "I was just thinking this after on the garret that I'd like you for my mother, to adopt you for it like people do with children when they have none and want some. I hear lots of people call you Aunty Bab—dare I call you Mother Bab?"

The woman laid a hand on the child's tumbled hair. Her voice trembled as she answered, "Yes, Phœbe, you can call me Mother Bab. I have no little girl so you may fill that place. Now ask Aunt Maria if you should wash your face and get fixed right again."

"Shall I, Aunt Maria?"

"Yes. Go get cleaned up. Fold all them clothes right and put 'em in the trunk and put your hair in two plaits again. If you're big enough to do such dumb things you're big enough to comb your hair." And Aunt Maria, peeved and hurt at the child's behavior, went back to her quilting while Phœbe hurried from the room alone.

The child scrubbed the three layers of decoration from her face, trudged up the stairs to the attic, took off the rose-sprigged gown and folded it away—a disconsolate, disillusioned prima donna.

When the attic was once more restored to its orderliness she closed the window and went down-stairs to wrestle with her curls. They were tangled, but ordinarily she would have been able to braid them into some semblance of neatness, but the trying experience of the past moments, the joy of gaining an adopted mother, set her fingers bungling.

"Ach, I can't, I just can't make two braids!" she said at length, ready to burst into tears.

Then she remembered David. "Mebbe he's on the porch yet. I'll go see once."

With the narrow brown ribbons streaming from her hand and a hair-brush tucked under one arm she ran down the stairs. She found David, for once a gloomy figure, on the back porch, just where she had left him.

"David," she said softly, "will you help me?"

"Why"—his face brightened as he looked at her—"you ain't"—he started to say "crying"—"you ain't mad at me for getting you into trouble with Aunt Maria?"

"Ach, no. And I ain't never going to be mad at you now for I just adopted your mom for my mom—mother. She's going to be my Mother Bab; she said so."

"What?"

He knitted his forehead in a puzzled frown. Phœbe explained how kind his mother had been, how she understood what little girls like to do, how she had promised to be Mother Bab.

"You don't care, Davie, you ain't jealous?" she ended anxiously.

"Sure not," he assured her; "I think it's kinda nice, for she thinks you're a dandy. But did they haul you over the coals in there?"

"Yes, a little, all but Granny Hogendobler and your mom— Mother Bab, I mean. Isn't it funny to get a mother when you didn't have one for so long?"

"Guess so."

"But, David, will you help me? I can't fix my hair and Aunt Maria is so mad at me she said I can just fix it myself. The plaits won't come right at all. Will you help me, please?" She asserted her femininity by adding new sweetness to her voice as she asked the uncommon favor.

"Why"—he hesitated, then looked about to see if any one were near to witness what he was about to do—"I don't know if I can. I never braided hair, but I guess I can."

"Be sure you can, David. You braid it just like we braid the daisy stems and the dandelion stems in the fields. You're so handy with them, you can do most anything, I guess."

Spurred by her appreciation of his ability he took the brush and began to brush the tangled hair as she sat on the porch at his feet.

"Gee," he exclaimed as the hair sprang into curls when the brush left it, "your hair's just like gold!"

"And it's curly," she added proudly.

"Sure is. Wouldn't Phares look if he saw it! I told him your hair is prettier than Mary Warner's and he said I was silly to talk about girls' hair."

"I don't want him to see it this way," she said, "for he'd say it's a sin to have curly, pretty hair, even if God made it grow that way! He's awful queer! I wouldn't want him for my adopted brother."

"Guess he'd keep you hopping," laughed David.

"Guess I'd keep him hopping, too," retorted Phœbe, at which the boy laughed.

"Now what do I do?" he asked when all the hair was untangled.

"Part it in the middle and make two plaits."

"Um-uh."

The boy's clumsy fingers fumbled long with the parting; several times the braids twisted and had to be undone, but after a struggle he was able to announce, "There now, you're fixed! Now you're Phœbe Metz, no more prima donna!"

"Thanks, David, for helping me. I feel much better around the head—guess curls would be a nuisance after all."

CHAPTER VII
"WHERE THE BROOK AND RIVER MEET"

When Phœbe adopted Mother Bab she did so with the whole-heartedness and finality characteristic of her blood.

Mother Bab—the name never ceased to thrill the erstwhile motherless girl whose yearning for affection and understanding had been unsatisfied by the matter-of-fact Aunt Maria.

At first Maria Metz did not seem too well pleased with the child's persistent naming of Barbara Eby as Mother Bab; but gradually, as she saw Phœbe's joy in the adoption, the woman acknowledged to herself that another woman was capable of mothering where she had failed.

Phœbe spent many hours in the little house on the hill, learning from Mother Bab many things that made indelible impressions upon her sensitive child-heart, unraveling some of the tangled knots of her soul, stirring anew hopes and aspirations of her being. But there remained one knot to be untangled—she could not understand why the plain dress and white cap existed, she could not reconcile the utter simplicity of dress with the lavish beauty of the birds, flowers—all nature.

"It will come," Mother Bab assured her one day. "You are a little girl now and cannot see into everything. But when you are older you will see how beautiful it is to live simply and plainly."

"But is it necessary, Mother Bab?" the child cried out. "Must I dress like you and Aunt Maria if I want to be good?"

"No, you don't have to. Many people are good without wearing the plain garb. A great many people in the world never heard of the plain sects we have in this section of the country, and there are good people everywhere, I'm sure of that. But it is just as true that each person must find the best way to lead a good life. If you can wear fine clothes and still be good and lead a Christian life, then there is no harm in the pretty clothes. But for me the easiest way to be living right is to live as simply as I can. This is the way for me."

"I'm afraid it's the way for me, too," confessed Phœbe. "I'm vain, awfully vain! I love pretty clothes and I'll never be satisfied till I get 'em—silk dresses, soft, shiny satin ones—ach, I guess I'm vain but I'll have to wait to satisfy my vanity till I'm older, for Aunt Maria is so set against fancy clothes."

It was true, Maria Metz compromised on some matters as Phœbe grew older, but on the question of clothes the older woman was adamant. The child should have comfortable dresses but there would positively be no useless ornaments or adornments, such as wide sashes, abundance of laces, elaborately trimmed ruffles. Fancy hats, jewelry and unconfined curls were also strictly forbidden.

Though Phœbe, even as she grew older, had much time to spend outdoors, there were many tasks about the house and farm she had to perform. The chest was soon filled with quilts and that bugbear was gone from her life. But there was continual scrubbing, baking, mending, and other household tasks to be done, so that much practice caused the girl to develop into a capable little housekeeper. Aunt Maria frankly admitted that Phœbe worked cheerfully and well, a matter she found consoling in the trying hours when Phœbe "wasted time" by playing the low walnut organ in the sitting-room.

During Miss Lee's first term of teaching on the hill she taught her how to play simple exercises and songs and the child, musically inclined, made the most of the meagre knowledge and adeptly improved until she was able to play the hymns in the Gospel Hymn Book and the songs and carols in the old Music Book that had belonged to her mother and always rested on the top of the old low organ.

So the organ became a great solace and joy, an outlet for the intense feelings of desire and hope in her heart. When her voice joined with the sweet tones of the old instrument it seemed to Phœbe as if she were echoing the harmony of the eternal music of all creation. Child though she was, she sang with the joy and sincerity of the true musician. She merely smiled when Aunt Maria characterized her best efforts as "doodling" and rejoiced when her father, Mother Bab or David praised her singing.

In school she progressed rapidly but her interest lagged when, after two years of teaching, Miss Lee resigned her position as teacher of the school on the hill and a new teacher took command. The entire school missed the teacher from Philadelphia, but Phœbe was almost inconsolable. She, especially, appreciated the gain of contact with the teacher she loved and she continued to profit by the remembrance of many things Miss Lee had taught her. The Memory Gems, alone, bore evidence of the change the teacher from the city had wrought in the rural school. Phœbe smiled as she thought how the poems had been sing-songed until Miss Lee taught the children to bring out the meaning of the words.

"Oh, my," she laughed one day as she and David were speaking of school happenings, "do you remember how John Schneider used to say Memory Gems? The day he got up and said, 'Have-you-heard-the-waters-singing-little-May—where-the-willows-green-are-bending-over-the-way—do-you-know-how-low-and-sweet-are-the-words-the-waves-repeat—to-the-pebbles-at-their-feet—night-and-day?'"

David laughed at the girl's droll imitation, the way she sing-songed the verse in the exact manner prevalent in many rural schools.

"And do you remember," he asked, "the day Isaac Hunchberger defined bipeds?"

"Oh, yes! I'll never forget that! It was the day the County Superintendent of Schools came to visit our school and Miss Lee was anxious to have us show off. Isaac showed off, all right, with his 'Bipets are sings vis two lex!' I guess Miss Lee decided that day that the Pennsylvania Dutch is ingrained in our English and hard to get out."

To Phœbe each Memory Gem of her school days became, in truth, a gem stored away for future years. Long after she had outgrown the little rural school scraps of poetry returned to her to rewaken the enthusiasm of childhood and to teach her again to "hear the lark within the songless egg and find the fountain where they wailed, 'Mirage!'"

Phœbe wanted so many things in those school-day years but

she wanted most of all to become like Miss Lee. So earnestly did she try to speak as her teacher taught her that after a time the peculiar idioms and expressions became more infrequent and there was only a delightfully quaint inflection, an occasional phrase, to betray her Pennsylvania Dutch parentage. But in times of stress or excitement she invariably slipped back into the old way and prefaced her exclamations with an expressive "Ach!"

Life on the Metz farm went on in even tenor year in and year out. Maria Metz never changed to any appreciable extent her mode of living or her methods of working, and she tried to teach Phœbe to conform to the same monotonous existence and live as several generations of Metzes had done. But Phœbe was a veritable Evelyn Hope, made of "spirit, fire and dew." The distinctiveness of her personality grew more pronounced as she slipped from childhood into girlhood and Maria Metz needed often to encourage her own heart for the task of rearing into ideal womanhood the daughter of her brother Jacob.

Phœbe had a deep love for nature and this love was fostered by her sturdy farmer-father. As she followed him about the fields he taught her the names of wild flowers, told her the nesting haunts of birds, initiated her into the circle of tree-lore, taught her to keep ears, eyes and heart open for the treasures of the great outdoors.

Phœbe required no urging in that direction. Her heart was filled with an insatiable desire to know more and more of the beautiful world about her. She gathered knowledge from every country walk; she showed so much "uncommon sense," David Eby said, that it was a keen pleasure to show her the nests of the thrush or the rare nests of the humming-bird. David and his mother, enthusiastic seekers after nature knowledge, augmented the father's nature education of Phœbe by frequent walks to field and woods. And so, when Phœbe was twelve years old she knew the haunts of all the wild flowers within walking distance of her home. With her father or with David and Mother Bab she found the first marsh-marigolds in the meadows, the first violets of the wooded slope of the hill, the earliest hepatica with its woolly buds, the first windflowers and spring beauties. She knew when the time was come for the bloodroot to lift its pure white petals about the golden hearts in the spot where the rich mould at the base of some giant tree nurtured the blooded plants. She could find the canopied Jack-in-the-pulpit and the pink azalea on the hill near her home. She knew the exact spot, a mile from the gray farmhouse, where, in a lovely little wood by a quiet road, a profusion of bird-foot violets and bluets made a carpet of blue loveliness each spring—so on, through the fleet days of summer, till the last asters and goldenrod faded, the child reveled in the beauties and wonders of the world at her feet and loved every part of it, from the tiny blue speedwell in the grass to the gorgeous orioles in the trees. What if Aunt Maria sometimes scolded her for bringing so many "weeds" into the house! With apparent unconcern she placed her flowers in a glass or earthen jar and secretly thought, "Well, I'm glad I like these pretty things; they are not weeds to me."

The buoyancy of childhood tarried with her into girlhood. Like the old inscription of the sun-dial, she seemed to "count none but sunny hours." But those who knew her best saw that the shadows of life also left their marks upon her. At times the gaiety was displaced by seriousness. Mother Bab knew of the struggles in the girl's heart. Granny Hogendobler could have told of the hours Phœbe spent with her consoling her for the absence of Nason, mitigating the cruel stabs of the thoughtless people who condemned him, comforting with the assurance that he would return to his home some day. Old Aaron loved the girl and found her always ready to listen to his hackneyed story of the battle of Gettysburg.

Phœbe was a student in the Greenwald High School when the war clouds broke over Europe and the world seemed to go mad in a whirl. She hurried to Old Aaron for his opinion on the terrible war.

"Isn't it awful," she said to him, "that so many nations are flying at each other's throats? And in these days of our boasted civilization!"

"Awful," he agreed. "But, mark my words, this is just the beginning. Before the thing's settled we'll be in it too."

She shrank from the words. "Oh, no, not America! That would be too terrible. David might go then, and a lot of Greenwald boys—oh, that would be awful!"

"Yes! But it would be far more dreadful to have them sit back safe while others died for the freedom of the world. I'd rather have my boy a soldier at a time like this than have him be ruler of a country."

The old man's words ended quaveringly. The pent-up agony of his disappointment in his son surged over him, and he bowed his head in his hands and wept.

Phœbe sent Granny to comfort him, and then stole away. The veteran's grief left an impression upon her. Were his words prophetic? Would America be drawn into the struggle? It was preposterous to dream of that. She would forget the words of Old Aaron, for she had important matters of her own to think about. In a few years she would be graduated from High School and then she would have her own life-work to decide upon. Her desire for larger experience, her determination to do something of importance after graduation was her chief interest. The war across the sea was too remote to bring constant fear to her. Dutifully she went about her work on the farm and pursued her studies. She was not without pity for the brave people of Servia and Belgium, not without praise for the heroic French and English. She added her vehement words of horror as she read of the atrocities visited upon the helpless peoples. She shared in the dread of many Americans that the octopus-arm of war might reach this country, and yet she was more concerned about her own future than about the future of battle-racked France or devastated Belgium.

CHAPTER VIII
BEYOND THE ALPS LIES ITALY

Phœbe's graduation from the Greenwald High School was her red-letter day. Several times during the morning she stole to the spare-room where her graduation dress lay spread upon the high bed. Accompanied by Aunt Maria she had made a special trip to Lancaster for the frock, though Aunt Maria had conscientiously bought a few yards of muslin and apron gingham.

The material was soft silky batiste of the quality Phœbe liked. The style, also, was of her choosing. She felt a glow of satisfaction as she looked at the dress so simply, yet fashionably, made.

"For once in my life I have a dress I like," she thought.

After supper, just as she was ready to dress for the great event, Phares Eby came to the gray farmhouse.

The years had changed the solemn, serious boy into a more solemn, serious man. Tall and broad-shouldered, he was every inch a man in appearance. He was, moreover, a man highly respected in the community, a successful farmer and also a preacher in the Church of the Brethren. The latter honor had been conferred upon him a year before Phœbe's graduation and had seemed to increase his gravity and endow him with true bishopric dignity. He dressed after the manner of the majority of men who are affiliated with the Church of the Brethren in that district. His chin was covered with a thick, black beard, his dark hair was parted in the middle and combed behind his ears. He looked ten years older than he was and gave an impression of reserved strength, indomitable will and rigidity of purpose in furthering what he deemed a good cause.

Phœbe felt a slight intimidation in his presence as she noted how serious he had grown, how mature he seemed. He appeared to desire the same friendship with her and tried to be comradely as of old, but there remained a feeling of restraint between them.

"Hello, Phares," she greeted him as cordially as possible on her Commencement night.

"Good-evening," he returned. "Are you ready for the great event?"

"Yes, if I don't have heart failure before I get in to town. If only I had been fourth or fifth in the class marks instead of second, then I might have escaped to-night with just a solo. As it is, I must deliver the Salutatory oration."

"Phœbe, you want to get off too easily! But I cannot stay more than a minute, for I know you'll want to get ready. I just stopped to give you a little gift for your graduation, a copy of Longfellow's poems."

"Oh, thanks, Phares. I like his poems."

"I thought you did. But I must go now," he said stiffly. "I'll see you to-night at Commencement. I hope you'll get through the oration all right."

"Thanks. I hope so."

When he was gone she made a wry face. "Whew," she whistled. "I'm sure Phares is a fine young man but he's too solemncoly. He gives me the woolies! If he's like that all the time I'm glad I don't have to live in the same house. Wonder if he really knows how to be jolly. But, shame on you, Phœbe Metz, talking so about your old friend! Perhaps for that I'll forget my oration to-night." With a gay laugh she ran away to dress for the most important occasion of her life.

The white dress was vastly becoming. Its soft folds fell gracefully about her slender young figure. Her hair was brushed back, gathered into a bow at the top of her head, and braided into one thick braid which ended in a curl. There were no loving fingers of mother or sister to arrange the folds of her gown, no fond eyes to appraise her with looks of approval, but if she felt the omission she gave no evidence of it. She seemed especially gay as she dressed alone in her room. When she had finished she surveyed herself in the glass.

"Um, Phœbe Metz, you don't look half bad! Now go and do as well as you look. If Aunt Maria heard me she'd be shocked, but what's the use pretending to be so stupid or innocent as not to appreciate your own good points. Any person with good sight and ordinary sense can tell whether their appearance is pleasing or otherwise. I like this dress——"

"Phœbe," Aunt Maria's voice came up the stairs.

"Yes?"

"Why, David's down. Are you done dressing?"

"I'll be down in a minute."

David Eby, too, was a man grown, but a man so different! Like his cousin, Phares, he was tall. He had the same dark hair and eyes but his eyes were glowing, and his hair was cut close and his chin kept smooth-shaven.

Between him and Phœbe there existed the old comradeship, free of restraint or embarrassment. He ran to meet her as her steps sounded on the stairs.

But she came down sedately, her hand sliding along the colonial hand-rail, a calm dignity about her, her lovely head erect.

"Good-evening," she said in quiet tones.

"Whew!" he whistled. "Sweet girl graduate is too mild a phrase! Come, unbend, Phœbe. You don't expect me to call you Miss Metz or to kiss your hand—ah, shall I?"

"Davie"—in a twinkling the assumed dignity deserted her, she was all girl again, animated and adorable—"Davie, you're hopeless! Here I pose before the mirror to find the most impressive way to hold my head and be sufficiently dignified for the occasion, and you come bursting into the hall like a tomboy, whistling and saying funny things."

"I'm awfully sorry. But you took my breath away. I haven't gotten it back yet"—he breathed deeply.

"David, will you ever grow up?"

"I'll have to now. I see you've gone and done it."

"Ach no," she lapsed into the childhood expression. "I'm not grown up. But how do I look? You won't tell me so I have to ask you."

"You look like a Madonna," he said seriously.

"Oh," she said impatiently, "that sounded like Phares."

"Gracious, then I'll change it! You look like an angel and good enough to eat. But honestly, Phœbe, that dress is dandy! You look mighty nice."

"Glad you think so. Shall I tell you a secret, David? I'm scared pink about to-night."

"You scared?" He whistled again.

"Don't be so smart," she said with a frown. "Were you scared on your Commencement night?"

"Um-uh. At first I was. But you'll get over it in a few minutes. The lights and the glory of the occasion dim the scary feeling when you sit up there in the seats of honor. You should be glad your oration is first."

"I am. Mary Warner is welcome to her Valedictory and the long wait to deliver it."

Phœbe stiffened a bit at the thought of the other girl. Since the days when the two girls attended the rural school on the hill and Mary Warner was the possessor of curls while Phœbe wore the despised braids the other girl seemed to have everything for which Phœbe longed.

"Ah, don't you care about the honor," said David. "Honors don't always tell who knows the most. Why, look at me; I was fifth in my class and I know as much any day as the little runt who was first."

"Conceit!" laughed Phœbe. "But I guess you do know more than he does. Bet he never saw an orioles' nest or found a wild pink moccasin. You're a wonder at such things, David."

"Um," came the sober answer, but there was a merry twinkle in his eyes, "I'm a wonder all right! Too bad only you and Mother Bab know it. But if I don't soon go you won't get to town in time to get the pink roses arranged just so for the grand march. The girls in our class primped about twenty minutes, patting their hair and fixing their ribbons and fussing with their flowers."

"David, you're horrid!"

"I know. But I brought you something more to primp with." He handed her a small flat box.

"For me?"

"From Mother Bab," he said.

"Oh, David, that's a beauty!" she cried as she held up a scarf of pale blue crepe de chine. "I'll wear it to-night. Tell Mother Bab I thank her over and over. But I'll see her to-night and tell her myself; she'll be in at Commencement."

"She can't come, Phœbe. She's sorry, but she has one of her dreadful headaches and you know what that means, how sick she really is."

"Oh, Davie, Mother Bab not coming to my Commencement—why, I'm so disappointed, I want her there"—the tears were near the surface.

"She's sorry, too, Phœbe, but she's too sick when those headaches get her. Her eyes are the cause of them, we think now."

"And I'm horribly selfish to think of myself and my disappointment when she is suffering. You tell her I'll be up to see her in the morning and tell her all about to-night. You are coming?"

"Sure thing! Aunt Mary is coming over to stay with mother,

64

but there is really nothing to do for her; the pain seems to have to run its course. She'll go to bed early and be perfectly all right when she wakes in the morning. Come on, now, cheer up, and get ready for that 'Over the Alps lies Italy.'"

"It's 'Beyond the Alps lies Italy,'" she corrected him. Her disappointment was softened by his cheerfulness.

"Ach, it's all the same," he insisted, and went off smiling.

To Phœbe that night seemed like a dream—the slow march down the aisle of the crowded auditorium to the elevated platform where the nine graduates sat in a semicircle; the sea of faces swathed in the bright glow of many lights; the perfume of the pink roses in her arm; the music of the High School chorus, and then the time when she rose and stood before the people to deliver her oration, "Beyond the Alps lies Italy."

She began rather shakily; the sea of faces seemed so very formidable, so many eyes looked at her—how could she ever finish! She spoke mechanically at first, but gradually the magic of the Italy of her dreams stole upon her, a singular softness crept into her voice, a mellowness like music, as she depicted the blue skies of the sunny land-of-dreams-come-true.

When she returned to her place in the semicircle a glow of satisfaction possessed her. She felt she had not failed, that she had, in truth, done very well. But later, when Mary Warner rose to deliver the Valedictory, Phœbe felt her own efforts shrink into littleness. The dark-eyed beautiful Mary was a sad thorn in the flesh for the fair girl who knew she was always overshadowed by the brilliant, queenly brunette. Involuntarily the country girl looked at David Eby—he was listening intently to Mary; his eyes never seemed to leave her face. Little, sharp pangs of jealousy thrust themselves into the depths of Phœbe's heart. Was it true, then, that David cared for Mary Warner? Town gossips said he frequented her house. Phœbe had met them together on the Square recently—not that she cared, of course! She sat erect and held her pink roses more tightly against her heart. It mattered little to her if David liked other girls; it was only that she felt a sense of proprietorship over the boy whose mother was her Mother Bab—thus she tried to console herself and quiet the demons of jealousy until the program was completed, congratulations received, and she stood with her aunt and father, ready for the trip back to the gray farmhouse.

Teachers and friends had congratulated her, but it was David Eby's hearty, "You did all right, Phœbe," that gave her the keenest joy.

"Did you walk in?" she asked him as she gathered her roses, diploma and scarf, preparatory to departure.

"Yes."

"Then you can drive out with us," her father offered.

"Yes, of course," she seconded the suggestion. "We have room in the carriage."

So it happened that Phœbe, the blue scarf about her shoulders, sat beside David as they drove over the country road, home from her graduation. The vehicle rattled somewhat, but the young folks on the rear seat could speak and hear above the clatter.

"I'm glad it's over," Phœbe sighed in relief. "But what next?"

"Mary Warner is going to enter some prep school this fall and prepare for Vassar," David informed the girl beside him.

"Lucky Mary"—Mary Warner—she was sick of the name! "I wish I knew what I want to do."

"Want to go away to school?"

"I don't know. Aunt Maria wants me to stay at home on the farm and just help her. Daddy doesn't say much, but he did ask me if I would like to go to Millersville. That's a fine Normal School and if I wanted to be a teacher I'd go to that school, but I don't want to be a teacher. What I really want to do is go away and study music."

"Well, can't you do it? That is not really impossible."

"No, but——"

"No, but," he mimicked. "But won't take you anywhere."

"You set me thinking, David. Perhaps it isn't so improbable, after all. I'm coming over to see Mother Bab to-morrow; she'll be full of suggestions. She'll see a way for me to get what I want; she always does."

"I bet she will," agreed David. "You'll be that primer donner yet," he mimicked, "I know you will."

"Oh, Davie, wouldn't it be great! But I wouldn't beautify my face with cream and beet juice and flour!"

They laughed so heartily that Aunt Maria turned and asked the cause of the merriment.

"We were just speaking of the time when I dressed in the garret and fixed my face—the time you had the quilting party."

"Ach," Aunt Maria said, smiling in the darkness. "You looked dreadful that day. I was good and mad at you! But I'm glad you're big enough now not to do such dumb things. My, now that you're done with school and will stay home with me we can have some nice times sewin' and quiltin' and makin' rugs, ain't, Phœbe?"

In the semi-darkness of the carriage Phœbe looked at David. The appealing wistfulness of her face touched him. He patted her

66

arm reassuringly and whispered to her, "Don't you worry. It'll come out all right. Mother Bab will help you."

CHAPTER IX
A VISIT TO MOTHER BAB

The next day as Phœbe walked up the hill to visit Mother Bab she went eagerly and with an unusual light in her eyes—she had transformed her schoolgirl braid into the coiffure of a woman! The golden hair was parted in the middle, twisted into a shapely knot in the nape of her neck, and the effect was highly satisfactory, she thought.

"Mother Bab will be surprised," she said gladly as she swung up the hill in rapid, easy strides. "And David—I wonder what David will say if he's home."

At the summit of the hill she paused and turned, looked back at the gray farmhouse and beyond it to the little town of Greenwald.

"I just must stand here a minute and look! I love this view from the hill."

She breathed deeply and continued to revel in the beauty of the scene. At the foot of the hill was the Metz farm nestling in its green surroundings. Like a tan ribbon the dusty road went winding past green fields, then hid itself as it dipped into a valley and made a sharp curve, though Phœbe knew that it went on past more fields and meadows to the town. Where she stood she had a view of the tall spires of Greenwald churches straggling through the trees, and the red and slate roofs of comfortable houses gleaming in the sunlight. Beyond and about the town lay fields resplendent in the pristine freshness of May greenery.

"Oh," she said aloud after a long gaze, "this is glorious! But I must hurry to Mother Bab. I'm wild to have her see me. Aunt Maria just said when I showed her my hair, 'Yes well, Phœbe, I guess you're old enough to wear your hair up.' Mother Bab is different. Sometimes I pity Aunt Maria and wonder what kind of childhood she had to make her so grim about some things."

The little house in which David and his mother lived stood near the country road leading to the schoolhouse on the hill. Like many other farmhouses of that county it was square, substantial and unadorned, its attractiveness being derived solely from its fine proportions, its colonial doorways, and the harmonious surroundings of trees and flowers. The garden was eloquent of the lavish love bestowed upon it. Mother Bab delighted in flowers and planted all the old favorites. The walks between the garden beds were trim and weedless, the yard and buildings well kept, and the entire little farm gave evidence that the reputed Pennsylvania Dutch thrift and neatness were present there.

Adjoining the farm of Mother Bab was the farm of her brother-in-law, the father of Phares Eby. This was one of the best known in the community. Its great barns and vast acres quite eclipsed the modest little dwelling beside it. David Eby sometimes sighed as he compared the two farms and wondered why Fate had bestowed upon his uncle's efforts an almost unparalleled success while his own father had had a continual struggle to hold on to the few acres of the little farm. Since the death of his father David had often felt the straining of the yoke. It was toil, toil, on acres which were rich but apparently unwilling to yield their fullness. One year the crops were damaged by hail, another year prolonged drought prevented full development of the fruit, again continued rainy weather ruined the hay, and so on, year in and year out, there was seldom a season when the farm measured up to the expectations of the hard-working David.

But Mother Bab never complained about the ill-luck, neither did she envy the woman in the great house next to her. Mother Bab's philosophy of life was mainly cheerful:

"I find earth not gray, but rosy,
Heaven not grim, but fair of hue.
Do I stoop? I pluck a posy.
Do I stand and stare? All's blue."

A little house to shelter her, a big garden in which to work, to dream, to live; enough worldly goods to supply daily sustenance; the love of her David—truly her Beloved, as the old Hebrew name signifies—the love of the dear Phœbe who had adopted her—given these blessings and no envy or discontent ever ventured near the white-capped woman. Life had brought her many hours of perplexity and several great sorrows, but it had also bestowed upon her compensating joys. She felt that the years would bring her new joys, now that her boy was grown into a man and was able to manage the farm. Some day he would bring home a wife—how she would love David's wife! But meanwhile, she was not lonely. Her friends and she were much together, quilting, rugging, comparing notes on the garden.

"Guess Mother Bab'll be in the garden," thought Phœbe, "for it's such a fine day."

But as she neared the whitewashed fence of the garden she saw that the place was deserted. She ran lightly up the walk, rapped at the kitchen door, and entered without waiting for an answer to her knock.

"Mother Bab," she called.

"I'm here, Phœbe," came a voice from the sitting-room.

"How are you? Is your headache all gone?" Phœbe asked as she ran to the beloved person who came to meet her.

"All gone. I was so disappointed last night—but what have you done to your hair?"

"Oh, I forgot!" Phœbe lifted her head proudly. "I meant to knock at the front door and be company to-day. I've got my hair up!"

"Phœbe, Phœbe," the woman drew her nearer. "Let me look at you." Her eyes scanned the face of the girl, her voice quivered as she spoke. "You've grown up! Of course it didn't come in a night but it seems that way."

"The May fairies did it, Mother Bab. Yesterday I wore a braid. This morning when I woke I heard the robin who sings every morning in the apple tree outside my window and he was caroling, 'Put it up! Put it up!' I knew he meant my hair, so here I am, waiting for your blessing."

"You have it, you always have it! But"—she changed her mood—"are you sure the robin wasn't saying, 'Get up, get up!' Phœbe?"

"Positive; it was only five o'clock."

"Now I must hear all about last night," said Mother Bab as they sat together on the broad wooden settee in the sitting-room. "David told me how nice you looked and how well you did."

"Did he tell you how pleased I am with the scarf? It's just lovely! And the color is beautiful. I wonder why—I wonder why I love pretty things so much, really pretty things, like crepe de chine and taffeta and panne velvet and satin. Oh, sometimes I think I must have them. When I go to Lancaster I want lots of lovely clothes and I hate ginghams and percales and serviceable things."

"I know, Phœbe, I know how you feel about it."

"Do you really? Then it can't be so awfully wicked. You are so understanding, Mother Bab. I can't tell Aunt Maria how I feel about such things for she'd be dreadfully hurt or worried or provoked, but you seem always to know what I mean and how I feel."

"I was eighteen myself once, a good many years ago, but I still remember it."

"You have a good memory."

"Yes. Why, I can remember some of the dresses I wore when

I was eighteen. But then, I have a dress bundle to help me remember them."

"What's a dress bundle?"

"Didn't Aunt Maria keep one for you?"

"I never heard of one."

"It's a long string of samples of dresses you wore when you were little. Wait, I'll get mine and show you."

She left the room and went up-stairs. After a short time she returned and held out a stout thread upon which were strung small, irregular scraps of dress material. "This is my dress bundle. My mother started it for me when I was a baby and kept it up till I was big enough to do it myself. Every time I got a new dress a little patch of the goods was threaded on my dress bundle."

"Oh, may I see? Why, that's just like a part of your babyhood and childhood come back!"

The two heads bent over the bundle—the girl's with its light hair in its first putting up, the woman's with its graying hair folded under the white cap.

"Here"—Mother Bab turned the bundle upside down and fingered the scraps with that loving way of those who are dreaming of long departed days and touching a relic of those cherished hours—"this white calico with the little pink dots was the first dress any one gave me. Grandmother Hoerner made it for me, all by hand. Funny, wasn't it, the way they used to put colored dresses on wee babies! See, here are pink calico ones and white with red figures and a few blue ones. I wore all these when I was a baby. Then when I grew older these; they are much prettier. This red delaine I wore to a spelling bee when I was about sixteen and I got a book for a prize for standing up next to last. This red and black checked debaige I can see yet. It had an overskirt on it trimmed with little ruffles. This purple cashmere with the yellow sprigs in it I had all trimmed with narrow black velvet ribbon. I'll never forget that dress—I wore it the day I met David's father."

"Oh, you must have looked lovely!"

"He said so." She smiled; her eyes looked beyond Phœbe, back to the golden days of her youth when Love had come to her to bless and to abide with her long beyond the tarrying of the spirit in the flesh. "He said I looked nice. I met him the first time I wore the purple dress. It was at a corn-husking party at Jerry Grumb's barn. Some man played the fiddle and we danced."

"Danced!" echoed Phœbe.

"Yes, danced. But just the old-fashioned Virginia reel. We had cider and apples and cake and pie for our treat and we went home at ten o'clock! David walked home with me in the moonlight and I guess we liked each other from the first. We were married the next year, then we both turned plain."

"Were you ever sorry, Mother Bab?"

"That I married him, or that I turned plain?"

"Yes. Both, I mean."

"No, never sorry once, Phœbe, about either. We were happy together. And about turning plain, why, I wasn't sorry either."

"But you had to give up Virginia reels and pretty dresses."

"Yes, but I learned there are deeper, more important things than dancing and wearing pretty dresses."

She looked at Phœbe, but the girl had bowed her head over the dress bundle and appeared to be thinking.

"And so," continued Mother Bab softly, "my bundle ended with that dress. Since I dress plain I don't wear colors, just gray and black. But I always thought if I had a girl I'd start a dress bundle for her, for it's so much satisfaction to get it out sometimes and look over the pieces and remember the dresses and some of the happy times you had when you wore them. But the girl never came."

"But you have David!"

"Yes, to be sure, he's been so much to me, but I couldn't make him a dress bundle. He wouldn't have liked it when he grew older—boys are different. And I wouldn't want him to be a sissy, either."

"He isn't, Mother Bab. He's fine!"

"I think so, Phœbe. He has worked so hard since he's through school and he's so good to me and takes such care of the farm, though the crops don't always turn out as we want. But you haven't told me what you are going to do, now that you're through school."

"I don't know. I want to do something."

"Teach?"

"No. What I would like best of all is study music."

"In Greenwald? You mean to learn to play?"

"No, to learn to sing. I have often dreamed of studying music in a great city, like Philadelphia."

"What would you do then?"

"Sing, sing! I feel that my voice is my one talent and I don't want to bury it."

"Well, don't Miss Lee live in Philadelphia? Perhaps she could help you to get a good teacher and find a place to board."

"Mother Bab!" Phœbe sprang to her feet and wrapped her arms about the slender little woman. "That's just it!" she cried. "I never thought of that! David said you'd help me. I'll write to Miss Lee to-day!"

"Phœbe," the woman said, smiling at the girl's wild enthusiasm.

"I'm not crazy, just inspired," said Phœbe. "You helped me, I knew you would! I want to go to Philadelphia to study music but I know daddy and Aunt Maria would never listen to any proposals about going to a big city and living among strangers. But if I write to Miss Lee and she says she'll help me the folks at home may consider the plan. I'll have a hard time, though"—a reactionary doubt touched her—"I'll have a dreadful time persuading Aunt Maria that I'm safe and sane if I mention music and Philadelphia and Phœbe in the same breath." Then she smiled determinedly. "At least I'm going to make a brave effort to get what I want. I'm not going to settle down on the farm and get brown and fat and wear gingham dresses all my life, and sunbonnets in the bargain! I never could see why I had to wear sunbonnets, I always hated them. Aunt Maria always tried to make me wear them, but as soon as I was out of her sight I sneaked them off. I remember one time I threw my bonnet in the Chicques and I had the loveliest time watching it disappear down the stream. But Aunt Maria made me make another one that was uglier still, so I gained nothing but the temporary pleasure of seeing it float away. And how I hated to do patchwork! It seemed to me I was always doing it, and I never could see the sense of cutting up pieces and then sewing them together again."

"But the sewing was good practice for you, Phœbe. Patchwork—seems to me all our life is patchwork: a little here and a little there; one color now, then another; one shape first, then another shape fitted in; and when it is all joined it will be beautiful if we keep the parts straight and the colors and shapes right. It can be a very beautiful rising sun or an equally pretty flower basket, or it can be just a crazy quilt with little of the beautiful about it."

"Mother Bab, if I had known that while I was patching I would have loved to patch! I had nothing to make it interesting; it was just stitching, stitching, stitching on seams! But those vivid quilts are all finished and I guess Aunt Maria is as glad about it as I am, for I gave her some worried hours before the end was sighted. Poor Aunt Maria, she should be glad to have me go to the city. I've led her some merry chases, but I must admit she was always equal to them, forged ahead of me many times."

"Phœbe, you're a wilful child and I'm afraid I spoil you more."

"No you don't! You're my safety valve. If I couldn't come up here and say the things I really feel I'd have to tell it to the Jenny Wrens—Aunt Maria hates to have me talk to myself."

"But she's good to you, Phœbe?"

"Yes, oh, yes! I appreciate all she has done for me. She has taken care of me since I was a tiny baby. I'll never forget that. It's just that we are so different. I can't make Phœbe Metz be just like Maria Metz, can I?"

"No, you must be yourself, even if you are different."

"That's it, Mother Bab. I feel I have the right to live my life as I choose, that no person shall say to me I must live it so or so. If I want to study music why shouldn't I do so? My mother left a few hundred dollars for me; it's been on interest and amounts to more than a few hundred, about a thousand dollars, I think. So the money end of my studying music need not worry Aunt Maria. I am determined to do it, wouldn't you?"

"I suppose I'd feel the same way."

"How did you learn to understand so well, Mother Bab? You have lived all your life on a farm, yet you are not narrow."

"I hope I have not grown narrow," the woman said softly. "I have read a great deal. I have read—don't you breathe it to a soul—I have often read when I should have been baking pies or washing windows!"

"No wonder David worships you so."

"I still enjoy reading," said Mother Bab. "David subscribes for three good magazines and when they come I'm so anxious to look into them that sometimes my cooking burns."

"That must be one of the reasons your English is correct. I am ashamed of myself when I mix my v's and w's and use a t for a d. I have often wished the Pennsylvania Dutch dialect would have been put aside long ago."

"Yes," the woman agreed, "I can't see the need of it. It has been ridiculed so long that it should have died a natural death. It's a mystery to me how it has survived. But cheer up, Phœbe, the gibberish is dying out. The older people will continue to speak it but the younger generations are becoming more and more English speaking. Why, do you know, Phœbe, since this war started in Europe and I read the dreadful crimes the Germans are committing I feel that I never want to hear or say, 'Yah.'"

"Bully!" Phœbe clapped her hands. "I said to old Aaron Hogendobler yesterday that I'm ashamed I have a German name and some German ancestors, even if they did come to this country before the Revolution, and he said no one need feel shame at that, but every American who is not one hundred per cent American should die from shame. I know we Pennsylvania Dutch can carry

73

our end of the burdens of the world and be real Americans, but I want to sound like one too."

Mother Bab laughed. "Just yesterday I said to David that the butter was all."

"I say that very often. I must read more."

"And I less. I haven't told you, Phœbe, nor David, but my eyes are going back on me. I went to Lancaster a few weeks ago and the doctor there said I must be very careful not to strain them at all. I think I'd rather lose any other sense than sight. I always thought it was the greatest affliction in the world to be blind."

"It is! It mustn't come to you, Mother Bab!"

The woman looked worried, but in a moment her face brightened.

"Anyhow," she said, "what's the use of worrying or thinking about it? If it ever comes I'll have to bear it just as many other people are bearing it. I'm glad I have sight to-day to see you."

Phœbe gave her an ecstatic hug. "I believe you're Irish instead of Pennsylvania Dutch! You do know how to blarney and you have that coaxing, lovely way about you that the Irish are supposed to have."

"Why, Phœbe, I am part Irish! My mother's maiden name was McKnight. David and I still have a few drops of the Irish blood in us, I suppose."

"I just knew it! I'm glad. I adore the whimsical way the Irish have, and I like their sense of humor. I guess that's one of the reasons I like you better than other people I know and perhaps that's why David is jolly and different from Phares. Ah," she added roguishly, "I think it's a pity Phares hasn't some Irish blood in him. He's so solemn he seldom sees a joke."

"But he's a good boy and he thinks a lot of you. He's just a little too quiet. But he's a good preacher and very bright."

"Yes, he's so good that I'm ashamed of myself when I say mean things about him. I like him, but people with more life are more interesting."

"Hello, who's this you like?" David's hearty voice burst upon them.

Phœbe turned and saw him standing in the sunlight of the open door. The thought flashed upon her, "How big and strong he is!"

He wore brown corduroys, a blue chambray shirt slightly open at the throat, heavy shoes. His face was already tanned by the wind and sun, his hands rough from contact with soil and farming implements, his dark hair rumpled where he had pulled the big straw hat from his head, but there was an odor of fresh spring earth about him, a boyish wholesomeness in his face, that attracted the girl as she looked at his frame in the doorway.

There was a flash of white teeth, a twinkle in his dark eyes, as he asked, "What did I hear you say, Phœbe—that you like me?"

"Indeed not! I wouldn't think of liking anybody who deceived me as you have done. All these years you have left me under the impression that you are Pennsylvania Dutch and now Mother Bab says you are part Irish."

"Little saucebox! What about yourself? You can't make me believe that you are pure, unadulterated Pennsylvania Dutch. There's some alien blood in you, by the ways of you. Have you seen Phares this afternoon?" he asked irrelevantly.

"Phares? No. Why?"

"He went down past the field some time ago. Said he's going to Greenwald and means to stop and ask you to go to a sale with him next week. He said you mentioned some time ago that you'd like to go to a real old-fashioned one and he heard of one coming off next week and thought you might like to go."

"I surely want to go. Don't you want to come, too, David? And Mother Bab?"

But David shook his head. "And spoil Phares's party," he said. "Phares wouldn't thank us."

Phœbe shrugged her shoulders. "Ach, David Eby, you're silly! Just as though I want to go to a sale all alone with Phares! He can take the big carriage and take us all."

"He can but he won't want to." David showed an irritating wisdom. "When I invite you to come on a party with me I won't want Phares tagging after, either. Two's company."

"Two's boredom sometimes," she said so ambiguously that the man laughed heartily and Mother Bab smiled in amusement.

"Come now, Phœbe," David said, "just because you put your hair up you mustn't think you can rule us all and don grown-up airs."

"Then you do notice things! I thought you were blind. You are downright mean, David Eby! When you wore your first pair of long pants I noticed it right away and made a fuss about them and it takes you ten minutes to see that my hair is up instead of hanging in a silly braid down my back."

"I saw it first thing, Phœbe. That was mean—I'm sorry——"

"You look it," she said sceptically.

"I'm sorry," he repeated, "to see the braid go, though you look fine this way. I liked that long braid ever since the day I braided it, the day you played prima donna. Remember?"

The girl flushed, then was vexed at her embarrassment and changed suddenly to the old, appealing Phœbe.

"I remember, Davie. You were my salvation that day, you and Mother Bab."

Before they could answer she added with seeming innocency, yet with a swift glance into the face of the farmer boy, "I must go now so I'll be home when Phares comes to invite me to that sale. I'm going with him; I'm wild to go."

"Yes?" David said slowly.

"Yes," she repeated, a teasing look in her eyes.

"Mommie, isn't she fine?" David said after Phœbe was gone and he lingered in the house.

"Mighty fine. But she is so different from the general run of girls; she's so lively and bright and sweet, so sensitive to all impressions. She's anxious to get to the city to study music. It would be a wonderful experience for her—and yet——"

"And yet——" echoed David, then fell into silence.

Mother Bab was thinking of her boy and Phœbe, of their gay comradeship. How friendly they were, how well-mated they appeared to be, how appreciative of each other. Could they ever care for each other in a deeper way? Did the preacher care for the playmate of his childhood as she thought David was beginning to care?

"Well, I must go again, mommie. I came in for a drink at the pump and heard you and Phœbe. Now I must hustle for I have a lot to do before sundown—ach, why aren't we rich!"

"Do you wish for that?"

"Certainly I do. Not wealthy; just to have enough so we needn't lie awake wondering if the dry spell or the wet spell or the hail will ruin the crops. I wish I could find an Aladdin's lamp."

"Davie"—the smile faded from her face—"don't get the money craze. Money isn't everything. This farm is paid for and we can always make a comfortable living. Money isn't all."

"No, but—but it means everything sometimes to a young, single fellow. But don't you worry; the crops are fine this year, so far."

The mother did not forget his words at once. "It must be," she thought, "that David wants Phœbe and feels he must have more money before he can ask her to marry him. Will men never learn that girls who are worth getting are not looking so much for money but the man. The young can't see the depth and fullness of love. I've tried to teach David, but I suppose there's some things he must learn for himself."

CHAPTER X
AN OLD-FASHIONED COUNTRY SALE

A week later Phares and Phœbe drove into the barnyard of a farm six miles from Greenwald, where the old-fashioned sale was scheduled to be held.

"We are not the first, after all," said the preacher as he saw the number of conveyances in and about the barnyard. He smiled good-humoredly as he led the way—he could afford to smile when he was with Phœbe.

All about the big yard of the farm were placed articles to be sold at public auction. It was a miscellaneous collection. A cradle with miniature puffy feather pillows, straw tick and an old patchwork quilt of pink and white calico stood near an old wood-stove which bore the inscription, Conowingo Furnace. Corn-husk shoe-mats, a quilting frame, rocking-chairs, two spinning-wheels, copper kettles, rolls of hand-woven rag carpet, old oval hat-boxes and an old chest stood about a huge table which was laden with jars of jellies. Chests, filled with linens and antique woolen coverlets, afforded a resting place for the fortunate ones who had arrived earliest. A few antique chairs and tables, a mahogany highboy in excellent condition and an antique corner-cupboard of wild-cherry wood occupied prominent places among the collection. Truly, the sale warranted the attention it was receiving.

"I'd like to bid on something—I'm going to do it!" Phœbe said as they looked about. "When I was a little girl and went to sales with Aunt Maria I coaxed to bid, just for the excitement of bidding. But she always made me tell what I wanted and then she bid on it."

"What do you want to buy?" asked the preacher.

"Oh, I don't know. I don't want any apple-butter in crocks, or any chairs. Oh, I'll have some fun, Phares! I'll bid on the third article they put up for sale! I heard a man say the dishes are going to be sold first, so I'll probably get a cracked plate or a saucer without a cup, but whatever it is, the third article is going to be mine."

"That is rather rash," warned Phares. "It may be a bed or a chest."

"You can't scare me. I'm going to have some real thrills at this sale."

The preacher entered into the spirit of the girl and smiled at her promise to bid on the third thing put up for sale.

"Oh, look at the highboy," she exclaimed to him.

"Do you like it?" he asked.

"Yes. See how it's inlaid with hollywood and cherry and how fine the lines of it are! I wonder how much it will bring. But Aunt Maria'd scold if I brought any furniture home, so I can't buy it."

"The price will depend upon the number of bidders and the size of their pocketbooks. If any dealers in antiques are here it may run way up. We used to buy homespun linen and fine old furniture very cheap at sales, but the antique dealers changed that."

By that time the number of people was steadily increasing. They came singly and in groups, in carriages, farm wagons, automobiles and afoot. Some of the curious went about examining each article in the motley collection in the yard.

Phœbe watched it all with an amused smile; finally she broke into merry laughter.

Phares looked up inquiringly: "What is it?"

"This is great sport! I haven't been to a good sale for several years. That old man has knocked his fist upon every chair and table, has tested every piece of furniture, has opened all the bureau drawers, even the case of the old clock, and just a moment ago he rocked the cradle furiously to convince himself that it is in good working condition. Here he comes with a pewter plate in his hand—let's hear what he has to say about it."

The old man's cracked harsh voice rose above the confusion of other sounds as he leaned against a table near Phœbe and Phares and spoke to another man:

"Here now, Eph, is one of them pewter plates that folks fuss so about just now, and I hear they put them in their dinin'-rooms along the wall! Why, when I was a boy my granny had a lot of 'em and we'd knock 'em around any way. Ha, ha," he laughed loudly, "I can tell you a good one, Eph, about one of them pewter dishes."

He slapped the plate against his knee, but the thud was instantly drowned by his quick, "Ach, Jimminy, I hit myself pretty hard that time! But I'll tell you about it, Eph. You heard of the fellows from the city who go around the country hunting up old relics, all old truck, and sell it again in the city? Well, one of them fellows come to my house the other week and asked if I had anything old-fashioned I would sell. Now if Lizzie'd been home we might got rid of some of the old things we have on the garret, but I was alone and I didn't know what I dared sell—you know how the women is. So I said, 'What kind of old things do you want?'

"'Oh,' he said, 'I buy old furniture, dishes, linen, pewter——'

"'Pewter?' I said. 'Who wants that?'

"'There is a great demand for it,' he said, 'and I will give you a good price for any you have.'

"'Well,' I laughed, 'I have just one piece of pewter.'

"'Where is it?'

"'Why, the cats have been eating out of it for a few years.'

"'May I see it?' he asks.

"So I took him out to the barn and showed him the big pewter bowl the cats eat out of and he said, 'I'll give you fifty cents for that dish.'

"Gosh, I said to him, 'Mister, I was just fooling with you. I know you don't want a cat-dish.'

"But he said again, 'I'll give you fifty cents for that dish.'

"So when I saw that he really meant it and wanted the dish I wrapped the old pewter dish in a paper and he gave me half a dollar for it. When I told Lizzie about it she laughed good and said the city folks must be dumb if they want pewter dishes when you can buy such nice ones for ten cents. Yes, Eph, that's the fellow's going to auctioneer. He's a good one, you bet; he keeps things lively all the time. All his folks is good talkers. Lizzie says his mom can talk the legs off an iron pot. But then he needs a good tongue in this business; it takes a lot of wind to be an auctioneer, specially at a big sale like this. He says it's going to be a wonderful sale, that he ain't had one like it for years. There's things here belonged to the family for three generations, been handed down and handed down and now to-day it'll get scattered all over Lancaster County, mebbe further. This saving up things and not using 'em is all nonsense. I tell Lizzie we'll use what we got and get new when it's worn out and not let a lot back for the young ones to fight over or other people to buy."

Here the auctioneer climbed upon a big box, clapped his hands and called loudly, "Attention, attention! This sale is about to begin. We have here a collection of fine things, all in good condition. The terms of the sale are cash. Now, folks, bid up fast and talk loud when you bid so I can hear you. We have here some of the finest antique dishes in the country, also some furniture that can't be duplicated in any store to-day. We'll begin on this cherry table."

He lifted a spindle-legged table in the air and went on talking.

"Now that's a fine table to begin with! All solid cherry, no screws loose—and that's more than you can say about some people—now what's bid for this table? Fine and good as the day it came out of a good workman's shop; no scratches on it—the Brubaker people knew how to take care of furniture. Who bids?

How much for it do you bid? Fifty cents—fifty, all right—make it sixty—sixty cents I'm bid. Sixty, sixty, sixty—seventy—go ahead, eighty—go on—ninety, one dollar, one dollar ten, twenty, thirty—keep on—one dollar thirty, make it forty, forty, forty, forty, I have a dollar forty for this table—all done? Going—all done—all done?"

All was said in one breathless succession of words. He paused an instant to gather fresh impetus, then resumed, "All done—any more? Gone at a dollar forty to——"

"Lizzie Brubaker."

"Sold to Lizzie Brubaker."

"There," whispered the preacher to Phœbe, "that's one."

She smiled and nodded her head.

"Here now," called the auctioneer, "here's a fine set of chairs. Bid on them; wink to me if you don't want to call out. My wife said she don't care how many ladies wink to me this afternoon at this sale, but after that she won't have it—now then; go ahead! Give me one of the chairs, Sam, so the people can see it—ah, ain't that a beauty! Six in all, all solid wood, too, none of your cane seats that you have to be afraid to sit in. All solid wood, and every one alike, all painted green and every one with fine hand-painted flowers on the back. Where can you beat such chairs? Don't make them any more these days, real antiques they are! Bid up now, friends; how much a piece? The six go together, it would be a shame to part them. Fifteen cents did I hear?—Say, I'm ashamed to take a bid like that! Twenty, that's a little better—thirty, thirty, forty over here? Forty cents I have, fifty, sixty, seventy, seventy-five, eighty, eighty, eighty cents I'm bid; I'm bid eighty cents—make it ninety—ninety I'm bid, make it a dollar—ninety, ninety—all done at ninety? Guess we'll let Jonas Erb have them at ninety cents a piece, and real bargains they are!"

"Here's where I bid," said Phœbe, her cheeks rosy from excitement.

"Shall I release you from your promise?" offered the preacher.

"No, I'll bid."

"Attention," called the auctioneer. "Attention, everybody! Here we have a real antique, something worth bidding on!"

Phœbe held her breath.

"Here now, Sam, give it a lift so everybody can see—ah, there you are!"

He shouted the last words as two men held above the crowd—the old wooden cradle!

Phœbe groaned and looked at Phares—he was smiling. The old aversion to ridicule swelled in her; he should not have reason to laugh at her; she would show him that she was equal to the occasion—she would bid on the cradle!

"Start it, hurry up, somebody. How much is bid for the cradle? Sam here says it's been in the Brubaker family for years and years. Think of all the babies that were rocked to sleep in it—it's a real relic."

Phœbe, unacquainted with the value of cradles, was silently endeavoring to determine the proper amount for a first bid. She was relieved to hear a woman's voice call, "Twenty-five cents."

"Twenty-five I have, twenty-five," called the auctioneer. "Make it thirty."

"Thirty," said Phœbe.

"Forty," came from the other woman.

"Make it fifty, Miss." He pointed a fat finger at Phœbe.

"Fifty," she responded.

"Fifty, fifty, anybody make it sixty? Fifty cents—all done at fifty? Then it goes at fifty cents to"—Phœbe repeated her name—"to Phœbe Metz."

He proceeded with the sale. Phœbe turned triumphantly to the preacher—"I kept my promise."

"You did," he said. "The cradle is yours—what are you going to do with it?"

"Gracious! Why, I never thought of that! I don't want it. I just wanted the fun of bidding. Can't I pay it and leave it and they can sell it over again?"

"You bid rashly," the preacher said, though his eyes were smiling and his usual tone of admonition was absent from his voice. "I think you may be able to sell it to the woman who was bidding against you."

"I'll find her and give it to her."

She elbowed her way through the crowd until she reached the place from which the opposing voice had come. She looked about a moment, then addressed a woman near her. "Do you know who was bidding on the cradle?"

"Yes, it was Hetty here, the one with the white waist. Here, Hetty, this lady wants to talk to you."

"To me?" echoed the rival bidder for the cradle.

"Did you bid on the cradle?" asked Phœbe.

"Yes, but I didn't get it. I only wanted it because it was in the family so long. I'm a Brubaker. I said I wouldn't give more than fifty cents for it, for it would just stand up in the garret anyway, and be one more thing to move around at housecleaning time. Yet I'd liked to have it. I don't know who got it."

"I did, but I don't want it. I'd like to give it to you."

"Why"—the woman was amazed—"what did you bid on it for?"

"Just for the fun of bidding," said Phœbe, laughing. "Will you let me give it to you?"

"I'll give you half a dollar for it," offered the woman.

"No, I mean it. I want to give it to you. I'll consider it a favor if you'll take it from me."

"Well, if you want it that way. But don't you want the quilt and the feather pillows?"

"No, take it just as it is."

"Why, thanks," said the woman as she went to the spot where the cradle stood. She soon walked away with the clumsy gift in her arm. "Now don't it beat all," she said as she set it down near her friends. "I just knew that I'd get a present to-day. This morning I put my stocking on wrong side out and I just left it for they say still that it means you'll get a present before the day is over, and here I get this cradle!"

With a bright smile illumining her face, Phœbe rejoined the preacher.

"I see you disposed of the cradle," he greeted her.

"Yes. But I felt like a hypocrite when she thanked me, for I was giving her what I didn't want."

Here the busy auctioneer called again, "Attention, everybody! This piece of furniture we are going to sell now dates back to ante-bellum days."

"Ach, it don't," Phœbe heard a voice exclaim. "That never belonged to any person called Bellem; that was old Amanda Brubaker's for years and she used to tell me that it belonged to her grandmother once. That man don't know what he's saying, but that's the way these auctioneers do; you can't believe half they say at a sale half the time."

Phœbe looked up at Phares; both smiled, but the loquacious auctioneer, not knowing the comments he was causing, went on serenely:

"Yes, sir, this is a real old piece of furniture, a real antique. Look at this, everybody—a chest of drawers, a highboy, some people call it, but it's pretty by any name. All of it is genuine mahogany trimmed with inlaid pieces of white wood. Start it up, somebody. What will you give for the finest thing we have here at this sale to-day? What's bid? Good! I'm bid five dollars to begin; shows you know a good thing when you see it. Five dollars—make it ten?"

"Ten," answered Phares Eby.

Phœbe gave a start of surprise as the preacher's voice came in answer to the entreaty of the auctioneer.

"Phares," she whispered, "I didn't mean that I want to buy it."

"I am buying it," he said calmly, an inscrutable smile in his eyes. "You like it, don't you?"

She felt a vague uneasiness at his words, at the new sound of tenderness in his voice.

"Yes, I like it, but——"

"Then we'll talk about that some other day soon," he returned, and looked again at the busy auctioneer.

"Ten dollars, ten, ten," came the eager call of the man on the box. "Who makes it fifteen? That's it—fifteen I have—sixteen, eighteen—twenty—twenty-five, thirty—thirty, thirty, come on, who makes it more? Not yet? Not going for that little bit? Who makes it thirty-five?"

"Thirty-five," said Phares.

"Thirty-five," the auctioneer caught at the words. "That's the way to bid."

"Thirty-eight," came a voice from the crowd.

"Thirty-eight," the auctioneer smiled broadly at the bid. "Some person is going to get a fine antique—keep it up, the highest bidder gets it—thirty-eight——"

"Forty," offered Phares.

"Forty, forty dollars—I have forty dollars offered for the highboy—all done at forty——"

There was a tense silence.

"Forty dollars—all done at forty—last call—going—going—gone. Gone at forty dollars to Phares Eby."

Phœbe turned to the preacher. "Did you bid just for the fun of bidding?" she asked.

"Well," he replied slowly, "the cases are not exactly alike. You like the highboy, don't you?"

"Yes—but what has that to do with it?" She looked up, but turned her head away quickly. What did he mean? Surely Phares was not given to foolishness or love-making to her!

She was glad that he suggested moving to the edge of the crowd after his successful bidding was completed. There a welcome diversion came in the form of the old man who had previously amused them by his talk about the pewter plate.

"There now, Eph," he was saying, "what do you think of paying forty dollars for that old chest of drawers? To be sure it's good and all the drawers work yet—I tried 'em before the sale commenced. But forty dollars—whew!"

83

The stupidity and extravagance of some people silenced him for a moment, then he continued: "My Lizzie, now, she knows better how to spend money. She bought ten dollars' worth of flavors and soap and things like that and she got in the bargain a big chest of drawers bigger than this old one, and it was polished up finer and had a looking-glass on the top yet. That man must have a lot of money to give forty dollars for one piece of furniture! Ach"—in answer to a remonstrance from his companion—"they can't hear me. I don't talk loud, and anyhow, they're listening to the auctioneer. That girl with him has a funny streak too. She bought the old cradle and then I heard her tell Hetty that she just bought it for fun and she gave it to Hetty. So, is that man Phares Eby from near Greenwald? Well, I thought he'd have too much sense to buy such a thing for forty dollars, but some people gets crazy when they get to a sale. Who ever heard of a person buying a cradle for fun and giving it away? But I guess that cradles went out of style some time ago. My girl Lizzie wasn't raised with funny notions like some girls have nowadays, but when she was married and had her first baby and we told her she could borrow the old cradle she was rocked in to put her baby in, she said she didn't want it, for cradles ain't healthy for babies, it is bad to rock babies! I guess that was her man's dumb notion, for he's a professor in the High School where they live, but he's just Jake Forney's John. They get along fine, but they do some dumb things. They let that baby yell till he found out that he wouldn't get rocked. It made her mom quite sick when we were up to visit them, and sometimes we'd sneak rocking it a little, just so the little fellow'd know there is such a thing as getting rocked. They don't want any person to kiss that baby, neither. Course I ain't in favor of everybody kissing a baby, but I can't see the hurt of its own people kissing it. We used to take it behind the door and kiss it good, and it's living yet. Ain't, Eph, it's a wonder we ever growed up, the way we were bounced and rocked and joggled and kissed! I say it ain't right to go back on cradles; they belong to babies. But look, Eph, there she's buying them old copper sheep bells! Wonder if she keeps sheep."

Phœbe, triumphant bidder for a pair of hand-beaten copper sheep bells, turned and looked at the farmer. The tenderness of a bright smile still played about her lips and the old man, interpreting the smile as a personal greeting to him, drew near and spoke to her.

"I can tell you what to take to clean them bells."

"Thank you," she answered cordially, "but I do not want to clean them."

"But you can make them shiny if you take——"

"You are very kind, but I really want to keep them just as they are."

The old man looked at her for a moment, then shook his head as though in perplexity and turned away.

Several more hours of vigorous work on the part of the noisy auctioneer resulted in the sale of the miscellaneous collection of articles.

The loquacious old farmer was often moved to whistle or to emit a low "Gosh" as the sale progressed and seemingly valueless articles were sold for high prices. A linen homespun table-cloth, woven in geometrical design, occasioned spirited bidding, but the man on the box was equal to the task and closed the bids at twenty dollars. Homespun linen towels were bought eagerly for seven, eight, nine dollars. A genuine buffalo robe was knocked down to a bidder at the price of eighty dollars. Cups and saucers and plates sold for from two to four dollars each. But it was an old blue glass bottle that provoked the greatest sensation. "Gosh, who wants that?" said the old man as the bottle was brought forth. "If he throws a cup or plate in with it mebbe somebody will give a penny for it."

But a moment later, as an antique dealer started the bid at a dollar the old man spluttered, "Jimminy pats! Why, it's just an old glass bottle!"

Some person enlightened him—it was Stiegel glass! After the first bid on the bottle every one became attentive. The two rival bidders were alert to every move of the auctioneer, the bids leapt up and up—ten dollars—eleven dollars—twelve dollars—thirteen dollars—gone at thirteen dollars!

It was late afternoon when Phœbe and the preacher turned homeward. The preacher's purchase had to be left at the farm until he could return for it in the big farm wagon, but Phœbe thought of the highboy as they rode along the pleasant country roads. She remembered the expression she had caught on the face of Phares and the remembrance troubled her. She sought desperately for some topic of conversation that would lead the man's thoughts from the highboy and prevent the return of the mood she had discovered at the sale.

"You—Phares," she began confusedly, "you are going to baptize this next time, Aunt Maria thought."

"Yes."

The preacher looked at the girl. The exhilarating influence of the early June outdoors was visible in her countenance. Her eyes sparkled, her cheeks glowed—she seemed the epitome of innocent, happy girlhood. The vision charmed the preacher and caused the blood to course more swiftly through his veins, but he bit his lip and steadied his voice to speak naturally. "Yes, Phœbe, I want to speak to you about that."

"Oh, dear," she thought, "now I have done it! Why did I start him on that subject!" Some of the excessive color faded from her face and she looked ahead as he spoke.

"Phœbe, the second Sunday in June I am going to baptize a number of converts in the Chicques near your home. Are you ready to come with the rest, and give up the vanities of the world?"

"Oh, Phares, why do you ask me? I can't wear plain clothes while I love pretty ones. I can't be a hypocrite."

"But surely, Phœbe, you see that a simple life is more conducive to happiness than a complex, artificial life can possibly be. It is my duty to strive for the saving of souls and we have been friends so long that I take a special interest in you and desire to see you safe in the shelter of the Church."

"Phares, I'll tell you frankly, if I ever wear plain garb it will be because I feel that it is the right thing for me to do, not because some person persuades me to."

"Of course, that is the only way to come. But can't you come now?"

"I can't. I hurt you when I say that, but I want you to be my good friend, as always, in spite of my worldliness. Will you, Phares?"

He opened his lips to speak, but she went on quickly: "Because I am learning every day how much I need the help and friendship of all my friends."

He longed to throw down the reins he was holding and tell her what was in his heart, but something in her manner, her peculiar stress on the word "friendship" restrained him. She was, after all, only a child. Only eighteen—too young to think of marriage. He could wait a while longer before he told her of his love and his desire to marry her.

"I will, Phœbe," he promised. "I'll be your friend, always."

"I thought so," she breathed deeply in relief. "I knew you wouldn't fail me. Look at that field, Phares—oh, this is a perfect day! There should be a superlative form of perfect for a day like this! Those fields have as many colors as the shades reflected on a copper plate: lilac, tan, purple, rose, green and brown."

The preacher answered a mere "Yes." She turned again and looked at the fields they were passing. "Perhaps," she thought, "before that corn is ripe I'll be in Philadelphia!" But she did not utter the thought, for she knew the preacher would not approve of her going to the city. He should know nothing about it until it was definitely settled.

The thought of studying music in Philadelphia left her restless. If only the preacher would be more talkative!

"It's just perfect to-day, isn't it, Phares?" she asked radiantly, resolved to make him talk. But his answers were so perfunctory that she turned her head, made a little grimace through the open side of the carriage and mentally dubbed him "Bump-on-log." Very well, if he felt indisposed to talk to her, she could enjoy the drive without his voice!

Suddenly she laughed outright.

"What——" he looked at her, puzzled.

"What's funny?" she finished. "You."

"I?"

"Yes, you. If sales affect you like this you must be careful to avoid them. You've been half asleep for the last half hour. I think the horse knows the way home; you haven't been driving at all."

"I have not been asleep," he contradicted gravely, "just thinking."

"Must be deep thoughts."

"They were—shall I tell them to you?"

"Oh, no, not to-day!" she cried. "I've had enough excitement for one day. Some other time. Besides, we are almost home."

After that he threw off his lethargic manner and entered the girl's mood of appreciation of the lavish loveliness of the June. Yet, as Phœbe alighted from the carriage at the little gate of the Metz farm, and after she had thanked him and started through the yard to the house, she said softly to herself, "If Phares Eby isn't the queerest person I know! Just like a clam one minute and just lovely the next!"

Maria Metz was dishing a panful of fried potatoes as Phœbe entered the kitchen.

"Hello, daddy, Aunt Maria," exclaimed the girl.

"So you come once?" said her aunt.

"Have a good time?" asked her father.

"Yes, it was a fine sale, a real old-fashioned one."

But Aunt Maria was impatient for her supper. "Hurry," she said, "and get washed to eat. I have everything out and it'll get cold, then it ain't good. Did Phares like the sale? What did he have to say?"

"Um, guess he liked it," said the girl with a shrug of her shoulders. "It's hard to tell what he likes—he's such a queer person. He said he's going to baptize the second Sunday of June and asked me if I want to come with the others."

"He did!" Aunt Maria could not keep the eagerness out of her voice. "Well, let's sit down and eat."

After a short grace she turned to the girl. "Now then," she said as she helped herself generously to sausage and potatoes and handed the dishes across the table to Phœbe, "tell us about it."

"There isn't much to tell. I just told him that I can't renounce the pleasures of the world before I had a chance to take hold of them. I'm not ready yet to dress plain."

"Why aren't you ready?" asked the woman.

"Ach, don't ask me," Phœbe replied, speaking lightly in an effort to conceal her real feeling. "I just didn't come to that state yet. I want some more fun and pleasure before I think only of serious things."

"You're just like a big baby," her aunt said impatiently. "You can hurt a good man like Phares Eby and come home and laugh about it."

"Now, Maria," interposed the father, "let her laugh; she'll meet with crying soon enough, I guess."

But the woman could not be easily silenced. "Some day, Phœbe, you'll wish you'd been nicer to Phares."

"Why, I am nice to him."

"Well, anyhow, I think it's soon time you give up the world and its vanities," said Aunt Maria.

The girl's teasing mood fled. "I think," she said slowly, "that the plain dress should not be worn by any one who does not realize all that the dress stands for. If I ever turn plain I'll do so because I feel it is the right thing to do, but just now vanity and the love of pretty clothes are still in my heart."

After the meal was over the women washed the dishes while Jacob went out to attend to the evening milking. Later, when the poultry houses and stables were locked he returned to the kitchen and read the weekly paper. After a while he turned to Phœbe.

"Will you sing for me this evening?" he asked.

"Yes," came the ready response.

"Then make the door shut," Aunt Maria directed as they went to the sitting-room. "I want to mark my rug yet this evening and your noise bothers me."

CHAPTER XI
"THE BRIGHT LEXICON OF YOUTH"

"What shall I sing?" Phœbe asked as her father sank into the big rocker and she took her place at the low organ.

"Ach, anything," he replied.

She smiled, turned the pages of an old music book, and began to sing, "Annie Laurie." Her father nodded approval and smiled when she followed that with several other old-time favorites. Then she hesitated a moment, a low melody came from the organ, and the words of the beautiful lullaby fell from her lips:

"Sweet and low, sweet and low,
Wind of the western sea;
Low, low,—breathe and blow,
Wind of the western sea;
Over the rolling waters go,
Come from the dying moon and blow,
Blow him again to me,
While my little one, while my pretty one sleeps."

Phœbe sang the lullaby as gently as if a tiny head were nestled against her bosom. She had within her, as has every normal, unspoiled woman, the loving impulses and yearning tenderness of motherhood. Her womanhood's star of hope shone brightly, though from a great distance; she devoutly hoped for the fulfillment of her destiny, but always dreamed of it coming in some time far removed from the present. Wifehood and motherhood— that was her goal, but long years of other joys and other achievements stretched between. Yet she felt an incomparable joy as she sang the lullaby. She sang it easily and sweetly and uttered each word with the freedom of one to whom music is second nature.

To the man who listened memory drew aside the curtains of twenty years. He beheld again the sweet-faced wife glorified with the blessed halo of motherhood. He thrilled at the remembrance of her intense rapture as she clasped her babe in moments of vivid ecstasy, or held it tenderly in her arms as she sang the slumber song. The man was lost in revery—the sweet voice of the mother had suddenly grown weak and drifted into silence—a silence which would have been intolerable save for the lisping of a child voice that was filled with the same indefinable sweetness the treasured, silenced voice had possessed. In those first days of bereavement Jacob Metz had clung to his motherless babe for comfort; her love and caresses had renewed his strength and touched him with a divine sense of his responsibility. His toil-hardened hands could not do the mother's tasks for her but his heart could love sufficiently to recompense, so far as that be possible, for the loss of the mother's presence. His own childhood had been stripped of all romance, hence he could not measure the value of the innocent pleasures of which Aunt Maria, in her stern and narrow discipline, deprived the little girl; but so far as he saw the light and so far as he was able, he quietly soothed where Aunt Maria irritated, and mitigated by his interest and sympathy the sternness of the woman's rule.

A fleeting retrospect of the past years crowded upon him as he heard Phœbe sing the mother's song. The two voices seemed strangely merged and blended; when she ended and turned her face to him she seemed the vivid reincarnation of that other Phœbe.

"That's a pretty song, isn't it, daddy? You like it?"

"Yes. Your mom used to sing you to sleep with it."

"I wish I could remember. I can't remember her at all," the girl said wistfully.

"I wish you could, too. You look just like her. I'm glad you do. We Metz people all have the black hair and dark eyes but you have your mom's light hair and blue eyes. I see her every time I look at you."

She seated herself near him. In a moment he spoke again, very deliberately, with his characteristic expressiveness:

"Phœbe, I want you to know more about your mom. You know she was plain, a member of our Church. I would like you to dress like she did but I don't want you to dress that way and then be dissatisfied and go back to the dress of the world. Not many people do that, but those that do are the laughing-stock of the world. I don't want you coaxed to be plain and then not stay plain. I tell you this because I can see that you are just like your mom was, you like pretty things so much. She came in the Church with some girls she knew; none of her people were plain. I knew her right after she joined, and I took her to Love Feasts and to Meetings and we were soon promised to marry each other. I saw that something was troubling her and she told me that she wanted pretty clothes again and wanted to go to parties and picnics like some of the other girls she knew. But because she cared for me and was promised to me she kept on dressing plain. So we were married. The second year you came and then she was satisfied without pretty dresses. She said to me once, 'Jacob, I was foolish to fret about pretty clothes and jewelry, they could not bring happiness, but this'—she looked down at you—'this is the most precious, most beautiful jewel any woman could have.' I knew then that the love of vanity was gone from her, that she would never be tempted to go back to the dress and ways of the world."

For a moment there was silence in the big room. The memory of the days when the home circle was unbroken left the father quiet and thoughtful and strangely touched Phœbe.

90

"I am glad you told me, daddy," she said presently. "To-day when Phares talked about the baptizing he seemed so confident and at peace in his religion, yet I could not promise to come into the Church and wear the plain dress. I am going to think about it——"

Here Aunt Maria called loudly, "Phœbe, come out here once."

Phœbe sighed, then turned from her father and entered the kitchen. The older woman was bending over an oblong frame and by the aid of a small steel hook was pulling tufts of cloth through the mesh of a piece of burlap, the foundation of a hooked rug.

"See once, Phœbe, won't this be pretty till it's done?"

"Yes, very pretty. I like the Wall of Troy design you are using, and the blues and gray will be a good combination. What are you going to do with it?"

"It's for your chest."

The girl laughed. "Aunt Maria, you'll have to enlarge that chest or buy a second one. This spring when we cleaned house and had all the things of that chest hung out to air, I counted eleven quilts, six rugs, five table-cloths, ten gingham aprons, ever so many towels, besides all the old homespun linen I have in that other chest on the garret. I'll never need all that."

"Why, you don't know. If you marry——"

"But if I don't marry?"

"Ach, I guess old maids need covers and aprons and things as well as them that marry. But now I guess I'll stop for to-night. I want to sew the hooks 'n' eyes on my every-day dress yet before I go to bed."

"But before you go I want to ask you, to talk with you and daddy," said Phœbe, determined to decide the matter of studying music in Philadelphia. The uncertainty of it was growing to be a strain upon her. If there was no possibility of her dreams becoming realities she would put the thoughts away from her, but she wanted the question settled.

"Now what——" Aunt Maria raised her spectacles to her forehead and looked at the girl, at her flushed cheeks, her eyes darkened by excitement.

"So," the woman chuckled, "Phares picked up spunk once and asked you——"

"Phares has nothing to do with it," Phœbe said curtly, her cheeks flushing deeper at the thought of the words she knew her aunt was ready to say. "This is my affair, and, of course, yours and daddy's." She turned to her father—"I want to study music."

"Music? How—you mean to learn to play the organ?" he asked.

"No. Oh, no! I mean to sing. Listen, please," she pleaded as she saw the bewildered look on his face. "You know I have always liked to sing. I have told you that many people have said my voice is good. So I'd like to go to Philadelphia and take lessons from a good teacher. May I? I can use the money I have in the bank, that my mother left me. I have about a thousand dollars. It won't take all of that for a few years' lessons. Daddy, if you'll only say I may go!" Her voice wavered suspiciously at the end.

Jacob Metz looked at his daughter, then at the little low organ in the other room. Another Phœbe had loved to sit at that instrument and sing—perhaps he was too easy with the girl—but if she wanted to go away and take lessons——

Before he could answer the plea Maria Metz found her voice and spoke authoritatively:

"Jacob Metz, goodness knows you're sometimes dumb enough to do foolish things, but you surely ain't goin' to leave Phœbe go off to learn singing! Throwing away money like that! And what good is to come of it, I'd like to know. Who put that dumb notion in her head, it just now vonders me! If she must go away somewheres to school, like all the young ones think they must nowadays, why not leave her go to Millersville or to Elizabethtown or to Lancaster to learn dressmakin'? But to Philadelphy—why, that's a big city! Anyhow, I can't see the use of all this flyin' around to school. We didn't get it when we was young, and we growed up, too. We was lucky if we got to the country school regular, and we got through the world so far!"

"But Maria," her brother spoke gently, "you know things have changed since we went to school. The world don't stay the same."

"But to learn music!" she placed a scornful accent on the last word. "What good will that do? And can't any one in Greenwald or Lancaster, even, learn her to sing? Anyhow, she don't need no lessons, she hollers too loud already. If she takes lessons yet what'll she do?"

"Oh, Aunt Maria," Phœbe said impatiently, "you don't understand! If my voice is worth training it is worth having a good teacher. A city like Philadelphia is the place to go to."

"But where would you stay down there? Mebbe you couldn't get a place with nice people. Abody don't know what kinda people live in a city."

"I've thought of that. I wrote to Miss Lee last week and asked her and she wrote back and said it would be a splendid thing for me. She offered to help me find a boarding place. I could see her often and would not be alone among strangers. Best of all, Miss Lee has a cousin who plays the violin and who lives with her and her mother and he will help me find a good teacher. Isn't that lovely?"

"Omph," sniffed Aunt Maria. "It'll cost you a lot of money for board, mebbe as much as four dollars a week! And your lessons will be a lot, and your car fare back and forth. Then I guess you'd want a lot more dresses and things—ach, you just put that dumb notion from your head."

"Maria," Phœbe's father spoke in significantly even tones, "you needn't talk like that. Phœbe has the money her mom left her and I guess I could send her to school if I wanted to. It won't hurt her to go study music and see something of the world. It'll do her good to get away once like other girls."

"Do her good," echoed Aunt Maria. "Jacob Metz! You know little of the dangers of the big cities! But then, men ain't got no sense! I never met one yet that had enough to fill a thimble!"

"Aunt Maria," the girl said gently, "I'm not a child. I'm eighteen and I'll be near Miss Lee and her friends."

"And the fiddler," added the woman tartly.

"Ach," Phœbe laughed. "Miss Lee will take care of me."

"Mebbe so," grumbled Aunt Maria.

"Now look here, Maria," Jacob spoke up, "Phœbe can go this fall once and try it and she can come home often and if she don't like it she can come home right away. It takes only three hours to go to there. So, Phœbe, you write to Miss Lee and tell her to expect you."

"Then I may go!" She threw her arms about her father's neck and kissed his bearded face. Demonstrations of affection were rare in the Metz household, but the father smiled as he stroked the girl's hair.

"You be a good girl, Phœbe, that's all I want," he said.

"I will, daddy, I will!"

"Then, Maria, you take Phœbe to Lancaster and get things ready so she can go in September. I'll let her take that thousand she has in the bank, but that must reach; it's enough for music lessons."

"I won't need all of it. What's left I'll save for next year."

"Next year! How many years must you go?" demanded Aunt Maria, still unhappy and sore.

"I don't know. But when the thousand is gone I'll earn more if I want to spend more."

"Ach, my," groaned the woman, "you talk like money grew

on trees! What's the world comin' to nowadays?" She rose and pushed her rugging frame into a corner of the kitchen.

"Maria," her brother suggested, "we can get a hired girl if the work's too much for you alone."

"Hired girl! I don't want no hired girl! Half of 'em don't do to suit, anyhow! I don't just want Phœbe here to help to work. It'll be awful lonesome with her gone."

Phœbe saw the glint of anguish in the dark eyes and felt that her aunt's protestations were partly due to a disinclination to be parted from the child she had reared.

"Aunt Maria," she said kindly, "I hate to do what you think I shouldn't do, for you're good to me. You mustn't feel that I'm doing this just to be contrary. You and I think differently, that's all. Perhaps I'm too young to always think right, but I don't want you to be hurt. I'll come home often."

"Ach, yes well," the woman was touched by the girl's tenderness, but was still unconvinced. "Not much use my saying more, I guess. You and your pop will do what you like. You're a Metz, too, and hard to change when you make up your mind once."

That night when Phœbe went to bed in her old-fashioned walnut bed she lay awake for hours, dreaming of the future. If Aunt Maria had known the visions that flitted before the girl that night she would have quaked in apprehension, for Phœbe finally drifted into slumber on clouds of glory, forecasts of the wonderful time when, as a prima donna in trailing, shimmering gown, she would have the world at her feet while she sang, sang, sang!

CHAPTER XII
THE PREACHER'S WOOING

There belonged to the Metz farm an old stone quarry which Phœbe learned to love in early childhood and which, as she grew older, she adopted as her refuge and dreaming-place.

Almost directly opposite the green gate at the country road was a narrow lane which led to the quarry. It was bordered on the right by a thickly interlaced hedge of blackberry bushes and wild honeysuckle, beyond which stood the orchard of the Metz farm. On the left of the lane a wide field sloped up along the road leading to the summit of the hill where the schoolhouse and the meeting-house stood. The lane was always inviting. It was the fair road to a fairer spot, the old stone quarry.

The old stone quarry banked its rugged height against the

side of a great wooded hill. Some twenty feet below the level of the lane was a huge semicircular base, and from this the jagged sides reared perpendicularly to the summit of the hill. The top and slopes of this hill were covered with a dense growth of underbrush and trees. Tall sycamores bordered the road opposite the quarry, making the spot sheltered and secluded.

To this place Phœbe hurried the morning after she had gained her father's consent to go to Philadelphia.

"I just had to come here," she breathed rapturously; "the house is too narrow, the garden too small, this June morning. They won't hold my dreams."

She stood under the giant sycamore opposite the quarry and looked appreciatively about her. Earth's warm, throbbing bosom thrilled with the universal joy of parentage and fruition. Shafts of sunlight shot through the green of the trees, odors of wild flowers mingled with the fresh, woodsy fragrance of the fields and woods, song sparrows flitted busily among the hedges and sang their delicious, "Maids, maids, maids, hang on your tea kettle-ettle-ettle!" From the densest portions of the woods above the quarry a thrush sang—all nature seemed atune with Phœbe's mood, blithe, happy, joyous!

Phares Eby, going to town that morning, walked slowly as he neared the Metz farm and looked for a glimpse of Phœbe. He saw, instead, the portly figure of Aunt Maria as she walked about her garden to see the progress of her early June peas.

"Why, Phares," she called, "you goin' to Greenwald?"

"Yes. Anything I can do for you?"

"Ach no. Phœbe was in the other day. But come in once, Phares, I'll tell you something about her."

"Where is Phœbe?" he asked as he joined Aunt Maria in the garden.

"Over at the quarry again. But I must tell you, she's goin' to Phildelphy to study singin'. She asked her pop and he said she dare."

"Philadelphia—singing!"

"Yes. I don't like it at all, but she's goin' just the same."

"It is a mistake to let her go," said the preacher. "It's a big mistake, Aunt Maria. She should stay at home or go to some school and learn something of value to her. In this quiet place she has never heard of many temptations which, in the city, she must meet face to face. It is the voice of the Tempter urging her to do this thing and we who are her friends should persuade her to remain in her good home and near the friends who care for her. Have you thought, Aunt Maria, that the people to whom she will go may dance and play cards and do many worldly things? Philadelphia is very different from Greenwald. Why, she may learn to indulge in worldly amusements and to love the vanities of the world which we have tried to teach her to avoid! She will be like a bird in a strange nest."

"I know, Phares, but I can't make it different. When Jacob says a thing once it's hard to change him, and she is like that too. They fixed it up last night and I had no say at all. All I said against her going did as much good as if I said it to the chairs in the kitchen. Phœbe is going to get Miss Lee, the one that was teacher on the hill once, to help her. And Miss Lee has a cousin that lives with her and he plays the fiddle and he is goin' to get a teacher for her."

Phares Eby groaned and gritted his teeth.

"I guess I'll go talk with her a while," he decided.

"Mebbe she'll come in soon, if you want to wait. I told her to bring me some pennyroyal along from the field next the quarry. You know that's so good for them little red ants, and they got into my jelly cupboard. She went a while ago and I guess she'll soon be back now."

"I think I'll walk over."

"All right, Phares. Tell her not to forget the pennyroyal."

With long strides the preacher crossed the road and started up the lane to the quarry. There he slackened his pace—he thought of the previous day when he had asked Phœbe about entering the Church. She had disappointed him, it was true, but she had seemed so eager to do right, so innocent and childlike, that the interview had not left him wholly unhappy or greatly discouraged. He had hoped last night that she would give the matter of her soul's salvation serious thought, that she would soon stand in the stream and be baptized by him. Over sanguine he had been—so soon she had forgotten serious things and planned a winter in Philadelphia studying music.

"I must act," he thought. "I must tell her of my love. All these years I have loved her and kept silent about it because I thought she was just a child. But I must tell her now. If she loves me she shall marry me soon and this great temptation will leave her; she will hearken to the voice of her conscience, and we will begin our life of happiness together."

With this resolution strong within him he went up the lane to the quarry and Phœbe.

She was seated on a rock under the giant sycamore and leaned confidingly against the shaggy trunk. The glaring sunshine that fell upon the fields and hills could not wholly penetrate the protecting canopy of well-proportioned sycamore leaves; only a few quivering rays fell upon the girl's upturned face.

As the preacher approached she looked around quickly but did not move from her caressing attitude by the tree.

"Good-morning, Phares. I'm glad you came. I was wishing for some one to share the old quarry with me this morning."

"Aunt Maria told me you were here—she is impatient for her pennyroyal." Now, that the supreme moment had arrived, he hesitated and grasped at the first straw for conversation.

"Oh, dear," she said childishly, "Aunt Maria expects me to remember ants and pennyroyal when I come here. Phares, I can't explain it, but this old quarry has a strange fascination for me. The beauty in its variegated stone with the sunlight upon it attracts me. Sometimes I am tempted to climb up the hill and hang over the quarry and look down into the heart of it."

"Don't ever do that!" cried the preacher.

"I won't," laughed Phœbe. "I don't want to die just yet. But isn't it the loveliest place! I come here often when the men are not blasting. It seems almost a desecration to blast these rocks when we think how long nature took in their making."

She paused . . . only the sounds of nature invaded the quiet of the place: the drowsy hum of diligent bees, the cattle browsing in a field near by, the ecstatic trill of a bird. The world of bustle and flurry with its seething vats of evil and corruption, its sordid discontent and petulance, its ways of pain and darkness, seemed far removed from that place of peace and calm solitude. Phœbe could not bear to think that across the seas men were lying in the filth of water-soaked trenches, agonizing and bleeding on the battlefields and suffering nameless tortures in hospitals that a peace like unto the peace of her quiet haven might brood undisturbed over the world in future generations. She dismissed the harrowing thought of war—she would enjoy the calm of her quarry.

The preacher had listened silently to the girl's rhapsodies— she suddenly awakened to the realization that he was paying scant attention to her enthusiastic words. She looked at him, her heart-beats quickened, some intuition warned her of the imminent declaration.

She rose quickly from the embrace of the sycamore tree, but the compelling eyes of the preacher restrained her from flight. She stood before him, within reach of his hands.

His first words reassured her somewhat: "Phœbe, your aunt has told me that you are going to Philadelphia to study music."

"Yes. Isn't it fine! I'm so happy——" she stopped.

Displeasure was written plainly upon his countenance. "Don't you think it's all right, Phares?"

"I think it is a great mistake," he said gravely. "Why not spend your time on something of value to yourself and your friends and the world in general?"

"But music is of great value. Why, the world needs it as it needs sunshine!"

"But, Phœbe, you must remember you do not come of a people who stand before the worldly and lift their voices for the joy of the multitude of curious people. Your voice is right as it is and needs no training. It is as God gave it to you and is made to be used in His service, in His Church and your home."

"But I have always wanted to learn to sing well, really well. So I am going to Philadelphia this winter and take lessons from a competent teacher."

"Phœbe," exhorted the preacher, "put away the temptation before it grips you so strongly that you cannot shake it off. You must not go!"

He spoke the last words in a tone of authority which the girl answered, "Phares, let us speak of something else. You know I have some of the Metz determination in my make-up and I can't be easily forced to give up a cherished plan. At any rate, we must not quarrel about it."

The preacher forbore to try further argument or persuasion. He became grave. His habitual serenity of mind was disturbed by shadowy forebodings—when the pebbles of doubt drop into the placid pool of content it invariably follows that the waters become agitated for a time. Hitherto he had been hopeful of winning Phœbe. Had he not known her and loved her all her life! What was more natural than that their friendship should culminate in a deeper feeling!

He stretched out his hand in a sudden rush of feeling—"Phœbe, I love you."

She stepped back a pace and his hand fell to his side.

"Don't, Phares," she began, but the next moment she realized that she could not turn aside his love without listening to him.

"Phœbe, you must listen—I love you, I have loved you all my life. Can't you say that you care for me?"

"Don't ask me that!" she pleaded. "I don't want to marry anybody now. All my life I have dreamed of going to a city and studying music and I can't let the opportunity slip away from me now when it is so near. To work under the direction of a master teacher has long been one of my dearest dreams."

"You mean that you do not love me, then. Or if you do, that you would rather gratify your desire to study music than marry me—which is it?"

"Ach, Phares, don't make it hard for me! I said I don't want to get married now. All my life I have lived on a farm and have thought that I should be wonderfully happy if I could get away from it for a while and know what it is to live in a big city. There I shall have a chance to see life in its broader aspects. I shall not be harmed by gathering new ideas and ideals, gaining new friends, and, above all, learning to sing well."

The man groaned in spirit. It was evident that she was thoroughly determined to go away from the farm.

"Phœbe," he pleaded again, not entirely for his own selfish desire, but worried about her love of worldliness, "do you know that the things for which you are going to the city are really not important, that all outward acquisitions for which you long now are transient? The things that count are goodness and purity and to be without them is to be pauperized; the things that bring happiness are love and home ties and to be without them is to be desolate. You want a larger, broader vision, but the city cannot always give you that."

There was no bitterness in his voice, only an undertone of sadness as he spoke. "Phœbe, tell me plainly, do you care for me?"

Her face was lamentably pathetic as she looked into his and read there the desire for what she could not give. "Not as you wish," she said softly. "But I don't really know what love is yet, I haven't thought about it except as something that will come to me some day, a long time from now. There are too many other things I must think about now. When I am through studying music I'll think about being married."

The preacher shook his head; his heart was too heavy for more words, more futile words.

"Let us go, Phares," she said, the silence becoming intolerable.

"Yes," he agreed. "And Phœbe," he added as they turned away from the quarry, "I hope you'll learn your lesson quickly and come back to us."

They stepped from the sheltered path into the sunshine of the lane. Long trails of green lay in their path as they went, but the eyes of both were temporarily blinded to the loveliness of the June. When they reached the dusty road the preacher said good-bye and went on his way to the town.

She stood where he left her; the suppressed feelings of the past half hour soon struggled to avenge themselves and she sped down the lane again, back to the refuge of the kindly tree, and there, under her sycamore, burst into passionate weeping.

Some time after Phares left the girl at the end of the lane David Eby came swinging down the hill and entered the Metz kitchen.

"Hello, Aunt Maria. Where's Phœbe?"

"Why, I guess over at the quarry. She went for pennyroyal long ago and then Phares came and he went over after her, but I saw him go on the way to town a bit ago, so I guess she's still over there. Guess she's stumbling around after a bird's nest or picking some weeds that ain't no good. I don't see why she stays so long."

"I'll go see," volunteered David.

"Yes well. And tell her to hurry with that pennyroyal. I want it for red ants, but they can carry away the whole jelly cupboard till she gets here."

"I'll tell her," said David, and went off, whistling.

Phœbe's paroxysm of grief was short-lived. The soothing quiet of the quarry calmed her, but her eyes showed telltale marks of tears as David's steps sounded down the lane.

She rose hastily, then sank back to her seat under the tree as she saw the identity of the intruder.

"Whew, Phœbe Metz," he said and whistled in his old, boyish way as he sat beside her, "you're crying!"

"I am not," she declared.

"Then you just have been! I haven't seen you in tears for many years. Phœbe"—he changed his tone—"what's gone wrong? Anything the matter?"

"Don't," she sniffed, "don't ask me or you'll have me at it again." She steadied her voice and went on, "I came over here so gloriously happy I could have shouted, because daddy said last night that I may go to Philadelphia this fall——"

"Gee whiz!" David grabbed her hand. "Why, I'm tickled to death. But what—why are you crying? Isn't that what you want?"

"Yes." She smiled, pleased by his interest and eagerness. "But just as I was happiest along came Phares and told me it was wicked to go. It's all a mistake to go, he said."

"Ach, the dickens with the old fossil!" David cried. "And I'm not going to take that back or be sorry for saying it. Hadn't he better sense than to throw a wet blanket on all your happiness!"

"Perhaps I needed it. I was just about burning up with gladness."

"Well, don't you care what he's thinking about it. You go learn music if you want to and your father lets you go. Did he see you cry?"

"Certainly not! I wouldn't cry before him. He would say that was foolish or wicked or something it shouldn't be. But you—you are so sensible I don't mind if you do see me with my eyes red."

"Ha, ha, that's a compliment. I have been told that I am happy-go-lucky and sort of a cheerful idiot, but no person ever told me that I'm sensible. Well, don't you forget me when you get to be that prima donna."

"I won't. You and Mother Bab rub me the right way."

"But won't she be glad when I tell her," said David. "I came down to see if you had decided about it, and I find it all arranged."

"And me in tears," added Phœbe, her natural poise and good humor again restored. "Tell Mother Bab I am coming up soon to tell her about it."

So, in happier mood, she walked beside David, down the green lane to the road, across the road to her own gate.

"So you come once!" Aunt Maria greeted her.

"Oh, I forgot your pennyroyal! I'll go get it."

"Never mind. You stayed so long I went over to the field near the barn and got some. But you look like you've been cryin', Phœbe. Did you and Phares have a fall-out?"

"No."

"You and David, then?"

"No—please don't ask me—it's nothing."

"Well, there ain't no man in shoe leather worth cryin' about, I can tell you that. They just laugh at your cryin'."

Phœbe smiled at her aunt's philosophy and resolved to forget the discouraging words of the preacher. She would be happy in spite of him—the future held bright hours for her!

CHAPTER XIII
THE SCARLET TANAGER

The days that followed were busy days at the gray farmhouse. Phœbe was soon deep in the preparations for her stay in the city. Her meagre wardrobe required replenishment; she wanted to go to Philadelphia with an outfit of which Miss Lee would not be ashamed. Much to her aunt's surprise the girl selected one-piece dresses of blue serge with sheer white collars for every-day wear in cold weather; a few white linens for warm days; and these, with her blue serge suit, her simple white graduation dress, and a plain dark silk dress, were the main articles of her outfit. Aunt Maria expressed her relief and wonder at the girl's choice—"Well, it wonders me that you don't want a lot of ugly fancy things to go to Phildelphy. Those dresses all made in one are sensible once. I guess the style makers tried all the outlandish styles they could think of and had to make a nice style once."

But when Phœbe purchased a piece of long-cloth and began to make undergarments, beautifying them by sprays of hand embroidery, Aunt Maria scoffed, "Umph, I'd be ashamed to put snake-doctors on my petticoats."

The girl laughed. "They aren't snake-doctors, they are butterflies," she said.

"Not much difference—both got wings. I don't see what for you want to waste time like that."

"It makes them prettier, and I like pretty things."

"Ach, you have dumb notions sometimes. I guess we better make your other dresses soon, then you won't have time for sewing snake-doctors or butterflies. You better get your silk dress made in Greenwald, it's so soft and slippery that I ain't going to bother my old fingers makin' it. Granny Hogendobler wants to come out and help to sew, and David's mom said she'll come down and help us cut and fit the serge dresses. She's real handy like that. If those dresses look as nice on you as they do on the pictures they will be all right. Granny and Barb dare just come and both help with your things—they both think it's so fine for you to go to the city! Granny Hogendobler spoiled her Nason by givin' him just what he wanted, and now what has she got for it? And I guess Barb is easy with that big boy of hers. Mebbe if she was a little stricter he'd be in the Church like Phares is, though David is a nice boy and I guess he don't give his mom any trouble."

"I just love Mother Bab; don't you say such things about her!" Phœbe exclaimed, her eyes flashing.

"Why, I like her too," the woman said. She looked at Phœbe in surprise. "You needn't be so touchy. For goodness' sake, don't take to gettin' touchy like some people are! Handling them's like tryin' to plane over a knot in wood; any way you push the plane is the wrong way. This here going to Philadelphy upsets you, I guess. You're gettin' as touchy as the little touch-me-nots we get on the hill; they all snap shut when you touch 'em—only you snap open."

Phœbe laughed. "I guess I am excited," she admitted. "I'm sewing too much for summer days and it makes me irritable. I think I'll let the butterflies wait and I'll go outdoors. Shall I weed the garden?"

"Weed the garden? Now you're talkin' dumb! Don't you know yet that abody don't weed a garden on Fridays? Ours always gets done on Monday. But if you want to get out you dare take some of the sand-tarts I baked yesterday up to David's mom, she likes them so much. And you ask her if she can come down next week to help with the dresses. But don't stay too long, for it's been so hot all day and I think it's goin' to storm yet."

"Don't worry about me if it rains. I won't start for home if it looks threatening. I'll wait till the storm is over."

Aunt Maria filled a basket with her delectable cookies and the girl started up the hill. It was, indeed, a hot day, even for August. Phœbe paused several times in the shelter of overhanging trees as she plodded up the steep road. On the summit she climbed the rail fence and perched in the cool shade for a little while and looked out over the valley where the town of Greenwald lay.

"It's lovely here, and I'm wondering how I can be happy when I know that I am going to leave it soon and go to the city for a long winter away from my home. But there's a voice calling to me from the great outside world and I won't be satisfied until I go and mingle with the multitude of a great city. It is life, life, that I want to see and know. And yet, I'm glad I'll have this to come back to! It gives me a comfortable feeling to know that this is waiting for me, no matter where I go—this is still my home. Sometimes I wonder if Aunt Maria could possibly be speaking wisely when she says it is all a waste of money to run off to the city and study music. But what is there on the farm to attract me? I don't want to marry yet"—the remembrance of Phares Eby's pleading came to her— "and if I do marry some time, it won't be Phares. No, never Phares! Ach, Phœbe Metz, you don't know what you want!" she said to herself as she jumped from the fence and ran down the road to the Eby farm.

At the gate she paused. Mother Bab stood among her flowers, her white-capped head bare of any other covering, the hot sunshine streaming upon her.

"Mother Bab," she cried, "you are simply baking in the sun!"

"No," the woman turned to Phœbe and smiled. "I'm forgetting it's hot while I look at the flowers. You see, Phœbe, I was in the house sewing and trying to keep cool and all of a sudden my eyes grew dim so I couldn't sew. The fear came to me, the fear that my sight is going, though I try not to strain them at all and never sew at night. Well, I just ran out here and began to look and look at my flowers—if I ever do go blind I'm going to have lots of memories of lovely things I've seen."

Phœbe drew Mother Bab's face to her and kissed it. "You just mustn't get blind! It would be too dreadful. There are many clever specialists in the city these days. Surely, there is some doctor who can help you."

"They all say there is little to be done in a case like mine. But, let's forget it; I can see and we'll keep on hoping it will last. I went to a doctor at Lancaster some time ago and I'm going to give him a fair trial. I guess it'll come out right."

Phœbe brightened again at the woman's words of contagious cheer and hope.

"Isn't the garden pretty?" asked Mother Bab as they looked about it.

"Perfect! Those zinnias are lovely."

"Yes, I like them. But I like their other name better—Youth and Old Age, my mother used to call them. She used to say that they are not like other flowers, more like people, for the buds open into tiny flowers and those tiny flowers grow and develop until they are large and perfect. I would think something fine were missing in my garden if I didn't have my Youth and Old Age every year. But you will be too hot in this sun; shall we go in?"

"No, please, not until I have seen the flowers. I need to gather precious memories, too, to take with me to Philadelphia. Oh, I like this"—she knelt in the narrow path and buried her face in fragrant lemon verbena plants.

"I like that, too. Mother used to call it Joy Everlasting. We always put it in our bureau drawers between the linens. David likes lavender better, so I use that now."

"How you spoil him," said Phœbe.

"You think so?" asked the mother gently.

Phœbe smiled in retraction of her statement. "We'll both be parboiled if we stay out here any longer," she said as she linked her arm into Mother Bab's. "Aunt Maria sent you some sand-tarts."

"Isn't she good!"

"Yes, but"—the blue eyes twinkled mischievously—"they are just a bribe. We want you to come down and help us with the dresses some day next week. You are not to sew, but if you are there to tell about the fit of them I'll feel better satisfied. Whew! If it's as hot as this I'll have a lovely time fitting woolen dresses!"

"You won't mind."

"I don't believe I shall, so long as the dresses are to be worn in Philadelphia. Granny Hogendobler is coming out, too. Will you come?"

"I'll be glad to. David can eat his dinner at his aunt's."

They entered the house and sat in the sitting-room, a room dear to both because of its association with many happy hours.

"I love this room," Phœbe said. "This must be one of my pleasant memories when I go."

"I like it better than any other room in the house," said Mother Bab. "I suppose it's because the old clock and the haircloth sofa are in it. Why, Davie used to slide down the ends of that sofa and call it his boat when he was just a little fellow. And that old clock"—her voice sank to the tenderness of musing retrospect—"why, Davie's father set it up the day we were married and came here and set up housekeeping and it's been ticking ever since. Davie used to say 'tick-tock' when he heard it, when he first learned to talk. I like that old clock most as much as if it were something alive. A man who comes around here to buy antique furniture came in one day and offered to buy it. I'll never forget how David told him it wasn't for sale. The very thought of selling the old clock made Davie cross."

"Davie cross! How could he keep the twinkle out of his eyes long enough to be cross?"

"Ach, it don't last long when he gets cross."

"Where is he now, Mother Bab?"

"Working in the tobacco field."

"In the hot sun!"

"He says he don't mind it. He's so pleased with the tobacco this summer. It looks fine. If the hail don't get in it now it'll bring about four hundred dollars, he thinks. That will be the most he has ever gotten out of it. But tobacco is an awful risk. If the weather is just so it pays about the best of anything around this part of the country, I guess, but so often the poor farmers work hard in the tobacco fields and then the hail comes along and all is spoiled. But ours is fine so far."

"I'm glad. David has been working hard all summer with it."

"Sometimes he gets discouraged; Phares's crops always seem to do better than David's, yet David works just as hard. But Phares plants no tobacco."

At that moment Phares Eby himself came into the room where the two sat. He appeared a trifle embarrassed when he saw Phœbe. Since the June meeting under the sycamore tree by the old stone quarry he had made no special effort to see her, and the several times they had met in that time he had greeted her with marked restraint.

"Good-afternoon," he murmured, looking from Phœbe to Mother Bab and back again to Phœbe. "I didn't know you were here, Phœbe. I—Aunt Barbara, I came in to tell you there's a bright red bird in the woods down by the cornfield."

"There is!" cried Phœbe with much interest. "Is it all red, or has it black wings and tail?"

"Why, I couldn't say. I know David and Aunt Barbara are always interested in birds and I heard David say the other day that he hadn't seen a red bird this summer, that they must be getting scarce around this section. So I thought I'd come up and tell you about it. I know it is bright red. Do you want to come out and try to find it again, Aunt Barbara?"

"Not now, Phares. I have been in the sun so much to-day that my head aches."

"Would you care to see it?" he asked Phœbe in visible hesitation.

She answered eagerly, her passionate love of birds mastering her embarrassment. "I'd love to, Phares! I am anxious to see whether it's a tanager or a cardinal. I have never seen a cardinal."

South of David Eby's cornfield stretched a strip of woodland. There blackberry brambles tangled about the bases of great oaks and the entire woods—trees and brambles—made an ideal nesting-place for birds.

"Perhaps it's gone," said the preacher as they went along to the woods.

"But it's worth trying for," she said.

They kept silent then; only the rustling of the corn was heard as the two went through the green aisle. When they reached the woodland a sudden burst of glorious melody came to them. Phœbe laid a hand impulsively upon the arm of the preacher, but she removed it quite as suddenly when he looked down at her and said, "Our bird!"

The bird, a scarlet tanager, aware of the presence of the intruders and eager to attract attention to himself and safeguard his hidden mate, flew to an exposed branch of an oak tree. There he displayed his gorgeous, flaming scarlet body with its touch of black in wings and tail.

"It's a tanager," said Phœbe. "Isn't he lovely!"

"Very fine," said the preacher. "What color is his mate? Is she red?"

"She's green, a lovely olive green. When she sits on the nest she's just the color of her surroundings. If she were red like her mate she'd be too easily destroyed."

"God's providence," said the preacher.

"It is wonderful—look, Phares, there he goes!"

The scarlet tanager made a streak of vivid color across the sky as he flew off over the corn.

"I wonder if he trusts us or if his mate is not about," Phœbe said. "He's a beauty, so is his mate in her green frock. A few minutes with the birds can teach us a great deal, can't it?"

"Yes, Phœbe, here, right near your home, are countless lessons to be learned and accomplishments to be acquired. Tell me, do you still wish to go away to the city?"

"Certainly. I am going in September."

"You remember the verse in the Third Reader we used to have at school:

"'Stay, stay at home, my heart and rest;
Home-keeping hearts are happiest.
For those who wander, they know not where,
Are full of trouble and full of care;
To stay at home is best.'"

"But I have ambitions, Phares. All my eighteen years of life have been spent on a farm, in the narrow existence of those whose days are passed within one little circle. I want to see things, I want to meet people, I want to live, I want to learn to sing—I can't do any of these things here. Oh, you can't understand my real sincerity in this desire to get away. It is not that I love my home and my people less than you love yours. I feel that I must get away!"

"But your voice, Phœbe, like the scarlet tanager's, is right as God made it. Because we are such old friends it grieves me to see you go. I was hoping you would change your mind—there is so much vanity and evil in the city."

"I'll try to keep from it, Phares. I shall merely learn to sing better, meet a few new people, and be wiser because of the experience."

"It is useless to try to persuade you, I suppose. I hoped you would reconsider it, that you would learn to care for me as I care."

"Phares, don't. You make me unhappy."

"Misery loves company," he quoted, trying to smile.

"But can't you see that marriage is the thing I am thinking least about these days? I am too young."

She looked, indeed, like a fair representation of Youth as she stood by the crude rail fence at the edge of the woods, one arm flung along the rough top rail, her hair tumbled from the walk through the cornfield, her eyes still gleaming with the joy of seeing the tanager, yet shadowy with the startled emotions occasioned by the preacher's wooing.

He looked at her—

"Oh, look! Our tanager is back!" she exclaimed.

"I guess she is too young," he thought as he saw how

quickly she turned from the question of marriage to watch the red bird.

Phœbe's lips parted in pleasure as she saw the tanager again take up his place on the oak and burst into song. So absorbed were man and maid that neither heard the rustle of parted corn nor were aware of the presence of a third person until a voice exclaimed, "Oh, I beg your pardon. I didn't know you were here."

As they turned David Eby stood before them, his expression a mingling of surprise and wonder. The flush on Phœbe's face, the awakened look in her eyes, troubled the man who had come through the corn and found the girl he loved standing with the preacher. The self-conscious look on the preacher's face assured David that he had stumbled through the field in an awkward moment, that his presence was unwelcome. He turned to go back, but Phœbe stepped quickly to him and took his hand.

"Ah," thought Phares with a twinge of jealousy, "she wouldn't do that to me. How quickly she dropped her hand a while ago. They are such good friends, she and David. It's wrong to be envious; I must fight against it—and yet—I want her just as much as David does!"

"David," Phœbe begged, "come back! Why, I was just wishing you were here! There's a scarlet tanager—see!" She pointed to the brilliant songster.

"I thought he was coming to this woods so I came to hunt him," said David, his irritation gone. "I saw that fellow over by the tobacco field and followed him here. I bet they have their nest in this very woods. We'll look better next spring and try to find it and see the little ones. Tut, tut," he whistled to the bird, "don't sing your pretty head off." His eyes turned to the sky and the smile left his face. "It looks threatening," he said. "I thought I heard thunder as I came through the corn."

"That so?" said Phares. "Then we better move in."

Even as they turned and started through the field the thunder came again—distant—nearer, rolling in ominous rumbles.

"Look at the sky," said David. "Clear yellow—that means hail!"

"Oh, David"—Phœbe stood still and looked at him—"not hail on your tobacco!"

He took her arm. "Come on, Phœbe, it's coming fast. We must get in. Come to our house, Phares, that's the nearest."

Just as they reached the kitchen door, where Mother Bab was looking for them, the hail came.

"It's hail, Mommie," David said. The three words held all the worry and pain of his heart.

"Never mind"—the little mother patted his shoulder. "It's hail for more people than we know, perhaps for some who are much poorer than we are."

"But the tobacco——" He stood by the window, impotent and weak, while the devastating hail pounded and rattled and smote the broad leaves of his tobacco and rendered it almost worthless.

"Won't new leaves grow again?" Phœbe tried to cheer him.

"Not this late in the summer. My tobacco was almost ready to be cut; it was unusually early this year."

"Well," spoke up the preacher, "I can't see why you always plant tobacco. Smoking and chewing tobacco are filthy habits. I can't see why so many people of this section plant the weed when the soil could be used to produce some useful grain or vegetable."

"Yes"—David turned and addressed his cousin fiercely—"it's easy enough for you to talk! You with your big farm and orchards and every crop a success! Your bank account is so fat that you don't need to care whether your acres bring in a big return or a lean one. But when you have just a few acres you plant the thing that will be likely to bring in the most money. You know many poor people plant tobacco for that reason, and that is why I plant it."

"Davie," the mother said, "Davie!"

"I know," he said bitterly. "I'm a beast when my temper gets beyond control, but Phares can be so confounded irritating, he rubs salt in your cuts every time."

"Just for healing," the mother said gently.

"David," said Phœbe, "I guess the temper is a little bit of that Irish showing up."

At that David smiled, then laughed.

"Phœbe," he said, "you know how to rub people the right way. If ever I have the blues you are just the right medicine."

"I don't want to be called medicine," she said with a shake of her head.

"Not even a sugar pill?" asked Mother Bab.

"No. I don't like the sound of pill."

David looked across at the preacher, who stood silent and helpless in the swift tide of conversation. "You may be right, Phares. It may be the wrath of Providence upon the tobacco. I'll try alfalfa in that field next and then I'll rub Aladdin's lamp. I'll make some money then!"

"Where do you find Aladdin's lamp?" asked Phœbe.

"I can't tell you now. But I know I'm tired of slaving and having nothing for my work, so I am going after the magic lamp."

CHAPTER XIV
ALADDIN'S LAMP

The morning after the hail storm dawned fair and sunshiny. David went out and stood at the edge of his tobacco field. All about him the hail had wrought its destruction. Where yesterday broad, thick leaves of green tobacco had stood out strong and vigorous there hung only limp shreds, punctured and torn into worthlessness.

"All wasted, my summer's work. I'll rub that magic lamp now. Fool that I was, not to do it sooner!"

A little later, as he walked down the road to town, his lips were closed in a resolute line, his shoulders squared in soldierly fashion. "I hope Caleb Warner is in his office," he thought.

Caleb Warner was in; he greeted David cordially.

"Good-morning, Dave. How are things out your way? Hail do much damage?"

"Some damage," echoed the farmer. "It hailed just about four hundred dollars' worth too much for me."

"What, you don't say so! That's the trouble with your farming."

Caleb Warner was an affable little man with a frank, almost innocent, look on his smooth-shaven face. Spontaneous interest in his friends' affairs made him an agreeable companion and helped materially to increase his clientele—Caleb Warner dealt in real estate and, incidentally, in oil stocks and gold stocks.

"That's just the trouble with your farming," he repeated. "You slave and break your back and crops are fine and you hope to have a good return for your labor, when along comes a hail storm and ruins your fruit or tobacco or corn, or along comes a dry spell or a wet spell with the same result. It sounds mighty fine to say the farmer is the most independent person on the face of the earth—it's a different proposition when you try it out. Not so?"

"I'm about convinced you speak the truth about it," said the farmer.

"I know I do. I used to be a farmer, but I have grown wiser. I think there are too many other ways to make money with less risk."

"That is why I came——" David hesitated, but the other man waited silently for the explanation. "Have you any more of the gold-mine stock you offered me some time ago?"

"That Nevada mine?"

110

"Yes."

"Just one thousand dollars' worth; the rest is all cleaned out. I sold a thousand yesterday. Listen, Dave, there's the chance of your life. You know how I worked on that farm of mine, how my wife had to slave, how even Mary had to work hard. Then one day a friend of mine who had gone west came to me and offered me some stock in a western gold mine. My wife was afraid of it, said I'd lose every cent I put in it and we'd have to go to the poorhouse—women don't generally understand about investments. But I went ahead and got the stock, and in a few years I sold out part of it for a neat sum and drew big dividends on what I kept. Then we moved to town; my wife keeps a maid, Mary goes to college, and we're living instead of slaving our lives away on a farm. And it's honestly made money, for the gold was put into the earth for us to use. It is just a case of running a little risk, but no person loses money because of your risk. Of course, there's lots of stock sold that's not worth the paper it's written on, but I don't sell that kind."

"People trust you here," said David.

If the man winced or had reason to do so, he betrayed no sign of it. "I hope so," he said. "You have known me all my life. If I ever want to work any skin game I'll go out of the place where all my friends are. This mine of which I speak is near the mine at Goldfield and some of the veins struck recently are richer than those of the renowned Goldfield. They are still striking deeper veins. I have sold stock in that mine to fifteen people in this town."

He mentioned some of the residents of Greenwald; people who, in David's opinion, were too shrewd to be entangled in any nefarious investment. The names impressed David—if those fifteen put their money into it he might as well be the sixteenth.

In a little while David Eby walked home with a paper representing the ownership of a number of shares of a certain gold mine in Nevada, while Caleb Warner patted musingly a check for five hundred dollars.

Mother Bab wondered at her boy's philosophical acceptance of his crop failure. "I'm glad you take it this way," she said as he came in, whistling, from his trip to Greenwald.

"What's the use of crying?" he answered gaily, though he felt far from gay. Had he been too hasty? Doubts began to assail him. It was going to be hard to deceive his mother, she was always so eager for his confidence. But, then, he was doing it for her sake as much as for his own. The war clouds were drawing nearer and nearer to this country; if the time came when America would enter the war he would have to answer the call for help. If the stock turned out to be what the other wise men of the town felt confident it would be then the added money would be a boon to his mother while he was away in the service of his country—and yet—it was a great risk he was running. Why had he done it? The old lines of the poem came back to him and burned into his soul,

"O what a tangled web we weave
When first we practice to deceive."

Then, again, swift upon that thought came the old proverb, "Nothing venture, nothing gain." Thus he was torn between doubt and satisfaction, but it was too late to undo the deed. He was the owner of the stock and Caleb Warner had the five hundred dollars!

CHAPTER XV
THE FLEDGLING'S FLIGHT

Phœbe found the packing of her trunk a task not altogether without pain. As she gathered her few treasures from her room a feeling of desolation seemed to pervade the place. Going away from home for the first long stay, however bright the new place of sojourn, brings to most hearts an undercurrent of sadness.

She smiled a bit wistfully at her few treasures—her books, an old picture of her mother, the little Testament Aunt Maria gave her to read, the few trinkets her school friends had given her from time to time, a little kodak picture of Mother Bab and David in the flower garden.

At last the dreary task was done, the trunk strapped, and she was ready for the journey. It was a perfect September day when she left the gray farmhouse, drove in the country road and stood with her father, Aunt Maria, Mother Bab, David and Phares at the railroad station in Greenwald and waited for the noon train to Philadelphia.

Jacob Metz and the preacher made brave, though visible, efforts to be cheerful; Maria Metz made no effort to be anything except very greatly worried and anxious; but Mother Bab and David were determined that the girl's departure was to be nothing less than pleasant.

"Now be sure, Phœbe," said Aunt Maria for the tenth time, "to ask the conductor at Reading if that train is for Phildelphy before you get on, and at Phildelphy you wait till Miss Lee fetches you."

"Yes, Aunt Maria, I'll be careful."

"And don't lose your trunk check—David, did you give it to her for sure?"

"Yes. She'll hold on to it, don't you worry."

"Phœbe will be all right," said Mother Bab.

"And," said David teasingly, "be sure to let me know when you need that beet juice and cream and flour."

"Davie! Now for that I won't write to you!"

"Yes you will!" His eyes looked so long into hers that she said confusedly, "Ach, I'll write. Mind that you take good care of Mother Bab and stop in sometimes to see how Aunt Maria and daddy are getting on without me."

"Ach, we'll be all right," said Aunt Maria. "Just you take care of yourself so far away from home. And if you get homesick you come right home. Anyway, you come home soon to see us; and be sure to write every week still."

"Yes, yes!"

A shrill whistle announced the approach of the train. There were hurried kisses and good-byes, a handshake for the preacher and, last of all, a handshake for David. He held her hand so long that she cried out, "David, you'll make me miss the train!"

"No—good-bye."

"Good-bye, David." Then she tugged at her hand and in a moment was hurrying to the train.

There were few passengers that day, so the train made a short stop. Phœbe smiled as the train started, leaned forward and waved till the familiar group was lost to her view, then she settled herself with a brave little smile and looked at the well-known fields and meadows she was passing. The trees on Cemetery Hill were silhouetted against the blue sky just as she had seen them many times in her walks about the country.

But soon the old landmarks disappeared and unknown fields lay about her. Crude rail fences divided acres of rustling corn from orchards whose trees were laden with red apples or downy peaches. Occasionally flocks of startled birds rose from fields freshly plowed for the fall sowing of wheat. Huge red barns and spacious open tobacco sheds, hung with drying tobacco, gave evidence of the prosperity of the farmers of that section. Little schoolhouses were dotted here and there along the road. Flowers bloomed by the wayside and in them Phœbe was especially interested. Goldenrod in such great profusion that it seemed the very sunshine of the skies was imprisoned in flower form, stag-horn sumac with its grape-like clusters of red adding brilliancy to the landscape—everywhere was manifest the dawn of autumnal glory, the splendor that foreruns decay, the beauty that is but the first step in nature's transition from blossom and harvest to mystery and sleep.

Every two or three miles the train stopped at little stations and then Phœbe leaned from her window to see the beautiful stretches of country.

At one flag station the train was signalled and came to a stop. Just outside Phœbe's window stood a tall farmer. He rubbed his fingers through his hair and stared curiously at the train.

"Step lively," shouted the trainman.

But the farmer shook his head. "Ach, I don't want on your train! I expected some folks from Lititz and thought they'd be on this here train. Didn't none get on——"

But the angry trainman had heard enough. He pulled the cord and the train started, leaving the old man alone, his eyes scanning the moving cars.

Phœbe laughed. "We Pennsylvania Dutch do funny things! I wonder if I'll seem strange and foolish to the people I shall meet in the great city."

At Reading she obeyed Aunt Maria's injunction and boarded the proper train. The ride along the winding Schuylkill was thoroughly enjoyed by the country girl, but the picture changed when the country was left behind, suburban Philadelphia passed, and the train entered the crowded heart of the city. They passed close to dark houses grimy with the accumulated smoke of many passing locomotives. Great factories loomed before the train, factories where girls looked up for a moment at the whirring cars and turned again to the grinding life of loom or machine. The sight disheartened Phœbe. Was life in the city like that for some girls? How dreadful to be shut up in a factory while outdoors the whole panorama of the seasons moved on! She would miss the fields and woods but she would make the sacrifice gladly if she might only see life, meet people and learn to sing. The thoughts awakened by the sight of the shut-in girls were not happy ones. She welcomed the call, "Reading Terminal, Philadelphia."

As she followed the stream of fellow passengers and walked through the dim train shed to the exit her heart beat more quickly—she was really in Philadelphia! But the noise, the stream of people rushing from trains past other people rushing to trains, bewildered her. She saw the sea of faces beyond the iron gates and experienced for the first time the loneliness that comes to a traveler who enters a thronged depot and sees a host of people but enters unwelcomed and ungreeted.

However, the loneliness was momentary. The next minute she caught sight of Miss Lee. A wave of relief and happiness swept over her—she was in Philadelphia, the land of her heart's desire!

CHAPTER XVI
PHŒBE'S DIARY

September 15.

I'm in Philadelphia—really, truly! Phœbe Metz, late of a gray farmhouse in Lancaster County, is sitting in a beautiful room of the Lee residence, Philadelphia.

What a lot of things I have to write in you, diary! I can scarcely find the beginning. Before I left home I thought about keeping a diary, how entertaining it would be to sit down when I'm old and gray and read the accounts of my first winter in the city. So I went to Greenwald and bought the fattest note-book I could find and I'm going to write in you all of my joys—let's hope there won't be any sorrows—and all of my pleasures and all about my impressions of places and people in this great, wonderful City of Brotherly Love. Of course, I'll write letters home and to David and Mother Bab and some of the girls, but there are so many things one can't tell others yet likes to remember. So you'll have to be my safety valve, confidant and confessor.

When I left the train at Philadelphia I was bewildered and confused. Such crowds I never saw, not even in Lancaster. Seemed like everybody in the city was coming from a train or running to one. I was glad to see Miss Lee. She's the dearest person! I love her as much as I did when I went to her school on the hill. I'm as tall as she is now. She dresses beautifully. I thought my blue serge suit was lovely but her clothes are—well, I suppose you'd call them creations. I'm so glad I'm going to be near her all winter and can copy from her.

As I came through the gates at the depot she caught me and kissed me. I thought she was alone, but a moment later she turned to a tall man and introduced him, her cousin, Royal Lee, the musician. If Aunt Maria could see him she'd warn me again, as she did repeatedly, not to "leave that fiddlin' man get too friendly." He's handsome. I never before met a man like him. His magnetic smile, his low voice attracted me right away.

After he piloted us through the crowded depot and into a taxicab Miss Lee began to ask me questions about Greenwald and the people she knows there. I felt rather timid, for I was conscious of the appraising eyes of her cousin. He didn't stare at me, yet every time I glanced at him his eyes were searching my face. Does he think me very countrified, I wonder? I do have the red cheeks country girls are always credited with, but I'm glad I'm not "buxom." I'd hate to be fat!

I wish I could describe Royal Lee. He's just as I pictured him, only more so. He has the lean, æsthetic face of the musician, the sensitive nostrils and thin lips denoting acute temperament. His eyes are gray.

As we rode through the streets of the city Miss Lee told me her mother would have me stay with them until we can find a suitable boarding place. To-morrow we're going in search of one.

Taxicabs travel pretty fast. We skirted past curbs so that I almost held my breath and shot past trucks and other cars till I thought we'd surely land in the street. But we escaped safely and soon stopped at the Lee residence, a big, imposing brownstone house. It looks bare outside, no yard, no flowers. But inside it's a lovely place, so inviting and attractive that I'd like to settle down for life in it.

Mrs. Lee is as charming as her daughter. She has been a semi-invalid for years, but even in her wheelchair she has the poise and manner of one well born. Her greeting was so cordial and gracious, but all I could answer was an inane, "Thank you, you are very kind." Will I ever learn to express my thoughts as charmingly as these people do, I wonder!

When Miss Lee took me up-stairs it was up a bare, polished stairway upon which I was half afraid to tread. And the room she took me to! I've heard about such rooms and read about them. Delft blue paper and rugs, white woodwork and furniture, blue hangings, white curtains—it's a magazine-room turned to real!

When I tried to express my gratitude for her goodness Miss Lee hushed me with a kiss and said she anticipated as much joy from my presence in the city as I did, that I was so genuine and refreshing that it would be a pleasure to have me around. I don't know just what she means. I'm just Phœbe Metz, nothing wonderful about me, unless it's my voice, and I hope that is. She said, too, that I would make her very happy if I'd let her be a real friend to me, and if I'd call her Virginia. Why, that's just what I've been wishing for! I told her so. She is just twelve years older than I am, so she's near the thirty mark yet, and I like a friend who is older. She seems just the same Miss Lee, no older than she was when I walked down the street of Greenwald in my gingham dress and checked sunbonnet and buried my nose in the pink rose David gave me. How lucky that little country girl is! I'm here in Philadelphia, in a beautiful house, with Virginia Lee for my friend, and glorious visions of music and good times flashing before my eyes. I put my hands to my head to keep it from going dizzy!

There's a little speck of cloud in the blue of my joy right now, though. I'm afraid I've blundered already. Miss Lee— Virginia, I mean—said as she turned to leave my room that they have dinner at six and I'd have plenty of time to get ready for it. I had to tell her that I couldn't change my dress, that I hadn't thought to bring any light dress in my bag but had packed them all in the trunk. She hurried to assure me that my dark skirt and white blouse would do very well, that she would not dress for dinner to-night. But I feel sure that she seldom appears at the dinner table in a blouse and tailored skirt. Guess Aunt Maria'd say I'm in a place too tony for me, but I know I can learn how to do here. I might have remembered that some people make of their evening meal a formal one. I've read about "dressing for dinner" and when my first opportunity comes to do so it finds me with all my dress-up dresses packed in a trunk in the express office! Perhaps it serves me right for wanting to "put on style," but I remember an old saying about "doing as the Romans do." At any rate, I'm going to make the best of it and quit worrying about it, or I'll be so fussed I'll eat with my knife or pour my coffee into my saucer!

Later in the evening.

What a whirl my brain is in! Things happen so fast that I scarcely know where to begin again to write about them. But it began with the dinner. That was the grandest dinner I ever tasted but I don't remember a single thing I ate, though I do know there was no bread or jelly. What would Aunt Maria think of that! The delicate china, fine linen and silver were the loveliest I have ever seen. There were electric lights with soft-colored shades and there was a colored waiter who seemed to move without effort. The forks and spoons for the different courses bothered me. I had to glance at Virginia to see which one to use. Once during the dinner I thought of the time Mollie Brubaker told Aunt Maria about a dinner she had in the home of a city relative. I remember how Aunt Maria sniffed, "Humph, if abody's right hungry you can eat without such dumb style put on. I say when you cook and carry things to the table for people you don't need to feed them yet, they can help themselves. Just so it's clean and cooked good and enough to go round, that's all I try for when I get company to eat." I felt like a fish out of water at the Lee dinner table, but Mrs. Lee and the others were so kind and tactful that I could not be embarrassed, not enough to show it. However, I thought to myself as we rose from the table, "Thank Heaven!"

Mrs. Lee asked me whether I like music. We were in the

sitting-room and Mr. Lee stood by the piano, his hand on his violin case.

"Yes, indeed!" I told her, for I was anxious to hear him play. I have never heard any great violinist but the sound of a violin sets me thrilling. I could listen to it for hours.

Mr. Lee smiled at my enthusiasm, lifted the instrument to his shoulder and began to play. If I live to be a hundred I'll never forget that music! Like the soothing winds of summer, the subtle fragrance of a wild rose, the elusive phantoms of our dreams, it stirred my soul. I sat as one dazed when he ended.

"You say nothing. Don't you like my music?" he asked me.

"Like your music? Like is too poor a word!" And I tried to tell him how I loved it. He smiled again, that calling, hypnotizing smile, that made me want to rush to him and ask him to be my friend. But I restrained myself and turned to listen to Virginia. The music haunted me. It sounded like the voice of a soul searching for something it could never find. I was still dreaming about it when I heard Mr. Lee say, "Now, Aunt, shall we have some cribbage?" I watched him uncomprehendingly as he arranged a small table and brought out cards and boards for a game. The full significance of his actions dawned upon me—they were going to play cards! I had never seen a game of cards, but Aunt Maria taught me long ago that cards are the instrument of the Evil One. My first impulse was to run from the room, away from the cards, but I hated to be so rude.

"Do you play cards?" Royal Lee asked me.

"No, oh, no!" I gasped.

"You should learn. I'm sure you would enjoy playing."

I know my face flushed. He did not notice my bewilderment and went on, "We'll teach you to play, Miss Metz." Then he turned to the game.

Virginia came to my rescue and drew me to a seat near her. She asked me questions about Greenwald. Goodness only knows what I answered her. My attention was a variant. Troubled thoughts distressed me. In Aunt Maria's category of sins dancing, card playing and theatre-going rank side by side with lying, stealing and idolatry. As I sat there I tried to reconcile my opinion of these worldly pleasures with the conduct of my new friends. The tangle is too complicated to unravel at once. I could feel blushes of shame staining my cheeks as the game progressed. What would Aunt Maria say, what would daddy say, what would even tolerant Mother Bab say, if they knew I sat passively by and watched a game of cards? After a little while I asked Virginia whether I could write a letter to Aunt Maria and tell her of my safe arrival. I just

118

had to get out of that room! I don't know if she saw through my ruse but she smiled as she put her arm around me and led me to the stairs. "There's a desk in your room, Phœbe. You can be undisturbed there. Tell your aunt we are going to help you find a comfortable home and that we are going to take care of you. I'll be up presently to visit with you."

When I got up-stairs I felt like crying. Those cards actually scared me. I shrank from being so near the evil things. But after a while as I came to think more calmly I decided that cards couldn't hurt me if I didn't play them. I promised myself to keep from being contaminated with the wickedness of the city the while I enjoyed its harmless pleasures. The first horror of the cards soon passed but it left me sobered. I wrote a long letter to Aunt Maria and then turned off the lights and looked down into the city street. It seemed wonderful to me to see so many lights stretched off until some of them were mere specks. There was a wedding across the street. I saw the guests and caught a glimpse of the bride, dressed all in white. But later, when Virginia came up to my room and I asked her about it she didn't know a thing about the wedding. Why, at home, if there's a big wedding and the neighbors don't know about it or are not invited to it, they feel slighted. But Virginia says a city is different, that you don't really have neighbors like in Greenwald.

Virginia told me, too, how she came to teach in our school on the hill. When she finished college she wanted to earn money, just to prove that she could. Her father wanted her to stay home and live the life of a butterfly, she says. One day he said, more in jest than earnest, that if she insisted upon earning money he'd give his consent to her being a teacher in a rural school. She accepted the challenge and through her cousin she secured the place on the hill and became my teacher. When her father died and her mother became a semi-invalid she gave up her work and took up the old life again. She said that as if it were not really a desirable life, this going to teas, dances, plays, musicals, lectures, and having no cares or worries. Of course I know many of her pleasures are forbidden fruit for me, but if I ever can wear pretty clothes like hers and go off to an evening musical or concert I know I'll be as excited as a Jenny Wren.

CHAPTER XVII
DIARY—THE NEW HOME

September 16.

I've dreamed my first dreams in Philadelphia. Such dreams as they were! Whatever it was I ate for supper it must have been richer than our Lancaster County sausage and fried mush, for I dreamed all night. My old-fashioned walnut bed with its red and green calico quilt seemed to swing before me while Mother Bab and Aunt Maria talked to me. A clanging trolley car woke me and I remembered that I had been dreaming of Phares and the tanager's nest. I slept again and heard the strains of Royal Lee's violin till another car clanged past and woke me. I woke once to find myself saying, "Braid it straight, Davie. Aunt Maria's awful mad." When I slept again I thought I heard Royal Lee say, "We'll teach you to play cards," and speared tails and horned heads seemed mixed promiscuously with little pieces of cardboard bearing red and black symbols and the words "I'll get you if you don't watch out" rang in my ears. "Ugh, what awful dreams," I thought as I lay awake and listened for sounds of activity in the house. I missed Aunt Maria's five o'clock call. The luxury of an eight o'clock breakfast couldn't be appreciated the first morning, as I was wide awake at five. I'll soon learn to sleep later. There are many things I shall learn before I go back to the farm.

This morning Virginia and I started out on a glorious adventure, looking for a boarding place. She laughed when I called it that.

"I like the uncertainty of it," I told her. "The charm of the unknown appeals to me. I do not know under whose roof I shall sleep to-night yet I'm happy because I know I am going to meet new people and see new things. Of course, if I did not have you to help me I would remember Aunt Maria's dire tales of the evils and dangers of a big city and should feel afraid. As it is, I feel only curious and gay. No matter where I find a place to live it's bound to be quite different from the farm, not better, necessarily, but different."

But my "high hopes of youth" received a jolt at the very first interview with a boarding-house mistress. She wouldn't take young ladies who were studying music, their practice would annoy the other boarders. I had never thought of that!

The second quest was equally unsatisfactory. One room was vacant, a pleasant room—at twelve dollars a week! The sum left me speechless. Virginia had to explain that the amount was a trifle more than I expected to pay.

The third proved to be a smaller house on a narrower street. A charming old lady led us into a sitting-room. All my life I've been accustomed to the proverbial cleanliness of the Pennsylvania Dutch but I'm certain I never saw a place as clean as that house. I said something like that to its mistress and she informed me with a gentle firmness I never heard before that she expected every guest in her house to help to keep it in that condition. She had several rules she wanted all to obey, so that the sunshine would not have a chance to fade the rugs and the dust from the street could not ruin things. I knew I would not be happy there. I like clean rooms, but if it's a matter of choosing between foul air without dust and fresh air with dust I'll take the dust every time. I'd feel like a funeral to live in a house where the curtains and shades were down every day, summer and winter, to keep the sunshine out of the rooms and prevent the jade-green and china-blue and old-rose of the rugs from fading.

The fourth place was in suburban Philadelphia, fifty minutes' ride from the heart of the city. It was a big colonial house set in a great yard, a relic of the days when gardens still flourished in the city and the breathing spaces allotted to householders were larger than at the present time. As we went up the shrubbery-bordered walk to the pillared porch I said, "I want to live here."

Mrs. McCrea, the boarding-house mistress, did not object to the music, provided I took the large room on the third floor and did all my practicing between the hours of eight and five, when the other boarders were gone to business. The price of the room is seven dollars a week.

I took the room at once, before Mrs. McCrea had any chance of changing her mind. I thought it was a very pleasant room, with its two windows looking out on the green yard.

But later, after Virginia had gone and I was left alone in the room, the queerest feeling came over me. I never knew what it meant to be homesick, but I think I had a touch of it this afternoon in this room. I hated this place for about half an hour. I saw that the paint is soiled, the rug worn, the pictures cheap, the bed and bureau trimmed with gingerbready scrolls and knobs. It's so different from the blue and white room I slept in last night, so different from my plain, old-fashioned room at home. "It's all right," I said to myself, half crying, "but it's so different."

Fortunately the word different struck a responsive chord in my memory. I remembered that I wanted different things, and smiled again and dashed the tears away. I arranged my own pictures and few belongings about the room and felt more at home. After I had dressed and stood ready to go down for my first dinner in my new home I felt happier. To be living, to be young and enthusiastic, to possess the colossal courage of youth, was enough to bring happiness into my heart again. I'm going to like this place. I'm going to work and play and live in this wonderful city.

Mrs. McCrea introduced the "New boarder" and I took my assigned place at a long table in the dining-room. I remembered that I once read that the average boarding-house is a veritable school for students of human nature. I wondered what I would learn from the people I met there. The fat man across the table from me gave me no opportunity for any mental ramblings. He launched me right into conversation by asking my opinion of the war in Europe and whether or not we would be dragged into the trouble.

"Really," I answered him, "I don't know much about it. I don't think of it any more than I can help."

Of course that was the wrong thing to say. It started a deluge. A studious-looking woman wearing heavy tortoise-shell rimmed spectacles took my answer as a personal affront. "Why not, Miss Metz?" she demanded. "Why should we not think about it? We women of America need to wake up! In this country we are lolling in ease and safety while other nations bleed and die that we might remain safe. We have no thoughts higher than our hats or deeper than our boots if the catastrophe across the sea does not waken in us an earnest desire to help the stricken nations."

Others took up the argument and I sat quiet and helpless, for I know too little about the cause and progress of the war to talk intelligently about it. A sense of responsibility grazed my soul. I wished I were able to help France and Belgium, but what can I do? The constant harping on the subject of war irritated me. I felt relieved when a young girl near me asked, "Miss Metz, do you like the movies? There's a place near here where they show fine pictures, funny ones to make you forget the war for several hours, at least."

On the whole, I think I'm going to like life at Mrs. McCrea's boarding-house. I hear the views of so many different sorts of people. And it certainly is different from my life on the farm.

CHAPTER XVIII
DIARY—THE MUSIC MASTER

September 19.

My four days in Philadelphia have just been one exclamation point after another! The most wonderful thing happened to me last night! Mrs. Lee invited me over for dinner. I glided through the courses a little more gracefully—one can learn if the will is there. I always loved dainty things. I suppose that is why I delight in the Lee home and am eager to adopt the ways of my new friends.

After dinner Mr. Lee played again. Of course I enjoyed that. When I praised his playing he said he heard I'm a real genius and asked me to sing for them. Mr. Krause, one of the best teachers of music in the city, is a friend of Royal and Virginia thinks he would be the very one to teach me. Mr. Lee wrote to Mr. Krause this summer and the music teacher promised to take me for a pupil if I have a voice worth the trouble. Virginia had prepared me for my meeting with him. Seems he's queer, odd, cranky and painfully frank. But he knows how to teach music so well that many would-be singers pray to be taken into his studio. Mr. Lee said yesterday that Mr. Krause was expected home from his vacation in a few days and then he'd arrange an interview. I trembled when he said that. What if the great teacher did not like my voice!

To-night when Mr. Lee asked me to sing I selected a simple song. As I sat down before the baby grand piano the words of the old song "Sweet and Low" came to me. I would sing that until I gained courage and confidence to sing a harder selection. I played from memory. As I sang I was back again at home, singing to my father at the close of the day.

As the last words died on my lips and I turned on the chair a man, a stranger to me, appeared in the room. He hurried unceremoniously to the piano and greeted me, "You can sing!"

I stared at him. He was an odd-looking, active little man of about fifty with keen blue eyes that bored into one like a gimlet.

Mr. Lee came toward us. "Mr. Krause," he exclaimed, and presented to me the music master, the teacher for whom I had dreaded so to sing! I was filled with inarticulate gladness.

"Mr. Krause," I cried, grasping his outstretched hand in my old impetuous way, "do you mean it? Can I learn to sing?"

"I said so—yes. You can sing. You need to learn how to use your voice but the voice is there."

123

"I'm so glad. I'll work——" I couldn't say any more. My joy was too great to be expressed in words. I looked mutely into the wrinkled face of the man.

"Royal said he had found a songbird," he went on smiling, "but I was afraid he didn't know the difference between that and an owl—I see he did. I'll be glad to have you for a pupil. Royal can bring you to my studio to-morrow at eleven."

Mr. Krause stayed a while longer and the sitting-room was gay with laughter and bright conversation. I think I heard little of it, though, for the words, "You can sing!" kept ringing in my ears and crowding out all other sounds.

I can sing! Mr. Krause has told me I can sing! And I will sing! Some day all the world may stop to hear!

CHAPTER XIX
DIARY—THE FIRST LESSON

September 20.

I had my first music lesson to-day. Mr. Lee called for me at the boarding-house and took me down-town to the studio. After he left I expected Mr. Krause to begin at once on the do, ra, me, fa, sol, la, si, do. But he thought differently!

He sat facing me, looking at me till I felt like running. "And so," he said quietly, "you want to learn to sing."

"Yes," was all I could say.

"Well, you have a voice. If you want to work like all great singers have had to work you can be a singer. You may not set the world afire with your fame but you'll be worth hearing. You are Pennsylvania Dutch?"

I nodded. What under the sun did Pennsylvania Dutch have to do with my becoming a singer? I was provoked. I didn't come to the city and pay a music teacher to ask me foolish questions.

"That is good," he went on calmly. "The Pennsylvania Dutch are not afraid of work and that is what you need. The road to success in music is like the road to success in any other thing, long and hard and up-hill most of the way. Now that Pennsylvania Dutch is a funny language. It is neither Dutch nor English nor German but is like hash, a little of this and a little of that. Do you speak it?"

I said I have spoken it all my life but wished I had never been taught it.

"Why?" he asked.

124

"Oh"—I couldn't quite veil my irritation—"it perverts our English."

"Nothing uncommon," he answered, smiling. "Every part of this great country has some peculiarities of speech common to that particular section and laughed at in the other sections. Now we will go on with the lesson."

When he really did begin to teach I found him a wonder. I'm going to enjoy, thoroughly enjoy, my music lessons.

Mr. Lee called for me after the lesson. I told him I could find the way back to the boarding-house alone, but he said he'd consider it a pleasure and privilege to call for me. He has the nicest manners! He never needs to flounder around for the right thing to say, it just slips from his tongue like butter. Aunt Maria always says, "look out for them smooth apple-sass talkers," but I'm sure Mr. Lee is a gentleman and just the right kind for a country girl to know.

When he called at the studio this morning I felt proud to walk away with him. He suggested riding home but I told him I'd rather walk, at least part of the way. We started up Chestnut Street. What a wonderful place that is! Such lovely stores I've never seen. I'm going to sneak away some day and visit every one that has women's belongings for sale. And the clothes I saw on Chestnut Street—on the women, I mean! My own wardrobe certainly is plain and ordinary compared with the things I saw women wear to-day. I couldn't help saying to Mr. Lee, "What lovely clothes Philadelphia women wear!" He smiled that wonderful smile and said, "Miss Metz, a diamond has no need of a glittering case, it has sufficient brilliancy itself." I caught his meaning, I couldn't help it—he meant me! Now I know I'm no beauty, but perhaps if I had clothes like those I saw to-day I'd be more attractive. I wonder if I'll get them; they must cost lots of money.

As we walked along Mr. Lee told me he knows I'll have a wonderful year in the city, and that he is going to help it be the gladdest, merriest one I've ever had.

"Oh, you're good," I said.

"It must be that goodness inspires goodness," he replied.

I didn't know what to answer. Men up home never say such things, at least I never heard them. Phares couldn't think of such things to say and David never made a "pretty speech" in his life. I know he thinks nice things about me sometimes but he wouldn't word them like Royal Lee does. I didn't want Mr. Lee to think I'm uncommonly good, I told him I'm not.

"Not good?" He laughed at the idea. "Why, you are just a sweet, lovely young thing knowing nothing of evil."

"Oh!" I said, feeling stupid before him, "you're too polite! I never met any one like you. But I want to ask you about cards, playing cards. I can't see that they are wrong but Aunt Maria and my father and all my friends up home think they are wicked. Aunt Maria would rather part with her right hand than play a game of cards."

Mr. Lee laughed and said he's surprised that I am willing to accept the beliefs of others; can't I decide for myself what is wrong or right? Did I want to be narrow and goody-goody?

Of course I don't want to be like that, and I told him so.

He laughed again, a low, soft laugh. I never heard a man laugh like that before. When daddy laughs he laughs out loud, the kind of laugh you join in when you hear it. And David laughs like that too, a merry laugh that sounds, as he says, like it's coming clean from his boots. But Mr. Lee's laugh is different. I don't like it as well as the other kind, though it fascinates me. He said he knows I can't change my ideas in a night but he depends upon my good sense to decide what is right for me to do. He asked if I thought Virginia and her mother are wicked. They have played cards, danced, gone to theatres, all their lives. If I hope to have a really enjoyable time in the city I must do the same. He said, too, that I'll soon see that many of the teachings of the country churches are antiquated and entirely too narrow for this day.

Dancing—I shuddered at the word, but I didn't tell him how I feel about it. Aunt Maria says dancing is even worse than playing cards. Why did he tempt me? I don't want to do wicked things, but when he mentioned forbidden pleasures I felt, somehow, that I wanted to do what Virginia does and have a good time with her and her friends. That would be dreadful! What am I thinking of! Is my head turned already? Can the evil of the world have exerted its influence upon me so soon? Of course, if I become a great singer I'll naturally have to live a life different from the narrow, restricted life of the farm. I must live a broader, freer life. But for a while, at least, I'll have to be the same old Phœbe Metz. I tried to tell Mr. Lee something like that, and he quoted,

"If you become a nun, dear,
A friar I will be;
In any cell you run, dear,
Pray look behind for me."

Are city men always free like that? Is it the way of the new world I have entered? Before I could think of a suitable answer he said lightly, "But before you turn nun let me buy you some flowers."

We stopped at a floral shop. Such flowers! I've never seen their equal! I exclaimed in many O's as I paused by the window, but I felt my cheeks flush at the idea of having him buy any of the lovely flowers for me.

"Come inside," he said. "What do you like?"

"I love them all," I told him as we stood before the array of blossoms. "I think I like the yellow rosebuds best, though. We have some at home on the farm but they bloom only in June."

I detected an odd smile on his lips. What was wrong? Had I committed a breach of etiquette? Was it wrong to mention farms in a city floral shop? But his courteous, attentive manner returned in an instant. He watched me pin the yellow roses on my coat, smiled, and led me outside again. I felt proud as any queen, for those were the first flowers any man ever bought for me.

CHAPTER XX
DIARY—SEEING THE CITY

October 2.

I have been seeing Philadelphia. Mr. Lee teasingly told me that most newcomers want to "do" the city so he and Virginia would take me round. They took me to see all the places I studied about in history class. I've done the Betsy Ross House, Franklin's Grave, Old Christ Church and Old Swede's Church. I like them all. Best of all I like Independence Hall, with its wonderful stairways and wide window sills and, most important, its grand old Liberty Bell and its history.

Yesterday Mr. Lee took me to Memorial Hall in Fairmount Park. I like the pictures and oh, I looked long at a white marble statue of Isaac, his hands bound for the sacrifice. The face is beautiful. Royal Lee was amused at my interest in it and took me off to see the rare Chinese vases. We wandered around among the cases of glassware and then I found a case with valuable Stiegel glass, made in my own Lancaster County. I was proud of that! We went through Horticultural Hall and stopped to see the lovely sunken gardens, with their fall flowers.

I like to go about with Royal Lee. He is so efficient. Crowds seem to fall back for him. He has the attractive, masterful personality that everybody recognizes. I feel a reflected glory from his presence. We have grown to be great friends in an amazingly short time. Our music, our appreciation of each other's ability, has strengthened the bond between us. Mrs. Lee sends me many invitations for dinner and week-ends in her beautiful home, so that Mr. Lee and I are already well acquainted. He has asked me to call him Royal and if he might call me Phœbe. I've told him all about my life on the farm, my friends up there, and the plans and dreams of my heart. He likes to tease me and call me a little Quakeress, but I don't enjoy that for he does it in a way I don't like. It sounds as if he's scoffing at the plain people. When I told him about the meeting house and described the service he laughed and said that a religion like that might do for a little country place but it would never do in a city. I bridled at that and tried to tell him about the wholesome, useful lives those people up home lead, how much good a woman like Mother Bab can do in the world. But he could not be easily convinced. He thinks they are crude and narrow. When I told him they are lovely and fine he challenged me and asked if I am willing to wear plain clothes and renounce all pleasures, jewelry and becoming raiment. I had to tell him I'm not ready for that yet, and he smiled triumphantly. He predicted I'll play cards and dance before the winter ends. I don't like him when he's so flippant. I want to be loyal to my home teaching but I see more clearly every day how great is the difference between the pleasures sanctioned by my people and those Virginia and her friends enjoy. There's a mystery somewhere I can't solve. Like Omar, I "evermore come out at the same door where in I went."

October 29.

To-day we went for a long drive along the Wissahickon. The woods are bronze and scarlet now. The wild asters made me homesick for Lancaster County. I wanted to get out of the car and walk but Virginia and her friends wouldn't join me. I wanted to bury my nose in the goldenrod and asters—and get hay fever, one of the girls told me—and I just ached to push my way through the tangled bushes along the road and let the golden leaves of the hickory and beeches brush my face. It seems that most city people I have met don't know how to enjoy nature. They have a nodding-from-a-motor-acquaintance with it but I like a real handshake-friendship with it. I just wished David were here to-day! He'd have taken my hand and run me to the top of the hill and picked a branch of scarlet maple to carry with my goldenrod and asters. Well, I can't have the penny and the cake. I want to be in the city, of course that's the thing I most desire at present—I really am having a good time.

In the evening we went to Holy Trinity Church. The organ

recital gripped my soul. I wanted it to last for hours. And yet when it was over and the rector stood before us and preached one of his impressive sermons I was just as much interested as I had been in the music. There's a feeling of restful calm comes to me in a big dim church with stained glass windows. We stopped in the Cathedral one day last week. That is a wonderful place, too. I like the idea of having churches open all the time for prayer and meditation. I'm learning so many new ideas these days. If I ever do wear the plain dress I'm sure of one thing, I'll be broad-minded enough to respect the beliefs of other persons.

November 11.

I can put another red mark on my calendar. I heard the great Irish Tenor! Glory, what a voice! It's the kind can echo in your ears to your dying day and follow you with its sweetness everywhere you go! I have been humming those lovely Irish songs all day.

But before the recital my heart was heavy. I have no evening gown, no evening wrap, so I couldn't join the box party to which one of Virginia's friends invited us. I meant to stay at home and not break up the party, but Royal insisted upon buying two tickets in a section of the opera house where a plainer dress would do. In the end I allowed myself to be persuaded by him and we two went to the recital alone. When that tenor voice sounded through the place I forgot all about my limited wardrobe. I could hear him sing if I were dressed in calico and think of nothing but his singing.

November 12.

I wrote letters to-day. Mother Bab and David write such lovely ones to me that I have to try hard to keep up my end of it. Sometimes David tells me he is anxious to supply me with the beet juice, cream and flour whenever I'm ready to begin the prima donna act. I can hear his laugh when I read the letter. Sometimes he's serious and talks about the crops of their farm and tells me the community news like an old grandmother. Phares Eby writes me an occasional letter, a stilted little note that sounds just like Phares. It always has some good advice in it. Aunt Maria's letters and daddy's come every week. I'd feel lost without them. I like to feel that everybody I care for at home is interested in and cares for me even if I am in Philadelphia.

CHAPTER XXI
DIARY—CHRYSALIS

December 3.

I'm as miserable as any mortal can be! Oh, I'm still having a good time going around seeing the city, visiting the stores and museums, practicing hard in music, pleasing my teacher. But just the same, I'm not happy. The reason is this: I want pretty gowns like Virginia wears, I want to dance and play cards and see real plays. I dare say I'm a contemptible sinner to want all that after the way I've been brought up. I ought to be satisfied with all the wonderful things I enjoy in this big city but I'm not.

Last week Virginia entertained the Bridge Club and tried to persuade me to learn to play and come to the party. Royal was provoked about it. He thinks I should learn to play. I told him I should have no peace if I learned to do such things.

"Peace," he scorned, "no one has peace these days. The whole world is in a turmoil. Do you think your little Quaker-like girls of Lancaster County have peace these days?"

"They have peace of mind and conscience."

"But that," he said, "is the peace that touches those who live in selfish solitude. The virtue that dwells in the hearts of those who retire into hermitages is a negative virtue."

"You speak like a seer, a philosopher," I told him.

"Like a rational human being, I hope," he said petulantly. "But the thoughts are not original. I am merely echoing the opinion of sane thinkers. I have no appreciation of the foolish and useless sacrifice you are persistently making. We were not put on this planet to be dull nuns and monks. We have red blood racing through our veins and were not intended for sluggishness."

"Yes—but——"

He went off peeved at my refusal to do as he wished.

What can I do? Shall I capitulate? I have wrestled with my desire for pleasure until I'm tired of the struggle. My old contentment has deserted me. I'm restless and dissatisfied, scarcely knowing what is right or wrong.

Next day.

I'm happy again. Being on the fence grows mighty uncomfortable after a while, so I jumped across. I have decided to become a butterfly!

I had luncheon to-day with Virginia. She had to run off to one of her Bridge Clubs so I offered to mend the lace on one of her gowns while she was gone. I was alone in the sitting-room that adjoins Virginia's bedroom. I love that little sitting-room. Virginia and I spend many happy hours in it when we want to get away from everybody and have a long chat. I like its big comfortable winged chairs by the cheery open fire.

I dreamed a while before the fire, the gown across my knees. It's a pink gown, that scarcely defined pink of a sea shell. Virginia had often tempted me to try it on and see how well I'd look in a dress of that kind. The temptation came to do it. I jumped up in sudden determination. I would put it on! I'd see for once how I looked in a real gown. I ran to Virginia's room to the low dressing table. My hands trembled as I opened the tight coils of my hair and shook it until it seemed to nod exultingly. I fluffed the curls loosely over my forehead and twisted the hair into a fashionable knot. Then I took off my plain blue serge dress and slipped the pink one over my head. The soft draperies clung to me, the gossamer lace lay upon my breast like a silken mist. I was beautiful in that gown and I knew it. It was my hour of appreciation of my own charm.

Later I lifted the dress and saw my plain calfskin shoes. I smiled but soon grew sober as I thought that the incongruity between gown and shoes was no greater than that between the gown and the girl—the girl who was reared to wear plain clothes and be honest and unpretentious. But honesty—that is the rock to which I cling now. I am going to be honest with myself and have my share of happiness while I'm young.

I went back again to the fire, still wearing the borrowed gown. Virginia found me there several hours later. When she came in and saw me, a gorgeous butterfly, she said, she was very happy. She would have me go down to her mother and Royal. I shrank from it but she said I might as well become accustomed to being stared at when I was so dazzling and beautiful. I went down, feeling almost as much of a culprit as I did the day Aunt Maria surprised me at playing prima donna and marched me in to the quilting party.

Mrs. Lee was lovely. She is sure I deserve to be happy in my youth. Royal went mad. "Ye Gods!" he cried as he ran to me and grasped my hands. "You take my breath away! You are like this!" He seized his violin and began to play the Spring Song. The quivering ecstasy of spring, the mating calls of robins and orioles, the rushing joy of bursting blossoms, the delicate perfume of violets and trailing arbutus, the dazzling shafts of sunlight pierced by silver showers of capricious April—all echoed in the melody of the violin.

"You are like that, that is you!" he said as he laid his

131

instrument aside. His words were very sweet to me. The future beckons into sunlit paths of joy.

So I have departed from the teachings of my childhood and turned to the so-called vanities of the world. I am going to grasp my share of happiness while I can enjoy them.

When I went up-stairs again to take off the borrowed gown I was already planning the new clothes I want to buy. I must have a pink crepe georgette, a pale, pale blue—just as I'm writing this there flashes to my mind one of those old Memory Gems I learned in school on the hill.

"But pleasures are like poppies spread,—
You seize the flower, its bloom is shed;
Or like the snow fall on the river,
A moment white, then melts forever."
I wonder, is there always a fly in the ointment!

CHAPTER XXII
DIARY—TRANSFORMATION

December 15.
A few days can make a difference in one's life. I'm well on the way of being a real butterfly. I have bought new dresses, a real evening gown and a lovely silk dress to wear to the Bridge Club. It's lucky I saved my money these three months and had a nice surplus to buy these new things.

Royal is teaching me to play cards. He says I take to them like a duck to water. Virginia and he are giving me dancing lessons. I love to dance! The same spirit that prompted me to skip when I wore sunbonnets is now urging me on to the dance. In a few weeks I'll be ready to join in the pleasures of my new friends. After the Christmas holidays the city will be gay until the Lenten season.

January 5.
I went home for Christmas and I suppose I managed to make everybody there unhappy and worried. I couldn't let them think I am the same quiet girl and not tell them about the cards and dancing. Daddy was hurt, but he didn't scold me. He said plainly that he does not approve of my course, that he thinks cards and dancing wicked. He added that I had been taught the difference between right and wrong and was old enough to see it. Perhaps he thinks I'll "run my horns off quicker" if I'm let go, as Aunt Maria often says about people. But she didn't say that about

me. She made up for what daddy didn't say. She begged him to make me stay at home away from the wicked influences of the city. I had the hardest time to keep calm and not say mean things to her. She's ashamed of me and afraid people up there will find out how worldly I am. I had to tell Mother Bab too. I know I hurt her. She was so gentle and lovely about it that I felt half inclined to tell her I'd give up everything she didn't approve of, just to please her. But I didn't. I couldn't do that when I know I'm not doing anything wrong. She changed the subject and inquired about my music. In that I was able to please her. She shared my joy when I told her of my critical music master's approval of my progress. I sang some of my new songs for her and she kissed me with the same love and tenderness she has always had for me. I wonder sometimes whether I could possibly have loved my own mother more. Somehow, as I sat with her in her dear, cozy sitting-room I hated the cards and the dancing and half wished I had never left the farm. But that's a narrow, provincial view to take. Now that I'm back again I'm caught once more in the whirl. Everybody is entertaining, as if in a frantic endeavor to be surfeited before Lent and thus be able to endure the dullness of that period of suspended social activities. The harrowing tales of suffering France and Belgium have occasioned Benefit Teas and Benefit Bridges and Benefit Dances, all for the aid of the war sufferers. Royal usually takes me to the social affairs. I enjoy being with him. He's the most entertaining man I ever met. He has traveled in Europe and all over our own country and can tell what he has seen. He attracts attention, whether he speaks or plays or is just silent. One day he said it would be a pleasure to travel with me, I enjoy things so and can appreciate their beauty. I could scarcely resist telling him how I'd enjoy traveling with a man like him. Oh, I dream wild dreams sometimes, but I really must stop doing that. The present is too wonderful to go borrowing joy from the future.

February 2.

I'm all in a fluster. I have to write here what happened to-day. If I had a mother she could help and advise me but an adopted mother, even one as dear and near as Mother Bab, won't do for such confidences.

Royal and I were sitting alone before the open fireplace. It's a dangerous place to be! The glowing fire sends such weird shadows flickering up and down. Its living fire is sometimes an entreating Circe waking undesirable impulses, then again it's a spirit that heals and inspires. I love an open fire but to-day I should have fled from it and yet—I think I'm glad I didn't.

I looked up suddenly from the gleaming logs—right into the eyes of Royal. His voice startled me as he said, with the strangest catch in his voice, that my eyes are bluer than the skies. I tried to keep my voice ordinary as I lightly told him that some other person once told me they are the color of fringed gentians—could he improve on that?

"You little fairy!" he cried. "I can beat that! They are blue as bluebirds!" Then he went on impetuously, telling me I was a real bluebird of happiness, a bringer of joy; that the ancients called the bluebird the emblem of happiness, but he knew the blue of my eyes was the real joy sign—or something like that he said. It startled me. I tried to tell him he must not talk like that but my words were useless. He went on to say that the world was bleak and unlovely till I came to Philadelphia and wouldn't I tell him I care for him.

Of course I value his friendship and told him so. But he laughed and said I was a wise little girl but I couldn't evade his question like that. He said frankly he doesn't want my friendship, he wants my love, he must have it!

I felt like a helpless bird. I couldn't answer him. He looked at me, a long, searching look. Then he pressed his thin lips together, and a moment later, threw back his head and laughed his low laugh.

"Little bluebird," he said softly, "I have frightened you and I wouldn't do that for worlds! We'll talk it over some other time, after you have had time to think about it. Shall I play for you?"

I nodded and he began to play. But the music didn't soothe me as it usually does. There were too many confused thoughts in my brain. Did Royal really love me? I looked at his white hands with the long tapering nails and the shapely fingers and couldn't help thinking of the strong, tanned hands of David Eby. I glanced at the handsome face of the musician with its magnetic charm—swiftly the countenance of my old playmate rose before me and then slowly faded: David, boyish and comradely; David, manly and strong, without ever a sneer or an unholy light upon his face. Could I ever forget him? Could I ever look into the face of any other man and call it the dearest in the whole world to me? Ach—I shook my head and gathered my recreant wits together! I'd forget what he said and attribute it to the weird influence of the firelight.

I was glad Virginia came before Royal finished playing. She looked at us keenly. I suppose my face was flushed. But Royal seldom loses his outward calm. He answered her remarks in his casual way and listened with seeming interest to her plans for a pre-Lenten masquerade dance she wants to give. She has asked me to go dressed in a plain dress and white cap like Aunt Maria wears. I hesitated about it but she has done so much for me that I hate to refuse. So I've promised to go to the dance dressed in a plain dress and cap.

A little later when Royal left us alone Virginia began to speak about him. She said she's so glad we have grown to be friends, in spite of the fact that he is so much older than I am. He's thirty-seven, she told me. I'm surprised at that. I never thought he's so much older. She mentioned something, too, about his being rather a gay Don Juan. I don't know just what she means. I'm sure he's a gentleman. Perhaps she expected me to tell her what Royal said to me, but how could I do that when I think it was just an impulsive burst that he's likely to forget by morning. If he really meant it—but I must stop dreaming all sorts of improbable dreams! I've had such a glorious time in Philadelphia just living and singing and working and playing that I wish it hadn't happened. I'm frightened when I think that any serious questions might confront me here.

February 10.
I guessed right when I thought that Royal would forget that foolish outburst. He has been perfectly lovely to me, taking me out and buying me flowers and telling me about his trips, but he hasn't said one word more of sentimental nature. I'm surely getting my share of fun and pleasure these days. There are so many things to enjoy, so much to learn from my fellow-boarders and every one I meet, that the days are all too short. Between times I'm making a dress and cap for the masquerade dance. I hate sewing. I lost all love for it during my years of calico patching. But I don't mind making the dress for I'm eager for the dance, my first masquerade party. I'm hoping for a good time.

CHAPTER XXIII
DIARY—PLAIN FOR A NIGHT

February 21.
Last night was the masquerade. I wore the plain gray dress, apron and cape and a white cap on my head. I felt rather like a hypocrite as I looked at myself in the glass, but Virginia said it was just the thing and certainly would not be duplicated by any other guest.

I was dressed early and started down the stairs, my black

mask swinging from my hand. As I rounded a curve in the stairway I glanced casually down the wide hall. The colored servant had admitted visitors. I looked in that direction—the mask fell from my hand and I ran down the steps and into the arms of Mother Bab! I couldn't say more than "Oh, oh!" as I kissed her over and over. When she got her breath she said happily, "Phœbe, you're plain!"

Oh, how it hurt me! I took her and David to a little nook off the library where we could be alone and then I had to tell her that I was wearing the plain dress and white cap as a masquerade dress. Even when I told her I learned to dance and do things she thinks are worldly there was no look of pain on her face like the look I brought there as I stood before her in a dress she reverenced and told her I wore it in a spirit of fun. I'll never get over being sorry for hurting her like that. But Mother Bab rallies quickly from every hurt. She soon smiled and said she understood. David came to my aid. He assured his mother that they knew I could take care of myself and would not do anything really wrong. I couldn't thank him for his kindness. I felt suddenly all weepy and tearful. But David began to talk on in his old friendly way and tell about the home news and about the Big Doctor he had taken Mother Bab to see in Philadelphia and how he hoped she would soon be able to see perfectly again. While he talked Mother Bab and I had a chance to recover a bit. I noted a quick shadow pass over her face as he spoke about her eyes—was she less hopeful about them than he was? Had the Big Doctor told her something David did not hear? But no! I dismissed the thought—Mother Bab could not go blind! She would never be asked to suffer that! I soon forgot my troublesome thoughts as she hastened to say that perhaps her eyes would improve more quickly than the doctor promised. Then she changed the subject—"Now, Phœbe, I hope I didn't hurt you about the dress. I guess I looked at you as if I wanted to eat you. I love you and wouldn't hurt you for anything."

"Mother Bab!" I gave her a real hug like I used to do when I ran barefooted up the hill with some childish perplexity and she helped me. "You're an angel! Mother Bab, David, having a good time won't hurt me. Our views up home are too narrow. It's all right to expect older people to do nothing more exciting than go to Greenwald to the store, to church every Sunday, to an occasional quilting or carpet-rag party, and to Lancaster to shop several times a year, but the younger generation needs other things."

"I guess you mean it can't be Lent all the time for you," she suggested with a smile.

"I just knew you'd understand."

Just then Royal began to play and the music floated in to us.

It was Traumerei. Mother Bab's tired face relaxed as she leaned back to listen to the piercingly sweet melody. David looked at me— I knew he was asking whether the player was Royal Lee.

"Oh, Davie," Mother Bab said innocently as the music ended, "if only you could play like that!"

"If I could," he said half bitterly, "but all I can do is farm. Are you coming home this spring?" he asked me, as if to forget the violin and its player.

"I don't know. I'll probably stay here until early June. I may go away with Virginia for part of the summer."

"Not be home for spring and summer!" he said dismally. "Why, it won't be spring without you! We can't go for bird-foot violets or arbutus."

Arbutus—the name called up a host of memories to me. "How I'd like to go for arbutus this spring," I told him.

"Then come home in April and I'll take you to Mt. Hope for some."

"Oh, David, will you?"

"I'd love to. We'll drive up."

"I'll come," I promised. "I'll come home for arbutus. Let me know when they're out."

"All right. But I think we must go now or we'll miss the train."

"Go?" I echoed. "You're not going home to-night? Can't you stay? Mrs. McCrea has vacant rooms. I've been so excited I forgot my manners. Let me take you to the sitting-room and introduce you to Mrs. Lee and Royal."

"Ach, no," Mother Bab protested. "We can't stay that long. We just stopped in to see you."

David looked at his watch. "We must go now. There's a train at eight-twenty-one gets to Lancaster at ten-forty-five and we'll get the last car out to Greenwald and Phares will meet us and drive us home."

I asked about the home folks as I watched David adjust Mother Bab's shawl. He looked older and worried. I suppose he was disappointed because the Big Doctor didn't promise a quick cure for Mother Bab's eyes.

As they said good-bye and left me I wanted to run after them and ask them to take me home, back to the simple life of my people. But I stayed where I was, the earthiest worldling in a dress of unworldliness.

"I—I believe I'll take it off," I thought as I stood in the doorway.

137

Just then Royal opened the door and saw me. "Ye Gods!" he exclaimed, "you look like a saint, Phœbe."

"But I'm not! I'm far from being a saint!"

"Don't be one, please. If you turn saint I shall be disconsolate. I don't like saints of women and I want to keep on liking you, little Bluebird. Remember, you promised me the first dance."

"I don't know—I don't feel like dancing."

"Oh, but you must! You look like a Quakeress but no one expects you to act like one to-night. I'm going up to dress—I'm going as a monk to match you."

He ran off, laughing, and I went in search of Virginia. My heart was heavy. The sudden appearance of Mother Bab and David brought me a vivid impression of the contrast between their lives and mine and the thoughts left me worried and restless. What was I doing? Was I shaping my life in such a way that it would never again fit into the simple grooves of country life? The dance lost its charm for me. I danced and made merry and tried to enter into the gay spirit of the occasion but I longed all the time to be with Mother Bab and David riding to Lancaster County.

CHAPTER XXIV
DIARY—DECLARATIONS

March 22.

Spring is here but I'd never know it if I didn't read the calendar. I haven't seen a robin or heard a song-sparrow. Just the same, I've had a wonderful time these past weeks. Of course my music gets first attention. I'm getting on well, though I'm beginning to see what a long, long time it will take before I become a great singer. Since I have heard really great singers I wonder whether I was not too presumptuous when I thought I might be one some day. I went to several big churches lately and heard fine music.

I thought Lent would be a dull season but it's been gay enough for me. There has been unusual activity, Virginia says, because of so many charitable affairs held for the benefit of the war sufferers.

I bought a new spring hat, a dream. Hope Aunt Maria never asks me what I paid for it. After wearing Greenwald hats all my life this one was coming to me.

But my thoughts are not all of frivolous matters. I have

taken advantage of some of the opportunities Philadelphia offers to improve my mind and broaden my vision. I've been to lectures and plays and enjoyed them all.

I asked Royal to-day why he never worked. He laughed and said I was an inquisitive Bluebird. Then he told me his parents left him enough money to live without working. He never did a solid hour's real work in his whole life. With his talent and his personal attractions he might become a famous musician if he had some odds to fight against or some person to encourage him and make him do his best. He said he knows he never developed his talent to the full extent but that since he knows me he is playing better than he did before. I wonder if I really am an inspiration to him. I suppose a genius does need a wife or sympathetic friend to bring out the best in him. He has been so lovely, showing his fondness for me in many ways, but he has never said anything sentimental like he did the day we sat by the fire. Sometimes he does say ambiguous things that I can't understand. He is surely giving me a long time to think it over. I like him but I'm afraid he's cynical, and it worries me.

There are other things, too, to dim the blue these days. War clouds are threatening. U-boats of Germany are sinking our vessels. Where will it all end?

April 7.

War has been declared. America is in it at last. I came home to-day feeling disheartened and sad. War was the topic everywhere I went. Papers, bulletin-boards flaunted the words, "The world must be made safe for democracy." People on the streets and in cars spoke about it, newsboys yelled till they were hoarse.

I stopped to see Virginia but she was out. Royal said he'd entertain me till she returned. He laughed at my tragic weariness about the war.

"I'll tell you, Bluebird," he whispered as he sat beside me, "we'll talk of something better. I love you."

The fire in his eyes frightened me. I couldn't look at him. "Why do you say such things?" I asked, and I couldn't keep my voice from trembling.

That didn't hush him—he said some more. He told me how he loves me, how he waited for me all his life and wants me with him. He quoted the verse I like so much, "Thou beside me singing in the wilderness—O wilderness were Paradise enow!" Then he asked me frankly if I loved him.

I couldn't answer right away. Now that the thing I had

dreamed of was actually happening I was dazed and stupid and sat like a bump-on-a-log.

He asked me again and before I knew what he was doing he had taken me into his arms and kissed me. "Say you love me," he pleaded.

I said what he wanted to hear and he kissed me again. We were both very happy. It is almost too wonderful to believe!

A few minutes later we heard Virginia enter the hall and we came back to earth. I know my cheeks still burned but Royal's ready poise served him well. He told his cousin he had been trying to make me forget about the war.

Virginia probably thought my excitement was due to the war. She began at once to speak about it. "America is in it and we can't forget it. Every true American must help."

"Do your bit, knit," chanted the musician.

She asked him if he is going to do his bit. He flushed and looked vexed, then explained that he can neither knit nor fight, that he is a musician.

Virginia argued that if he could play a violin he could learn to play a bugle, that many of the men who will fight for the flag are men who have never been taught to fight. She spoke as if she thought Royal should enlist in some branch of government service at once.

I resented her words. "Do you want Royal to go to war and be killed?" I asked her.

"My dear," she said solemnly, "have you ever heard that there is such a thing as losing one's life by trying to save it?"

That startled me. I realized then that the war is going to be a very serious matter, that there will be work for each one of us to do. But Royal laughed and made me forget temporarily every solemn, sad thing. He told Virginia that she was over-zealous, that she need not worry about him. He'd be a true American and give his money to help protect the flag. We began to play Bridge then and I thought no more about the war for an hour or two.

April 12.

I have learned to knit. Virginia has taught me and we are elbow-deep in gray and khaki wool. I have wound it and purled it and worked on the thing till I'm tasting fuzz. But I do want to do the little bit I can to help my country. This war is a serious matter. Already people are talking about who is going to enlist—what if David would go! I hope he won't—yet I don't want him to be a coward. Oh, it's all too confusing and terrible to think long about. I try to forget it for a time by remembering that Royal Lee cares for me. He has told me over and over that he loves me. Love must be blind, for he thinks I am beautiful and perfect. I'm glad I look like that to him. We should be happy when we are married, for we are so congenial, both loving music and things of beauty. It's queer, though, I have thought of it several times—he has never mentioned our marriage. I suppose he's too happy in the present to make plans for the future. But I know he is a gentleman, therefore his words of love are synonymous with an offer of marriage. All that will come later. It's enough now just to know we care for each other.

CHAPTER XXV
DIARY—"THE LINK MUST BREAK AND
THE LAMP MUST DIE"

April 13.

I'm in sackcloth and ashes. My dream castles have tumbled down upon my head and left me bruised and sorrowful. I'm awake at last! I'd like to bury my face in my old red and green patchwork quilt and ask forgiveness for being a fool. But I must compose myself and write this last chapter of my romance.

Last night the "Singer with the Voice of Gold" gave a recital in the Academy of Music. Royal and I helped to make up a merry box party. I felt festive and gay in my lovely white crepe georgette gown. Royal said I looked like a dream and that made me radiant, I know.

As we sat down I whispered to him that I was excited because hearing that great singer has always been one of my dearest dreams and now the dream was coming true. He whispered back that more of my dreams would soon come true. I made him hush, for several people were looking at us. But his words sent my heart thrilling.

The Academy became quiet as the singer appeared, then the audience gave her a real Brotherly Love welcome and settled once more into silence as her beautiful voice rose in the place. The operatic selections were beautifully rendered. I thought her voice was most captivating in the simple songs everybody knows. Annie Laurie had new charm as she sang it. When she sang that Royal whispered, "That is what I feel for you." I smiled into his eyes, then turned again to look at the singer. Could I ever sing like that? Would the dreams of my childhood come true? It seemed improbable and yet—I had traveled a long way from the little girl of the tight braids and brown gingham dresses, I thought. Perhaps the future would bring still more wonderful changes.

The hours in the Academy of Music passed like a beautiful dream. I shrank from the last song, though. It was too much like some fatal, dire prophecy:

"The cord is frayed, the cruse is dry,
The link must break, and the lamp must die—
Good-bye to hope! Good-bye, good-bye!"

I told Royal I didn't like it, it was too much like Cassandra.

He laughed and said she generally sings it, but that it couldn't hurt us—was I superstitious?

"No, oh, no," I declared. But I wished I could forget the words of that song.

Some of the party decided that a proper ending to the delightful evening would be a visit to a fashionable café. I didn't care to go. Royal urged me till I consented and I soon found myself in a beautiful place where merry groups of people were seated about small tables. Any desire for food I might have had left me as I heard Royal and the other men order wines and highballs.

"What will you have, Phœbe?" Royal asked me.

I gasped—"Why—nothing."

"Be a sport," he urged, "look around and do as the 'Romans do.'"

I looked around. Some of the women were smoking, others were drinking.

"Oh," I said, "this is dreadful. Let's go."

Royal laughed and the others teased me. One of the girls said I'd be doing all those things before the year ended. When I declared I would not Royal reminded me that I had said the same about cards and dancing. His words silenced me. I felt engulfed in shame and deeply hurt. How could Royal be amused at my discomfiture if he loved me! Did he love me? Did I want him to? Could I promise to honor and love him all my life? But perhaps he was teasing me—ah, that was it! I breathed more easily again. Royal was teasing me, sure of my refusal to indulge in any intoxicant. The others ate and made merry while I toyed idly with the glass of ginger ale the waiter brought me against my wish. I mused and dreamed—would Royal like my people? Somehow, he seemed an incongruity among the dear ones at the gray farmhouse in Lancaster County. What would he say when we ate in the kitchen and daddy came to the table in his shirt sleeves? Love can bridge greater chasms than that, I thought. When we are married——

"Royal Lee, are you ever going to marry?" The question broke into my revery.

I looked at Royal. There was no rise of color in his handsome face. He returned my look dispassionately then turned to his teasing, inquisitive friend.

"I'm a bachelor forever," he declared. "But that does not keep me from loving. Women I care for have too much good sense to think that marriage always follows love. Ye Gods, I think love goes when marriage comes, so you'll have no chance to see my love interred."

I clenched my hands under the table. I felt my lips go white. How could he hurt me so? Of course our love was not a thing to be paraded in a public place but if he really cared for me as I thought he did he could have answered differently. An evasive answer would have served. An hour ago he had whispered tender words to me and now he frankly informed all present that he was a bachelor forever. I could not grasp the full significance of his words at once. I was dazed by the shock of them. I wanted to get away and be alone, to cry, to think, to determine what he had meant by his demonstrations of love if he did not hope to win me for his wife.

But later, when I went to bed in the pretty blue and white room next Virginia's, I did not cry. I lay wide awake thinking over and over, "How could he do it? Why is he heartless? Was he only playing?"

When morning came I had partially decided that I had been a ready, silly fool; that Royal Lee had merely whiled the hours away more pleasantly because of my love. I felt tempted to denounce him but I thought that would afford him additional amusement and make me not a whit less miserable. I was eager to get away from him. I desired but one little moment alone with him to satisfy myself that I did not judge him unjustly. Fortunately he came to the sitting-room as I sat there staring at the page of a magazine.

"Alone?" he asked.

"Yes."

"Phœbe"—he drew nearer and I rose and stood away from him. "My Bluebird! You look unhappy. Are you still shocked at the smoking and drinking you saw last night? It's all in the game, you know. Why not be happy along with the rest of us, why be a prude?"

I shivered. Couldn't he know why I was unhappy! How false and fickle he was! I wouldn't wear my heart on my sleeve for him to read and laugh about. All my Metz determination rose in me.

"Why," I lied, "I'm not unhappy. I'm just tired. Late hours don't agree with me."

He stretched out his arm but I eluded him. "Don't," I said lightly; "we've been foolish long enough."

"Why"—he looked at me keenly. But I was determined he should not read my feelings. I smiled in spite of my contempt for him. "Why, Phœbe," he said tenderly, "what has changed you? Why shouldn't I kiss you when I love you? Love never hurt any one."

"No—but——"

"But what?" he asked.

"Oh, nothing," I said, stepping farther away from him. "I'm in a hurry this morning. Good-bye." And for the first time I saw a look of chagrin mar the handsome face of Royal Lee. Before he could recover his customary equanimity I was gone from the house.

I walked, caring not where the way led. My brain was in a whirl. I felt as though I were fleeing from a crumbling precipice. In a flash I understood Virginia's tactful attempts at warning. She had tried to make me understand but my head was too easily turned by the fine speeches and flattering attentions of the musician. I have been vain and foolish but I've had my lesson. It still hurts and yet I can see the value of it. I'll be better qualified after this to discriminate between the false and true.

I am going home to-day! It came to me suddenly as I went back to my boarding-house after my long walk. I promised David I'd come home for arbutus and the inspiration came to go home for the whole spring and summer. I'll write a note to Mr. Krause and one to Virginia. Dear Virginia, she has been so good to me and helped me in so many ways! I can never thank her enough. These eight months in Philadelphia have been a liberal education for me. I'll never regret them. I hope to come back in the fall and go on with the music lessons. By that time Royal Lee will have found another to make love to.

So I'm going home to-day, back to Lancaster County. The trees are green and the flowers are out—oh, I'm wild to get back!

CHAPTER XXVI
"HAME'S BEST"

Lancaster County never before looked so fertile, so lovely, as it did that April day when Phœbe returned to it after a long winter in Philadelphia.

As she came unexpectedly there was no one to meet her at Greenwald. She started across the street and was soon on the dusty road leading to the gray farmhouse.

"Let me see," she thought, "this is Friday afternoon and Aunt Maria will be scrubbing the kitchen floor."

But when the girl reached the kitchen of the gray house and tiptoed gently over the sill she found the big room in order and Aunt Maria absent.

"Why," she thought, "is Aunt Maria sick?" She opened the door to the sitting-room and there, seated by a window, was Aunt Maria with a ball of gray wool in her lap and five steel knitting needles plying in her hands.

"Aunt Maria!"

"Why, Phœbe!"

The exclamations came simultaneously.

"What in the world are you doing? I mean why aren't you cleaning the kitchen? Oh, Aunt Maria, you know what I mean! I never saw you sitting down early on a Friday afternoon."

Aunt Maria laughed. "I ain't sick! You can see what I'm doin'; I'm knittin'. Ain't you learned to do it yet? I can learn you."

"Why, I know how. But what are you knitting? For the Red Cross?"

"Why not? You think the ladies in Phildelphy are the only ones do that? There's a Red Cross in Greenwald and they are askin' all who can to help. I used to knit all my own stockings still so I thought I'd pitch right in. I let the cleanin' slide a little this week so I could get a good start on this once."

The girl gasped and looked at her aunt in wonder. All the days of her life she had never known her aunt to "let the cleanin' slide," if the physical strength were there to do the work. Aunt Maria was working for the Red Cross! While she, who had scorned the country folks and called them narrow, had knitted half-heartedly and spent the major part of her time in the pursuit of pleasure, the people of the little town and surrounding country had been doing real work for humanity.

"I think you're splendid, Aunt Maria, to help the Red Cross," she said with enthusiasm.

The woman looked up from her knitting. "Why, how dumb you talk! I guess abody wants to help. Them soldiers are fightin' for us. Now you can get yourself something to eat. It vonders me, anyhow, why you come home this time of the year. You said you'd stay till June."

"I came because I want to be here."

"So. Then I guess you got enough once of the city."

"Yes," said Phœbe, laughing. "But how is everybody?"

"All pretty good. But a lot of boys from round here went a'ready to enlist. I ain't for war, but I guess it has to come sometimes. But it's hard for them that has boys."

"David?" Phœbe asked. "Has he gone?"

"Ach, no, not him. He's got his mom to take care of."

Phœbe remembered Virginia's words, "We can't get away from it, we're in it." The thought of them made her feel depressed. "I'm going to forget the war," she thought after a moment, "I'm going to forget it for to-morrow and have one perfect day in the mountains hunting arbutus."

CHAPTER XXVII
TRAILING ARBUTUS

It was a balmy day in April when Phœbe and David drove over the country roads to the mountains where the trailing arbutus grow.

"Spring o' the year," called the meadow-larks in clear, piercing tones.

"It is spring o' the year," said Phœbe. "I know it now. But last week I felt sure that the calendar was wrong and I wondered whether God made only English sparrows this year; that was all I could see. Then I saw a few birds early this week when we went along the Wissahickon for a long walk. Oh, no," she said in answer to the unspoken question in his eyes, "I did not go alone with a man. In Philadelphia one does not do that. I went properly chaperoned by Mrs. Hale. Virginia and Royal and several others were in the party. You should have been there; you would have enjoyed it for you know so much about birds and flowers. Royal didn't know a spring beauty from a bloodroot, and when we heard a song-sparrow he said it was a thrush."

David threw back his head and laughed. "Some nature student he must be! But it must be fine along the Wissahickon. I have read about it."

"It is fine, but this is finer."

"You better say so!"

"Oh, look, David, the soil is pink!" She pointed to a tilled field whose soil was colored a soft old rose color. "I'm always glad to see the pink soil."

"So am I. It means that we are getting near the mountains. We'll drive over to Hull's tavern and leave the carriage there, then we can go to the patch of woods near the tavern where we used to find the great beauties, the fine big ones. There's the old tavern now." He pointed to a building with a fine background of wooded hills.

Hull's tavern, a rambling structure erected in 1812, is still an interesting stopping-place for summer excursionists and travelers through that mountainous section of Pennsylvania. Situated on the south side of the beautiful South Mountains and overlooking the richest of hills, it has long been a popular roadhouse, accommodating many pleasure parties and hikers.

Phœbe wandered about on the long porches while David took the horse to the stable.

"Now then," he said as he joined her, "give me the lunch box and we'll be off."

They walked a short distance in the loamy soil of the mountain road and then turned aside and scrambled up a steep bank to a tract of woodland. Phœbe sank on her knees in the dry, brown leaves and pushed aside the leaves. "There," she cried in triumph a moment later, "I found the first one!" She lifted a small cluster of trailing arbutus and gave it to David.

"Um-ah," he said, in imitation of a little girl of long ago.

"Little Dutchie," she answered. "But you can't provoke me to-day. I'm too happy to be peevish. Come, kneel down, you'll never find arbutus when you stand up."

"I'm down," he said as he knelt beside her. "I'd go on my knees to find arbutus any day."

"So would I—— Oh, look at this—and this! They are perfect." She fairly trembled with joy as she uncovered the waxlike flowers of dainty pink and white. "I could bury my nose in them forever."

"They are perfect," agreed the man. "Fancy living where you never saw any arbutus or had the joy of picking them."

"I don't want to fancy that, it's too delicious being where they do grow. Won't Mother Bab love them?"

"Yes. She'll keep them for days in water. That flower you gave her in Philadelphia lasted four days."

"These are better," Phœbe said quickly, anxious to shut out all thoughts of the city. Now that she was in the woods again she knew how hungry she had been for them. "I am going to pick a bunch of big ones for Mother Bab."

"She would like the small ones every whit as much," the man declared.

"Perhaps better," she mused. "She would say they are just as sweet and pretty. David, I don't know what I should have done without Mother Bab! My life was different, somehow, after she allowed me to adopt her."

"She's great, isn't she?"

"Wonderful! I have many friends, many new ones, many dear ones, but there is only one Mother Bab."

The man's hands trembled among the arbutus—did the admiration touch Mother Bab's son? Could the dreams of his heart ever come true?

"You know," Phœbe went on, "if I could always have her near me, in the same house, I'd be less unworthy of calling her Mother Bab."

It was well that she bent over the dry leaves and blossoms and missed the look that flooded the face of the man for a moment. She wanted to be with Mother Bab—should he tell her of his love? But the very fact that she spoke thus was evidence that she did not love him as he desired. And the war must change his most cherished plans for the future, change them greatly for a time. If he went and never returned it would be harder for her if he went as her lover. As it was he was merely her old comrade and friend; he could read from her manner that no deeper feeling had touched her—not for him, but he wondered about the musician——

The spell was broken when Phœbe spoke again: "Do you know, Davie, I read somewhere that arbutus can't be made to grow anywhere except in its own woods, that the most skilful hand of man or woman can't transplant it to a garden where the soil is different from its native soil."

"I never heard that before, but I remember that I tried several times and failed. I dug up a big box of the soil to make it grow, but it lasted several months and died. Let us go along this path and find a new bed; we have almost cleaned this one."

"See"—she raised her bunch of flowers—"I didn't take a single root, so next year when we come we shall find as many as this year. They are too altogether lovely to be exterminated."

They moved about the woods, finding new patches of the fragrant flowers, until they declared it would be robbery to take another one.

"Let's eat," she suggested; "I'm hungry as a bear."

"Race you to that big rock," cried David and began to run. Phœbe followed through the brush and dry leaves, but the farmer covered the distance too quickly for her.

"Now I'm hungry," she said, panting; "I'll eat more than my share of the lunch."

She climbed to the top of the boulder and they sat side by side, the lunch box resting on David's knees.

"Now anything you want ask for," said he.

"I will not!" She delved into the box and brought out a sandwich. "It's mine as much as yours."

"Going in for Woman's Suffrage and Rights and the like?" he asked, laughing.

"Ugh," she wrinkled her nose, "don't mention things like that to-day. I don't want to hear about war or work or problems or anything but just pure joy this day! I earned this perfect day this year. This is to be a day of all-joy for us. Have another sandwich? I'm going to—this makes only four more left for each. Aunt Maria knew what she was doing when she made me take this big box of lunch for just us two. Now, aren't you glad that I brought lunch in a box instead of eating our dinner at Hull's as you suggested?" she said as she kicked her feet, little girl fashion, against the side of the boulder.

"Of course I am glad. I was afraid you might like dinner at the tavern better, that is why I suggested it."

"Don't you know me better than that? Why, we can eat in dining-rooms three hundred and sixty-four days in every year. This is one day when we eat in the birds' dining-room."

"I am enjoying it, Phœbe. It is the first picnic I have had for a long time. I can't tell how I'm drinking in the joy of it."

"Now," said Phœbe later, when the last crumb had been taken out of the lunch box, "we can pack the arbutus in this box. If you find some damp moss I'll arrange them."

She laid the flowers on the cushion of moss, covered them with a few damp leaves and closed the box. "That will keep them fresh," she said. "Now for our drink of mountain water, then home again."

Farther in the woods they found the spring. In a little cove edged with laurel bushes and overhung with chestnut trees and tall oaks it sent up a bubbling fountain of cold water.

"I'm sorry the picnic is over," said Phœbe as she leaned over the clear water and drank the cold draught.

"There is still the lovely drive home," he consoled her.

"Yes," she said as they turned and walked back through the woods to the road again, "and I shall remember this day for a long time. In the spring it's dreadful to be shut in the city."

"I believe you are growing tired of Philadelphia."

"Yes and no. I love the many things to do and see there, but on a day like this I think the country is the place to really enjoy the spring. I wish you could come down some time to the city; there are many places of interest you would like to visit."

"Yes." He opened his lips to tell her that he was soon to be in the service of his country, then he remembered that she had said she did not want to hear the word war on that day, it must be a day of all joy, so he closed his mouth resolutely and merely smiled in answer as she entered the carriage for the ride home. They spoke of many things; she was gay with the childish happiness she always felt in the woods or open country roads. He answered her gaiety, but his heart ached. What did the future hold for him? Would she, perchance, love another before he could return—would he return?

"Look," Phœbe said after they had driven several miles, "it is going to storm—see how dark! We are going to have an April storm."

Even as they looked up black clouds moved swiftly across the sky. They turned and looked toward the mountains behind them—the summits were shrouded in dense blackness; the whole countryside was being enveloped in a gloom like the gloom of late twilight. There was an ominous silence in the air, living things of the fields and woods scurried to shelter; only a solitary red-headed woodpecker tapped noisily upon a dead tree trunk.

Suddenly sharp flashes of lightning darted in zigzag rays through the gloom.

Phœbe gripped the side of the carriage. "The storm is following us," she said. "Look at the hills—they are black as night. Can we get home before the storm breaks over us?"

"Hardly. It travels faster than we can, and we still have four more miles to go."

The horse sniffed the air through inflated nostrils and sped unbidden over the country road. The lightning grew more vivid and blinding and darted among the hills with greater frequency; loud peals of thunder echoed and reëchoed among the mountains. Then the rain came. In great splashes, which increased rapidly, it poured its cool torrents upon the earth.

Phœbe laughed but David shook his head. "We'll have to stop some place till it's over. You're getting wet. I'll drive in this barnyard."

Amid the deafening crashes of thunder and the steady downpour of rain they ran through the barnyard and up the path that led to the house. As they stepped upon the porch a door was opened and a woman appeared.

"Why, come right in!" she greeted them. "This is a bad storm."

"If you don't mind," Phœbe began, but the woman was talkative and broke in, "Now, I just knowed there'd be company come to-day yet! This after when I dried the dishes I dropped a knife and fork and that's a sure sign. Mebbe you don't believe in signs?"

"They come true sometimes," said Phœbe.

"Ach, yes, my granny used to plant her garden by the signs in the almanac. Cabbage, now, must be planted in the up-sign. But mebbe you're hungry after your drive? I'll get some cake."

"We had lunch——"

"Ach, if your man's like mine he can eat cake any time." She opened a door that led to the cellar and soon returned with a plate piled high with cake. "Now eat," she invited. "But, ach, I just thought of it—you said you come from Greenwald—then I guess you know about Caleb Warner dying, killing himself, or something."

"Caleb Warner dying!" David echoed. He half started from his chair, then sank with a visible effort at self-control.

"Yes. I guess you know him. My mister was in to dinner a while ago and he said it went over the 'phone at Risser's and Jacob Risser told him that Caleb Warner of Greenwald was dead. It was from gas or something funny like that. It's the Warner that sold that oil stock and gold stock. You know him?"

David nodded, his lips dry.

"Well, I guess now a lot of people will lose money. There's a lady lives near here that gave him almost all her money for some of his stock. For a while she got big interest from it, but then it stopped and now she ain't got hardly enough money to live. And I guess a lot will lose money. My mister had no time for that stock. But if the man's dead now we should let him rest, I guess."

"Yes——" David braced himself. "The rain is over. Phœbe, we must go."

He smiled to the little woman as he gripped her hand. "You have been very kind to us and we appreciate it."

"Yes, indeed," echoed Phœbe. "I hope we have not kept you from your work."

"Ach, I can work enough to-day yet. I like company and I don't have much of it week-days. Um, ain't it good smelly after the rain?" She sniffed, smiling, as she followed Phœbe and David down the path to the barnyard.

"Good-bye," she called as they drove off. "Safe home."

"Thank you. Good-bye," Phœbe called over the side of the carriage. Then, as they entered again upon the country road, she turned to her place beside David.

She looked up at him. All the light and joy had faded from his face; he stared straight head, though he must have felt her eyes' intent gaze upon him.

151

"David," she said softly, "what is wrong?"

"Nothing," he lied.

"Seems you look different," she persisted. "Is it anything about Caleb Warner's death?"

"I'm not much of a stoic, Phœbe. I should have hidden my worry. But you must forget it; we must not let it spoil our perfect day. It really is no great matter. I am affected, in some way you can't know, by his death, but I'll get over it," he tried to treat the matter lightly.

But Phœbe felt a sudden heaviness of heart. She was almost certain that David had had no money to buy any stock from Caleb Warner, therefore, she jumped to the conclusion, it must be that David cared for Mary Warner, as town gossip said he did, and that the death of the girl's father would affect him. She felt hurt and baffled and sorely rebuffed at the withholding of David's confidence and was worried as she saw the marks of worry in the face of the man. Womanlike, she felt certain that the other girl was not good enough for David. Mary Warner, beautiful, aristocratic in bearing and manner—what had she to do with a man like David Eby! Was an incipient engagement with Mary Warner the Aladdin's lamp David had mentioned several times as being on the verge of rubbing and thus become rich? The thought left her trembling; she shivered in the April sunshine. When David spoke it was with an abstracted manner, and the girl beside him finally said, "Oh, don't let us talk. Let us just sit and look at the fields and enjoy the scenery."

She said it calmly enough, but the man beside her could not know that it required the last shreds of her courage to keep her voice from breaking. She would not let David see that she cared if he did care for Mary Warner! Of course, she didn't want to marry him, it was merely that she knew Mary was too haughty for him. Mother Bab would also say that he was too different from Mary, that he was too fine for her. Then she remembered that Mother Bab had said on the previous evening that the Warners had taken David to Hershey recently in their fine new car. She shook herself in an effort at self-control. "Phœbe," she thought, "you're selfish! You go to Philadelphia and you go out with Royal Lee and dance with other young men, and yet, when David pays attention to another girl you have a spasm!"

But the self-administered discipline failed to correct her attitude. She knew their day of all-joy was changed for her as it had been changed for David. The jealousy in her heart could not be quite overcome. She was glad when they reached familiar fields and were on the road near Greenwald.

"Will you come in?" she invited as she left the carriage.

"No. I better go right home."

"I'll divide the flowers, David."

"Oh, keep them all."

"No, indeed. Mother Bab would be disappointed if you brought her none."

She opened the box, separated half of the arbutus from their mates and laid them in the uplifted corner of her coat. "There," she said, "the rest are yours and Mother Bab's. It was perfect in the woods to-day. Thank you——"

But he interrupted her. "It is I who must say that, Phœbe! This has been a great day. I'll never forget the glorious hour when we were on our knees and pushed away the leaves and found the arbutus. That is something to take with one, to remember when the days are not perfect as this one."

He laid his fingers a moment on her hand as she held the corner of her coat to keep the flowers from falling, then he turned and jumped into the carriage.

"Give my love to Mother Bab," she said.

He turned, smiled and nodded, then started off. Phœbe stood at the gate and watched the carriage as it went slowly up the steep road by the hill. Her thoughts were with the man who was going home to his mother, going with trailing arbutus in his hands and some great unhappiness in his heart.

"Is it always so?" she thought. "We carry fragrance in our hands, but what in our hearts?" For the time she was once more the old sympathetic, natural Phœbe, eager to help her friend in need, feeling the divine longing to comfort one who was miserable. "Oh, Davie, Davie," she thought as she went into the house, "I wish I could help you."

CHAPTER XXVIII
MOTHER BAB AND HER SON

When David drove over the brow of the hill and down the green lane to the little house he called home he caught sight of his mother in her garden. He whistled. At the sound Mother Bab rose from the soft earth in which she was working and straightened, smiling. She raised a hand to shade her eyes and waited for the coming of her boy, dreaming of a possible separation from him, dreaming long mother-dreams while he took the horse and carriage to the barn.

153

When he returned he had mustered all his courage and was smiling—he would be a stoic as long as he could, but he knew that his mother would soon discover that all was not well with him.

"Here, mother." He gave her the box of arbutus.

"Then you got some, Davie!" She buried her face in the cool, sweet blossoms. "Oh, how sweet they are! Did you and Phœbe have a good time? Did she enjoy it as much as she always used to enjoy a day in the woods?"

She looked up suddenly from the flowers and caught him unawares. "What is wrong?" she asked with real concern. "Did you and Phœbe fall out?"

"No," he shook his head. He knew that attempts at subterfuge and evasion would be vain. "No, mommie, no use trying to deceive you any longer—I fell out with myself—I wish I could keep it from you," he added slowly; "I know it's going to hurt you."

"You tell me, Davie. I've lived sixty years and never yet met a trouble I couldn't live through. Tell me about it."

She placed the box of arbutus in the garden path and laid her hand on his arm.

"Oh, mommie," he blurted out, almost sobbing, "I'm ashamed of myself! You'll be ashamed of your boy."

"It's no girl——" the mother hesitated.

He answered with a vehement, "No!"

"Then tell me," she said softly. "I can look in your eyes and hear you tell me most anything so long as you need not tell me that you have broken the heart or spoiled the soul of a girl."

She spoke gently, but the man cried out, "Thank God, I have nothing like that to confess! You know there is only one girl for me. I could never look into her eyes if I had betrayed the trust of any girl. I have dreamed of growing into a man she could love and marry, but I failed. I wanted to offer her more than slavery on a farm, I wanted to have something more than the few hundreds I scraped together. I took the five hundred dollars we skimped for and bought stock of Caleb Warner—you heard that he died?"

"Phares told me."

"I guess the five hundred dollars is gone with him! I heard of other men getting rich by buying gold and oil stock so I took a chance and staked all the spare money I had."

"It was your money, Davie."

"You called it mine, but you helped to earn and save it. Caleb promised me he would sell half of the stock for me at a great profit in a week or two, and I could keep the other half for the big dividends it would pay me soon—now he's dead, and the stock is probably worthless."

154

He looked miserably at her troubled face. She flung her arm about him and led him to a seat under the budded cherry tree. "We must sit down and talk it over," she said. "Perhaps it isn't so bad as you think. Are you sure the stock is worth nothing? Perhaps you can get something out of it."

"Perhaps I can." He brightened at the suggestion.

"Well," she went on, "I can't say that I think you did right to buy the stock and try to get rich quick. You know that money gotten that way is tainted money, more or less. To earn what you have and have a little is better and safer than to have much and get it in such a way. But it's too late to preach about that now—I guess I didn't tell you that often enough and hard enough before this, or else you wouldn't have wanted to buy the stock. It is partly my fault, for I thought some time ago you talked as though you were getting the money craze, but I thought it would soon wear off. You did a foolish thing, but there's no use crying about it. You see you did wrong and are sorry, so that is all there is to it. I'm not sorry you lost on the stock, for if you made on it the craze would go deeper. I can live without the few extra things that money would buy."

"Don't be so forgiving, mother! Scold me! I'd feel less like a criminal. But here comes Phares; he'll give me the scolding you're saving me."

The preacher crossed the lawn and advanced to the seat under the cherry tree.

"Aunt Barbara," he began, then noted the troubled look on the face of David and asked, "What is wrong?"

"Nothing," said David, "except that I have some of Caleb Warner's stock."

"You do? Whatever made you buy that?"

David spoke as calmly as possible. "I wanted to be rich, that's all. But I guess I was never intended to be that."

"I'm afraid you are going to be sorry," said the preacher very soberly. "I just came from town and they say things look bad for the investors. They said first that Warner was asphyxiated accidentally, but he was so deep in a hole with investing and re-investing other people's money and his own and he had lost so much that people think this was the easiest way out of it all for him. I suppose it will be hushed up and no one will ever know just how he died. There are at least twenty people in town and farms near here who are worried about their money since he died. Did you have much stock?"

"Five hundred dollars' worth."

"If people were as eager to lay up treasures in heaven——" the preacher said thoughtfully.

"If they were," said David, struggling to keep the wrath from his words and voice. "I know, Phares, you can't understand why everybody should not be as good as you. I wish I were—mother should have had a son like you. I'm the black sheep of the Eby family, I suppose."

"No, no!" cried Mother Bab. "We all make mistakes! You are good and noble, David. I am proud of you, even if you do err sometimes."

"We must make the best of it," said the preacher. "Perhaps the stock is not quite worthless. If I were you I'd go to the lawyer in Lancaster. He'll see you at his house if you 'phone in."

"Mighty good to think of that for me," said David, gripping the hand of his cousin. "I'll go in to-night."

Several hours later David Eby sat before a lawyer and waited for the verdict. "I'm sorry," the lawyer shook his head. "The stock is worthless. Six months ago you might have sold it; now it's dead as a door-nail."

"Guess it was a wildcat scheme," said David.

A few minutes later he went out to the street. His Aladdin's lamp was smashed! What a fool he had been!

When he reached home Mother Bab read the news in his face. "Never mind," she said bravely, "we'll get along without that money."

"Yes—but"—David spoke slowly, as if fearing to hurt her further—"I hoped to have a nice bank account for you to draw on when—when I go."

"You mean——" Mother Bab stopped suddenly. Something choked her, but she faced him squarely and looked up into his face.

"Yes, mother, I mean that I must go. You want me to go, don't you?"

"Yes." The word came slowly, but David knew how truly she felt it. "You must go. I knew it right away when I saw that we were called of God to help in the fight for world peace and righteousness. You must go; there is nothing to keep you. Phares will look after the little farm. I spoke to him about it last week——"

"Mother, you knew then!"

"I saw it in your face as soon as war was declared. Phares was lovely about it and said he could just as well take your few acres in with his and pay a percentage to me for the crops he'll get from them. Phares is kind; he has a big heart, for all his queer ways and his strict views."

"Phares is too good to be related to me, mommie. I'm ashamed of myself."

"Ach, you two are just different, that's all. I can go over and stay at their house. Did you tell Phœbe you are going?"

He shook his head. "I couldn't tell her yesterday. We had such a great day in the woods finding the arbutus, eating our lunch on a rock and acting just like we used to when we were ten years younger. She never mentioned war and I could not seem to break into that day of gladness to speak about the subject. I meant to tell her all about it when we got home, but then that storm came up and we stopped at a farmhouse and I heard about Caleb Warner. It struck me so hard I was just no good after that. I'll be a dandy soldier, won't I?"

He laughed and took the little woman in his arms. When, some moments later, he held the white-capped mother at arms' length and smiled into her face neither knew if the wet lashes were caused by laughter or tears.

"Some soldier you'll make," she said as she looked at him, tall, broad of shoulder, straight of spine. "Some soldier or sailor you'll make!"

CHAPTER XXIX
PREPARATIONS

The days following the death of Caleb Warner were days of anxiety to other inhabitants of the little town who, like David, had purchased stock with glorious visions of sudden gain. In a short time the list of Warner's unfortunate investors was known and they were accorded various degrees of sympathy, rebuke or ridicule. The thing that hurt David was not so much the knowledge that some were speaking of him in condemnation or pity as the fact that he merited the condemnation.

But he had neither time nor inclination for self-pity. His country was calling for his services and he knew his duty was to offer himself. He could not conscientiously say his mother had urgent need of him for he knew that the little farm would supply enough for her maintenance.

Phares Eby, although a preacher among a sect who, as a sect, could not sanction the bearing of arms, accepted the decision of his cousin with no show of disapproval. "I don't believe in wars," he said gravely, "but there seems to be no other way this time. One of the Eby family should go. I'll be glad to keep up your farm and help look after your mother while you are gone. The most I can do here will be less than you are going to do, but I'll raise the best crops I can and help in the food end of it."

"You'll do your part here, Phares, and it will count. You're a bona-fide farmer. You'll have our little place a record farm when I get back. You're a brick, Phares!" For the first time in months he felt a genuine affection for his preacher cousin. Preaching, prosaic Phares, how kind he was!

Lancaster County measured up to its fair standard in those first trying days of recruit gathering. The sons of the nation answered when she called. Pennsylvania Dutch, hundreds of them, rallied round the flag and proved beyond a doubt that the real Pennsylvania Dutch are not German-American, but loyal, four-square Americans who are keeping the faith. Two hundred years ago the ancestors of the present Pennsylvania Dutch came to this country to escape tyranny, and the love of freedom has been transmitted from one generation to another. The plain sects, so flourishing in some portions of the Keystone State, consider war an evil, yet scores of men in navy blue and army khaki have come from homes where the mother wears the white cap, and have gone forth to do their part in the struggle for world freedom.

As David Eby measured the days before his departure he felt grateful to Mother Bab for refraining from long homilies of advice. Her whole life was a living epistle of truth and nobility and she was wise enough to discern that what her son wanted most in their last days together was her customary cheerfulness—although he knew that at times the cheerfulness was a bit bluffed!

News travels fast, even in rural communities. The people on the Metz farm soon learned of David's loss of money and of his desire to enter the navy.

"Why didn't you tell me about the stock?" Phœbe chided him.

"I couldn't. It knocked me out—it changed some of my plans. I knew you'd despise me and I couldn't stand that too that day."

"Despise you! How foolish to think that. Of course it's better to earn your money, but I think you learned your lesson."

"I have. I'll never try to get rich quick."

"And you're going to war!" The words were almost a cry. "What does Mother Bab say? How dreadful for her!"

"Dreadful?" he asked gently. "Phœbe, think a minute—would you rather be the mother of a soldier or sailor than the mother of a slacker?"

"I would," she cried. "A thousand times rather!" She clutched his sleeve in her old impetuous manner. "I see now what it means, what war must mean to us! We must serve and be glad to do it. Your going is making it real for me. I'm proud of you and I know Mother Bab must be just about bursting with pride, for she always did think you are the grandest son in the wide world."

"Phœbe, you always stroke me with the grain."

"That sounds as if you were a wooden pussy-cat," she said merrily. "But you are just being funny to hide your deeper feelings. I know you, David Eby! Bet your heart's like lead this minute!"

"'I have no heart,'" he quoted. "'The place where my heart was you could roll a turnip in.'"

She laughed, then suddenly grew sober. "I've been horribly selfish," she said. "Having fine clothes and a good time and dreaming of fame through my voice have taken all my time during the past winter. I have taken only the husks of life and discarded the kernels. I'm ashamed of myself."

"You mustn't condemn yourself too much. It's natural to pass through a period when those things seem the greatest things in the world, but if we do not shake off their influence and see the need of having real things to lay hold on we need to be jolted. I was money-mad, but I had my jolt."

"Then we can both make a fresh beginning. And we'll try hard to be worthy of Mother Bab, won't we, David?"

David was mute; he could merely nod his head in answer. Worthy of Mother Bab—what a goal! How sweet the name sounded from Phœbe's lips! Should he tell her of his love for her? He looked into her face. Her eyes were like clear blue pools but they mirrored only sisterly affection, he thought. Ah, well, he would be unselfish enough to go away without telling of the hope of his heart. If he came back there would be ample time to tell her; it was needless to bind her to a long-absent lover. If he came back crippled—if he never came back at all—— Oh, why delve into the future!

CHAPTER XXX
THE FEAST OF ROSES

In the little town of Greenwald there is performed each year in June an interesting ceremony, the Feast of Roses.

The origin of it dates back to the early colonial days when wigwam fires blazed in many clearings of this great land and Indians, fashioned after the similitude of bronze images, stole among the stalwart trees of the primeval forests. In those days, about the year 1762, a tract of land containing the present site of the little town of Greenwald fell into the hands of a German, who was so charmed by the fertility and beauty of the fields encircled by the winding Chicques Creek that he laid out a town and proceeded to build. The erection of those early houses entailed much labor. Bricks were imported from England and hauled from Philadelphia to the new town, a distance of almost one hundred miles.

Some time later the founder built a glass factory in the new town, reputed to have been the first of its kind in America. Skilled workmen were imported to carry on the work, and marvelously skilful they must have been, as is proven by the articles of that glass still extant. It is delicately colored, daintily shaped, when touched with metal it emits a bell-like ring, and altogether merits the praise accorded it by every connoisseur of rare and beautiful glass.

Tradition claims that the founder of that town was of noble birth, but his right to a title is not an indisputable fact. It is known, however, that he lived in baronial style in his new town. His red brick mansion was a treasure house of tapestries, tiles and other beautiful furnishings.

However, whether he was a baron or an untitled man, he merits a share of admiration. He was founder of a glass factory, builder of a town, founder of iron works, religious and secular instructor of his employees and citizens, and earnest philanthropist.

The last rôle resulted in his financial embarrassment. There is an ominous silence in the story of his life, then comes the information that the man who had done so much for others was left at last to languish in a debtors' jail, die unbefriended and be buried in an unknown grave.

In the days of his prosperity he gave to the congregation of the Lutheran Church in his town a choice plot of ground, the consideration being the sum of five shillings and an annual rental of one red rose in June.

Years passed, the man died, and either through forgetfulness or negligence the annual rental of one red rose was unpaid for many years. Then, one day a layman of the church found the old deed and the people prepared to pay the long-neglected debt once more. Since that renewal there is set apart each June a Sabbath day upon which the rose is paid to the nearest descendant of the founder of the town. They give but one red rose, but all around are roses, roses, and it seems most fitting to call the unique occurrence the Feast of Roses.

If ever the little town puts on royal garb it is on the Feast of Roses Sabbath. For days before the ceremony the homes of Greenwald are beehives of industry. That day each train and trolley, every country road, is crowded with strangers or old acquaintances coming into the town. A heterogeneous crowd swarms through the street. The curious visitor who comes to see, the dreamer who is attracted by the romance of the rose, the careless youth who rubs his sleeve against some portly judge or senator; the tawdry, the refined, the rich, the poor—all meet in the crowd that moves to the red brick church in which the Feast of Roses is held.

The old church of that early day has been removed and in its place a modern one has been erected, but by some happy inspiration of the builders the new church is devoid of the garish ornamentation that is too often found in churches. Harmonious coloring, artistic beauty, make it a fitting place for a Feast of Roses.

When Phœbe Metz entered the church to keep her promise to sing at the service she found an eager crowd waiting for the opening. Every available space was occupied; people stood in the rear aisles, others waited in the churchyard by the open windows and hoped to catch there some stray parts of the service.

Phœbe pushed her way gently through the crowd at the door and stood in the aisle until an usher saw her and directed her to a seat near the organ. The pink in her cheeks grew deeper. "I'll sing my best for Greenwald and the Feast of Roses," she thought. "And for David! He's in the crowd. He said he's coming to hear me sing."

At the appointed hour the pipe-organ pealed out. The June sunlight streamed through the open windows, fell upon the banks of roses, and gleamed upon the fountain that played in the midst of the crimson flowers. Peace brooded over the place as the last strains of music died. There was silence for a moment, then a prayer, a hymn of adoration, and then the chosen speaker stood before the crowd and delivered his message.

Phœbe listened to him until he uttered the words, "True life must be service, true love must be giving. No man has reached true greatness save he serves, and he who serves most faithfully is greatest in the kingdom."

After those words she fell to thinking. Many things that had been dark to her suddenly became light. She seemed to see Royal Lee fiddling while the world was in travail, but beside him rose a vision of David in sailor's blue, ready to do his whole duty for his country.

"Oh," she thought, "I've been blind, but now I see! It's David I want. He's a man!"

She heard as in a dream the words of the one who presented the red rose to the heir. "Once more the time has come to pay our debt of one red rose. It is with cheerfulness and reverence we pay our rental. Amid these bright surroundings, in the presence of the many who have come to witness this unique ceremony, do we give to you in partial payment of the debt we owe—one red rose."

The heir received the flower and expressed her appreciation. Then silence settled upon the place and Phœbe rose to sing.

As the organ sent forth the opening strains of music the people in the church looked at each other, surprised, disappointed. Why, that was the old tune, "Jesus, Lover of my soul." The tune they had heard sung hundreds of times—was Phœbe going to sing that? With so many impressive selections to choose from no soloist need sing that old hymn! Some of the town people thought disdainfully, "Was that all she could sing after a whole winter's study in Philadelphia!"

But Phœbe sang the old words to the old tune. She sang them with a new power and sweetness. It touched the listeners in that rose-scented church and revealed to them the meaning of the old hymn. The dependence upon a divine guide, the utter impotence of mortal strength, breathed so persuasively in the second verse that many who heard Phœbe sing it mentally repeated the words with her.

"Other refuge have I none,
Hangs my helpless soul on Thee:
Leave, ah! leave me not alone,
Still support and comfort me;
All my trust on Thee is stayed;
All my help from Thee I bring;
Cover my defenceless head
With the shadow of Thy wing."

Then the hymn changed—hope displaced hopelessness, faith surmounted fear.

"Plenteous grace with Thee is found,
Grace to cleanse from every sin;
Let the healing streams abound,
Make and keep me pure within;
Thou of life the fountain art,
Freely let me take of Thee:
Spring Thou up within my heart,
Rise to all eternity."

The people in that rose-scented church heard the old hymn sung as they had never heard it sung before. A subdued hum of approval swept over the church as the girl sat down. She felt that she had sung well; her heart was in a tumult of happiness. She was glad when one man rose and lifted his hands in benediction.

Again the organ throbbed with glad melodies. The eager crowd fell into line and walked slowly to the altar to lay their roses there. Children with half withered blossoms, maidens with bunches of crimson flowers, here and there a stranger with gorgeous hot-house roses, older men and women with the products of the gardens of the little town—all moved to the spot where lay a bank of fragrant roses and placed their tributes there.

Phœbe added her roses to the others on the altar and left the church. Friends and acquaintances stopped to tell her how well she sang. But the words that one short year ago would have filled her with overwhelming pride in her own talent were soon crowded from her thoughts and there reigned there the words of the speaker, "No man has reached true greatness save he serves." She had learned great things at that Feast of Roses service. She had looked deep into her own heart and on its throne she had found David.

He was waiting for her outside the church.

"You sang fine, Phœbe," he told her as they went down the street together.

"Yes? I'm glad you liked it."

Then they spoke of other things, of many things, but not one word of the thoughts lying deepest in the heart of each.

Aunt Maria and Jacob were eating supper in the big kitchen when Phœbe reached home.

"Well," greeted the aunt, "did you come once! We thought that Feast of Roses would been out long ago. But when you didn't come for so long and supper was made we sat down a while. Did you sing?"

"Yes," the girl said as she removed her hat and gloves and drew a chair to the table.

"Now," cautioned the aunt, "put your apron on! That light goods in your dress is nothin' for wear; everything shows on it so. And if you spill red-beet juice or something on it it'll be spoiled."

"I forgot." Phœbe took a blue gingham apron from a hook behind the kitchen door. "There, if I spoil it now you may have it for a rug."

"Well, I guess that would be housekeepin'! And everything so high since the war!"

"Tell me about the Feast of Roses," said the father. "Was the church full?"

"Packed! It was a beautiful service."

"Well," spoke up Aunt Maria, "I'm glad it's over and so are

many people. Of course that Feast of Roses don't do no harm, but I think it's so dumb to have all this fuss just to give somebody a rose. If that man wanted to give the church some land why didn't he give it and done with it? It's no use to have this pokin' around every year to find the best red rose to give to some man or lady that's related to him. The rose withers right away, anyhow. And this Feast of Roses makes some people a lot of bother. I heard one woman say in the store that she has to get ready for a lot of company still for every person she knows, most, comes to visit her that Sunday and she's got to cook and wash dishes all day. I guess she's glad it's over for another year."

CHAPTER XXXI
BLINDNESS

David Eby had spent the day at Lancaster and returned to Greenwald at seven-thirty. He started with springing step out the country road in the soft June twilight. It was a twilight pervaded by blended perfumes and the sleepy chirp of birds. David drew in deep breaths of the fresh country air.

"Lancaster County," he said aloud to himself, "and it's good enough for me!"

Scarcely slackening his pace he started up the long road by the hill. He paused a moment on the summit and looked back at the town of Greenwald, then almost ran down the road to his home.

He whistled his old greeting whistle.

"Here, David, I'm on the porch," came his mother's voice.

"Mommie," he cried gaily as he took her into his arms, "I knew you'd be looking for me."

Then for the first time since his father's death he heard his mother sob. "Oh, mother," he asked, "is my going away as hard as all that? Or are you only glad to see me?"

"Glad," she replied, restraining her emotion. "Sit down on the bench, Davie."

"Why—I didn't notice it first—you're wearing dark glasses again! Are your eyes worse?"

"Sit down, Davie, sit down," she said nervously. "That's right," she added as he sat beside her and put one arm about her.

"Now tell me," he said imperiously. "Are you sure you're all right? You're not worrying about me?"

"No, I'm not worrying about you; I quit worrying long ago.

But I must tell you—I wish I didn't have to—don't be scared—it's just about my eyes."

"Tell me! Are they worse?"

She laid her hand on his knees. "Don't get excited—but—I can't see."

"Can't see!" He repeated the words as though he could not understand them. Then he put his hands on her cheeks and peered into her face in the semi-darkness of the porch. "Not blind? Oh, mommie, not blind?"

She nodded, her lips trembling. "Yes, it's come. I'm blind."

The words, fraught with so much sorrow, sounded like claps of thunder in his ears. "Mother," he cried again, "you can't be blind!"

"But I am. I knew it was coming. The light was getting dimmer every day. I could hardly see your face this morning when you went."

"And I went away and you stayed here and went blind!" He broke into sobs and she allowed him to cry it out as they sat together in the darkness.

"Come," she said at length, "now you mustn't take on so. It's not as awful as you think. I said to Phares to-day that I'm almost glad it's here, for it was awful to know it's coming."

"But it's awful," he shuddered. "Come in to the light and let me see you—but oh, you can't see me!"

"Yes I can." She reached a hand to his face. "This is the way I see you now. The same mouth and chin, the same mole on your left cheek—that's good luck, Davie—the same nose with its little turn-up."

"Mommie"—he grabbed her hands and kissed them— "there's not another like you in the whole world! If I were blind I'd be groaning and moaning and making life miserable for everybody near me, and here you are your same cheerful self. You're the bravest of 'em all!"

"But you mustn't think that I haven't rebelled against this, that I haven't cried out against it! I've had my hours of weakness and tears and rebellion."

"And I never knew it."

"No. Each one goes to Gethsemane alone."

"But isn't it almost more than you can bear—to be blind?"

"It's dreadful at first. I stumble so and every little sill and rug seems a foot high. But I'll soon learn."

"Is there nothing to do? What did Dr. Munster say about your eyes when we were down to see him?"

"He told me then I'd be blind soon. And he said the only

thing might save my sight or bring it back was a delicate operation that would be a big risk, for it probably wouldn't help at any rate. So I'm not thinking of ever trying that. Now I don't want you to think I'm brave about it. I've cried all my tears a month ago, so don't put me on any pedestal. It seems hard not to see the people I love and all the beautiful things around me, but I'm glad I have the memory of them. I'm glad I know what a rainbow is, and a sunset."

"Yes, but I think it's awful to know what they look like and never see them again. I can't, just can't, realize that you're blind!"

"You will when you come back from war and have to fetch and carry for me. Your Aunt Mary and Phares are just lovely about it and willing to help in every way. I was going to live over with them at any rate."

"I wish I could stay with you, mommie. You need me, but I guess Uncle Sam needs me too. I'm to go soon, you know."

"You go, even if I am blind. I'm not helpless. It will be awkward for a while but there are many things I can do. I can knit without seeing."

"You're a wonder! But is there no hope?"

"Hope," she repeated softly. "No hope of the kind you mean, except that very severe operation that would cost big money and then perhaps not help. But this world isn't all. I've always liked that part of Isaiah, 'The eyes of the blind shall be opened, and the ears of the deaf shall be unstopped. Then shall the lame man leap as an hart, and the tongue of the dumb sing.' I know now what it'll mean to us. It seems like the afflicted will have a special joy in that time."

David was silent for a moment; his mother's words stirred in him emotions too great for ready words.

Presently she continued, "But, Davie, this isn't heaven yet! And I'm concerned just now about helping myself to live the rest of this life the best way I can. I can knit like a machine and I like to knit socks——"

The remainder was left unsaid for the strong arms of her boy surrounded her and held her close while his lips were pressed upon her forehead.

"Such a mother," he breathed, as if the touch of her forehead bestowed a benediction upon him. "Such a mother!"

In the morning he brought the news to the Metz farmhouse.

"Blind?" Phœbe cried.

David nodded.

"Blind! Mother Bab blind? Oh, it's too awful!"

"My goodness," Aunt Maria said with genuine sorrow, "now that's too bad! Her blind and you goin' off to war soon!"

166

"I'm going up to see her," said Phœbe, and went off with David.

Mother Bab heard the girl's step and called gaily, "Phœbe, is that you? I declare, it sounds like you!"

Phœbe ran to the room where Mother Bab sat alone. The girl could not speak at first; she twined her arms about the woman while her heart ached with its poignant grief. Again it was the afflicted one who turned comforter. "Come, Phœbe, you mustn't cry for me. Laugh like you always did when you came to see me."

"Laugh! Oh, Mother Bab, I can't laugh!"

"But, Phœbe, I'll want you to come up to see me every day when you can and you surely can't cry every time and be sad, so you might as well begin now to be cheerful."

"But, Mother Bab, can't something be done?"

"Dr. Munster, the big doctor I saw in Philadelphia, said that only a big operation might help me, but he's not sure that even it would do any good. And, of course, we have no money for it and at my age it doesn't matter so much."

Later, as Phœbe walked down the hill again, she kept revolving in her mind what Mother Bab had said about the operation. An inspiration suddenly flashed to her. The wonder of it made her stand still in the road.

"I know! I'll buy sight for Mother Bab! I will! I must! If it's only money that's necessary, if there's any wonderful doctor can operate on her eyes and make her see again she's going to see! Oh, glory! What a happy thought! I'm the happiest girl since that idea came to me! The money I meant to spend on more music lessons next winter will be put to better use; it will give Mother Bab a chance to see again! Why, I'd rather have her see than be able to call myself the greatest singer in the world! But she'll never let me spend so much money for her. I know that. I'll have to make her believe the operation will be free. I can fool her in that, dear, innocent, trusting Mother Bab! She'd believe me against half the world. But I'm afraid I can't fool David so easily. I must wait till he goes, then I'll write to Dr. Munster and start things going!"

CHAPTER XXXII
OFF TO THE NAVY

Phœbe was glad when David came to her with the news that he had been accepted for the navy and was going to Norfolk.

"That's so far away he won't come home soon," she thought.

"It'll give me a chance to arrange for the operation. I hope he goes soon. That's a dreadful thing to say! The days are all too short for Mother Bab, I know."

If the days seemed Mercury-shod to the blind mother she did not complain.

"It's hard to let you go," she said to her boy, "but it would be harder to see you a slacker. Phœbe is going to read to me now when you go. She'll be up here often."

"Yes, that makes it easier for me to go, mommie."

"Don't you worry about me. Phœbe will be good company for me and she'll write my letters for me. We'll send you so many you'll be busy reading them."

"I'm going to make her promise that," he declared with a laugh.

He exacted the promise as Mother Bab and Phœbe stood with him and waited for the train to carry him away. "Mother, you and Phœbe must take me to the train," he had said. "I want you to be the last picture I see as the train pulls out." Phœbe had assented, though she thought ruefully of the deficiency of the English language, which has but one form for singular you and plural you. She wondered whether he included her in the picture he wanted to cherish in his memory. Now, when he was going away from her she knew that she loved her old playmate, that he was the one man in the world for her. She loved David, she would always love him! She wanted to run to him and tell him so, but centuries of restriction had bequeathed to her the universal fear of womanhood to reveal a love that has not been sought. She felt that in all her life she had never wanted anything so keenly as she wanted to hear David Eby tell her that he loved her, that her face would be with him in whatever circumstances the future should place him. But David could not read the heart of his old playmate, and while his own heart cried out for its mate his words were commonplace.

"Mother has promised that I'm to have so many letters that I can't read them all. As you're to be private secretary, you'll have to promise to carry out her promise."

"David," she met him with equal jest, "you have as many promises in that sentence as a candidate for political office."

"But I want them better kept than that," he said, laughing. "Will you promise, Phœbe?"

"Promise what?" she asked, the levity fading suddenly.

"To write often for mother."

"Yes—I promise to write often for Mother Bab," she said, and the man could not know the effort the simple words cost her.

"Oh, Davie," she thought, "it's not for Mother Bab alone I want to write to you! I want to write you my letters, letters of a girl to the man she loves. How blind you are!"

The moment was becoming tense. It was Mother Bab who turned the tide into a normal channel. "Now, don't you worry, Davie. I can make Phœbe mind me."

The train whistled. Phœbe drew a long breath and prayed that the train would make a short stop and speed along for she could not endure much more. She looked at Mother Bab. The hysteria was turned from her. She knew she would have to be brave for the sake of the dear mother.

"I'll take care of Mother Bab, David," she promised as the train drew in, "and I'll write often."

"Phœbe, you're an angel!" He grasped both hands in his for a long moment. Then he turned to his mother, folded her in his arms and kissed her.

"There he is," Phœbe cried as the train moved. She was eyes for Mother Bab. "Turn to the right a bit and wave; that's it! He's waving back—— Oh, Mother Bab, he's waving that box of sand-tarts Aunt Maria gave him! They'll be in pieces!"

"Sand-tarts," said the other, still waving to the boy she could not see. "Well, he'll eat them if they are broken. Davie is crazy for cookies."

"I'm going to need you more than ever now, Phœbe," Mother Bab said as they started home. "Aunt Mary and Phares are so busy and I feel it's so lovely of them to have me there when I can do so little to help, that I don't want to make them more trouble than I must. So if you'll take care of the writing to David for me I'll be glad." Ah, blind Mother Bab, you had splendid vision just then!

"I'll write for you. I'll love to do it. Mother Bab——" She hesitated. Should she broach the subject of the operation now? Perhaps it would be kind to divert the thoughts of the mother from the recent parting. "Mother Bab, I've thought about what you said, and I think you should have that operation. The doctor said there was a chance."

"Ach, a very slim one. One chance in—I don't know how many!"

"But a chance!"

"Yes"—the woman thought a moment—"but it would cost lots of money, I guess. I didn't ask the doctor, but I know operations are dear. I have fifty dollars saved, but that wouldn't go far."

"But don't you know," the girl said guilelessly, "that all big hospitals have free rooms and do lots of work for nothing? Many rich people endow rooms in hospitals. If you could get into one like that and pay just a little, would you go?"

A light seemed to settle upon the face of the blind woman. "Why," she answered slowly, "why, Phœbe, I never thought of that! I didn't remember—why, I guess I would—yes, of course! I'd go and make a fight for that one chance!"

"I knew you'd be brave! You'll have that operation, Mother Bab! I'll write to Dr. Munster right away. But don't you let Phares write and tell David. We'll surprise him!"

"Ach, but won't he be glad if I can see when he comes home!"

"Won't he though! I'll make all the arrangements; don't you worry about it at all."

"My, you're good to me, Phœbe!"

"Good—after all you've done for me!"

"Good," she thought after Mother Bab had been left at the home of Phares and Phœbe turned homeward. "She calls me good the first time I deceive her. I've begun that tangled web and I know I'll have to tell a whole pack of lies before I'm through with it."

CHAPTER XXXIII
THE ONE CHANCE

Phœbe lost no time in carrying out her plans. When she mentioned the operation to Phares Eby he looked dubious.

"I'm afraid it's no use," he said gravely. "Those operations very often fail."

"But there's a chance, Phares! If it were your eyes wouldn't you snatch at any meagre chance?"

"Why, I guess I would," he admitted, wondering at her insight into human nature and admiring her devotion to the blind woman.

Aunt Maria also was sceptical. "Ach, Phœbe, it vonders me now that Barb'll spend all that money for carfare and to stay in the city and then mebbe it's all for nothin'. There was old Bevy Way and a lot of old people I knowed went blind and they died blind. When abody gets so old once it seems the doctors can't do much. I guess it just is to be."

"Oh, Aunt Maria," Phœbe said hotly, "I don't believe in that is-to-be business! Not until you've done all you can to make things better."

170

"Well, mebbe, for all, it's worth tryin'. I guess if it was my eyes I'd do most anything to get 'em fixed again."

Mother Bab said little about the hopes Phœbe had raised, but the girl knew how the woman built upon having sight for a glad surprise for David.

"I'm afraid the fifty dollars won't reach," she said the day before they were to take the trip to Philadelphia.

"Don't worry about that. Those big doctors usually have hearts to match. I told you there are generous people who give lots of money to hospitals."

"And I guess the hospitals pay the doctors then," offered the woman.

"I guess so," Phœbe agreed. Her conscience smote her for the deception she was practicing on the dear white-capped woman. "But what's the use of straining at every little gnat of a falsehood," she thought, "when I'm swallowing camels wholesale?"

She managed to secure a short interview with Dr. Munster before the examination of Mother Bab's eyes.

"I want to ask you what the operation is going to cost, hospital charges and all," she said frankly.

"At least five hundred dollars."

Phœbe's year in the city had taught her many things. She showed no surprise at the amount named. "That will be satisfactory, Dr. Munster. But I want to ask you, please don't tell Moth—Mrs. Eby anything about it. I—it's to be paid by a friend. I know Mrs. Eby would almost faint if she knew so much money was going to be spent for her. She knows that many hospitals have free rooms and thinks some operations are free. I left her under that impression. You understand?"

The big doctor understood. "Yes, I see. Well, we'll run this one chance to cover and make a fight. I wish I could promise more," he said.

"Thank you. I know you'll succeed. I'm sure she'll see again!"

True to his promise Dr. Munster answered Mother Bab so tactfully that she came out of his office feeling that "the physician is the flower of our civilization, that cheerfulness and generosity are a part of his virtues."

The optimism in Phœbe's heart tinged the blind woman's with its cheery faith. "I figure it this way," the girl said; "we'll do all we can and then if we fail there's time enough to be resigned and say it's God's will."

"Phœbe, you're a wonderful girl! Your name means shining,

171

and that just suits you. You're doing so much for me. Why, you didn't even want to let me pay your carfare down here!"

The girl winced again. "I must learn to wince without showing it," she thought, "for after she sees she'll keep saying such things and I can't spoil it all by letting her know the truth."

Perhaps the optimistic words of Phœbe rang in the ears of the big doctor as he bent over Mother Bab's sightless eyes and began the tedious operation. His hands moved skilfully, with infinite precision, cutting to the infinitesimal fraction of an inch.

Afterward, when Mother Bab had been taken away, he sought Phœbe. "I hope," he said, "that your faith was not unwarranted, though I can't promise anything yet."

"Oh, I'm surer now than ever!" the girl said happily.

But at times, in the days of waiting, her heart ached. What if the operation had failed, what if Mother Bab would have to bear cruel disappointment? All the natural buoyancy of the girl's nature was required to bear her through the trying days of waiting. With the dawning of the day upon which the bandage should be removed and the truth known Phœbe's excitement could not be restrained.

"I can't wait!" she exclaimed. "I want to be right there when he takes it off. I want you to see me first, since David isn't here."

Long after that day it seemed to her that she could hear Mother Bab's glad, sweet voice saying, "I can see!"

"I can see!" The words were electric in their effect. Phœbe gave an ecstatic "Oh!" then hushed as her lips trembled.

"You win," the big doctor said to her.

"Oh, no, not I! You! But I knew she'd see again!"

"She sees again, but," he cautioned, "Mrs. Eby, there must be no reading or sewing or any close work to strain your eyes."

"Oh, doctor, it's enough just to see again! I can do without the reading and writing, for Phœbe, here, does all that for me. And I'll not miss the sewing. I'm glad I can potter around the garden again and plant flowers and see them and"—her voice broke—"I think it's wonderful there are men like you in the world!"

CHAPTER XXXIV
BUSY DAYS

The news of the operation spread quickly and with it spread the interesting information that Mother Bab was keeping her sight as a surprise for David. So it happened that no letters to him

172

contained the news, that even the town paper refrained from printing the item of heart interest and David's surprise was unspoiled.

His letters to Mother Bab were long and interesting and always required frequent re-reading for the mother.

"I wanted to read that letter awful bad," she confessed to Phœbe one day, "but I didn't. I'm not taking any chances with my eyes. I'm too glad to be able to see at all. The letter came this morning and Phares read it for me, but I want to hear it again. Will you read it, Phœbe? Did David write to you this week yet?"

"No." The girl felt the color surging to her cheeks. "He doesn't write to me very often. He knows I read your letters."

"Ach, yes. I guess he's busy, too. It's a big change for him to be learning to be a sailor when he always had his feet on dry land. But read the letter; it's a nice big one."

Phœbe's clear laughter joined Mother Bab's at one paragraph: "Do you remember the blue sailor suits you used to make for me when I was a tiny chap? And once you made me a real tam and I was proud as a peacock in it. Well, since I'm here and wearing a sailor suit I feel like a masculine edition of Alice in Wonderland when she felt herself growing bigger and bigger and I wonder sometimes if I'll shrink back again and be just that little boy."

Another portion of the letter set Phœbe's voice trembling as she read, "I must tell you again, mother, how thankful I am that you made it so much easier for me to go than I dreamed it could be. You are so fine about it. With a mother as plucky as you I can't very well be a jelly-fish. It's great to have a mother one has to reach high to live up to."

"Just like David," said Phœbe as she laid the letter aside. "Of course I think war is dreadful, but the training is going to do wonders for many of the men."

"Yes," said the white-capped woman. "Out of it some good will come. Selfishness is going to be erased clean from the souls of many people by the time war is over."

"But we must pay a big price for all we gain from it."

"Yes—I wonder—I guess Davie will be going over soon. He said, you know, that if we don't hear from him for a while not to worry. I guess that means he thinks he'll be going over."

When, at length, news came from the other side it was Phœbe who was the bringer of the tidings.

"Oh, Mother Bab," she cried breathlessly one day in autumn as she ran back from the gate after a visit from the postman, "it's a letter from France!"

Phares Eby and his mother ran at the news and the four stood, an eager group, as Phœbe opened the letter.

"Read it, Phœbe! He's over safely!" Mother Bab's voice was eager.

"I—I can't read it. I'm too excited. I can't get my breath. You read it, Phares."

The preacher read in his slow, calm way.

"Somewhere in France.

"Dear Mother:

"You see by the heading I'm safe over here. I can't tell you much about the trip—no use wearing out the censor's pencils. The sea's wonderful, but I like dry land better. I'm on dry land now, in a quaint French village where the streets run up hill and the people wear strange costumes. The women wash their clothes by beating them on stones in the brook—how would the Lancaster County women like that?"

It was a long, chatty letter and it warmed the heart of the mother and interested Phœbe and the others who heard it.

"He's a great David," the preacher said as he handed the letter to Phœbe. "I suppose you'll have to read it over and over to Aunt Barbara."

He looked at the girl as he spoke. Her high color and shining eyes spoke eloquently of her interest in the letter. "Ah," he thought, "I believe she still likes Davie best. I'm sure she does."

The preacher had been greatly changed by the events of the past year. He would always be a bit too strict in his views of life, a bit narrow in many things. Nevertheless, he was changed. He was less harsh in his opinions of others since he had seen and heard how thousands who were not of his religious faith had gone forth to lay down their lives that the world might be made a decent place in which to live. He, Phares Eby, preacher, had formerly denounced all that pertained to actors and the theatre, yet tears had coursed down his cheeks as he had read the account of a famous comedian who had given his only son for the cause of freedom and who was going about in the camps and in the trenches bringing cheer to the men. As the preacher read that he confessed to himself that the comedian, familiar as he was with footlights, was doing more good in the world than a dozen Phares Ebys. That one incident swept away some of the prejudice of the preacher. He knew he could never sanction the doings so many people indulge in but he felt at the same time that those same pleasures need not have a damning influence upon all people.

Phœbe noted the change in him. She felt like a discoverer of hidden treasure when she heard of the influence he was exerting in behalf of the Red Cross and Liberty Loans. But she was finding hidden treasures in many places those days. Strenuous, busy days they were but they held many revelations of soul beauty.

Every link with Phœbe's former life in Philadelphia was broken save the one binding her to Virginia. That friendship was too precious to be shattered. The country girl had written a long letter to the city girl, telling of the decision to give up the music lessons. "My dear, dear friend," she wrote frankly, "you tried to keep me from being hurt, but I wouldn't see. How I must have worried you and how foolish I was! I know better now. I do not regret my winter in the city and I do appreciate all you did for me, but I am happy to be back on the farm again. I'm afraid I tried to be an American Beauty rose when I was meant to be just some ordinary wild flower like the daisy or even the common yarrow. I owe so much to you. We must always be friends."

One day in late summer Phœbe fairly radiated joy as she hurried up the hill and ran down the road to the garden where Mother Bab was gathering larkspur seeds.

"Oh, Mother Bab, I've such good news about Granny Hogendobler and Old Aaron!"

"Come in, tell me!"

"I've been to town and stopped to see Granny. You know Old Aaron and their boy Nason fell out years ago about something the boy said about the flag and was too stubborn to take back."

"Yes, I know."

"It was foolishness on the part of the father, of course, for he should have known boys say things they don't mean. Well, the two kept on acting all these years like strangers. The old man grew bitter. Last year when the boys went to Mexico he said that if he had a son instead of a blockhead he'd be sending a boy to do his share down there. It almost killed him to think of his boy sitting back while others went and defended the flag. Well, Granny said yesterday she was in the yard and she heard the gate click. She didn't pay any attention for she knew Old Aaron was in the front yard under the arbor. But then she heard a cry and ran to see, and there was Old Aaron with his arms around a big fellow dressed in a soldier uniform, and when the man turned his head it was Nason! Granny said it was the greatest day in their lives and paid up for all the unhappy days when Old Aaron was cross and said mean things about Nason. Nason had just a day to stay, but they made a day of it. Granny said, 'I-to-goodness, but we had a time! Aaron wanted to kill a chicken, for Nason likes chicken so much, but I knew that Aaron was so excited he'd like as not only cripple the poor thing, so I said I'd kill it while they talked. I made stuffing with onions in, like Nason likes, and I had just baked a snitz pie and I tell you we had a good dinner. But I bet them two didn't know what they ate, for they were all the time talking about the war and bombs and Gettysburg and France till I didn't know what they meant.'"

"My, I'm glad for Granny and Old Aaron," Mother Bab said.

"And what do you think!" Phœbe went on. "They are changing the name of Prussian Street, and some are talking of changing the name of the town, but I hope they won't do that."

"No, it would be strange to have to call it something else after all these years."

"I think it's a grand joke," said Phœbe, "that this little town was founded by a German and yet the town is strong American and doing its best to down the Potsdam gang. The people of Lancaster County are loyal to Old Glory and I'm glad I belong here."

She appreciated her goodly heritage, not with any Pharisaical exultation but with honest gratitude.

"I have learned many things, Mother Bab, and this is one of the big things I've learned lately: to be everlastingly thankful to Providence for setting me down on a farm where I could spend a childhood filled with communications with nature. I never before realized what blessings I've had all the years of my life. Why, I've had chickens to play with and feed, cows and wobbly calves to pet, birds to love and learn about, clear streams to wade in and float daisies on, meadows to play in, hills to run down while the dust went 'spif' under my bare feet. And I've had flowers, thousands of wild flowers, to find and carry home or, if too frail to bear carrying home, like the delicate spring beauty and the bluet, just to look at and admire and turn again to look at as I went out of the woods. My whole childhood has been a wonderful one but I was too blind to see the wonder of it. I see now! But, Mother Bab, I don't see, even yet, that I should wear plain clothes. I've been thinking about it lately. I do believe, though, that the plain way is a good way. Many people enjoy the simple service of the meeting-house more than they would enjoy a more complex form of worship. I feel so restful and peaceful when I'm in a meeting-house, so near to the real things, the things that count."

Mother Bab answered only a mild "Yes," but her heart sang as she thought, "I believe she'll be plain some day, she and David. Perhaps they'll come together. But I'll not worry about them; I know their hearts are right."

176

CHAPTER XXXV
DAVID'S SHARE

Another June came with its roses and perfume, but there was no Feast of Roses in Greenwald that June of 1918. Phœbe regretted the fact, for she felt that even in a war-racked world, with the multiple duties and anxiety and suffering of many of its people, there should still be time for a service as beautiful and inspiring as the Feast of Roses.

But all thoughts of it or similar omissions were crowded into the background one day when the news came to Mother Bab that David had been wounded in France.

The official telegram flashed over the wire and in due time came a letter with more satisfying details. The letter was characteristic of David: "I suppose you heard that the Boche got me, but he didn't get all of me, just one leg. What hurts me most is the fact that I didn't get a few Huns first or do some real thing for the cause before I got knocked out. I know you'll feel better satisfied if I tell you all about it. Several of the other boys and I left the town where we were stationed and went to Paris for a few days. It was our first pleasure trip since we came to this side. We gazed upon the things we studied about in school—Eiffel Tower, Notre Dame, and so forth. Later we went to a railroad station where refugees were coming in, fleeing from the invading Huns. I can't ever forget that sight! Women and children they were, but such women and children! Women who had gone through hell and children who had seen more horror in their few years that we can ever dream possible. Terror and suffering have lodged shadows in their eyes till one wonders if some of them will ever smile or laugh again. Many of them were wounded and in need of medical care. They carried with them their sole possessions, all of their belongings they could gather and take with them as they rushed away from the hordes of the enemy soldiers. We helped to place them into Red Cross vans to be taken to a safe place in the southern part of the country. As we were putting them into the vans the signal came that an air raid was on. The subways are places for refuge during the raids, so we hurried them out of the vans and into subways. They all got in safely but I was a bit too slow. I got knocked out and my right leg was so badly splintered that I'm better off without it. The thing worries me most is that I'll be sent home out of the fight before I fairly got into it."

"Oh, Mother Bab," Phœbe said sobbingly, "his right leg's gone!"

"It might be worse. But—I wish I could be with him."

"But isn't it just like him," said Phœbe proudly, "to write as though it was carelessness caused the accident, when we know he got others to safety and never thought of himself. He was just as brave as the boys who fight."

"Yes. There is still much to be thankful for. Many mothers will get sadder news than mine. You must write him a long letter."

It was a long letter, indeed, that the mother dictated to her boy. When it was written Phœbe added a little postscript, "David, I'm mighty proud of you!" To this he responded, "Thank you for your pride in me, but don't you go making a hero of me; I can't live up to that when I get home. Guess I'll be sent back as soon as my leg is healed. Uncle Sam has no need of me here since I bungled things and left a leg in Paris. I'll have to do the rest of my bit on the farm. I wasn't a howling success as a farmer when I had two legs, but perhaps my luck has turned. I'm going to raise chickens and do my best to make the little farm a paying one."

"He's the same cheerful David," thought the girl, "and we'll have to keep cheerful about it, too."

But it was no easy matter to continue steadfast in cheerfulness during the long days of the summer. Phœbe and Mother Bab shared the anxiety of many others as the news came that the armies of the enemy were pushing nearer to Paris, nearer, and nearer, with the Americans and their allies fighting like demons and contesting every inch of the ground. A fear rose in Phœbe—what if the Germans should reach Paris, what if they should win the war! "But it can't be!" she thought.

Her confidence was not unwarranted. Soon came the turn of the tide and the German drive was checked. One July day shrieking whistles, frenzied ringing of bells, impromptu parades and waving flags, spread the news that "America's contemptible little army" was helping to push the Germans back, back!

"It's the beginning of the end for the Germans," said Phœbe jubilantly as she ran to Mother Bab with the news. "If they once start running they'll sprint pretty lively. We'll have to tell David about the excitement in town when the whistles blew—but, ach, I forgot! He won't think that was much excitement after he's been in real excitement."

Mother Bab laughed with the girl. "But we'll have lots to tell him when he comes back," she said. "And won't he be glad I can see!"

CHAPTER XXXVI
DAVID'S RETURN

It was October of 1918 when David Eby alighted from the train at Greenwald and started out the country road to his home. He could not resist the temptation to run into the yard of the gray farmhouse and into the kitchen where Aunt Maria and Phœbe were working.

"David!"

"Why, David!"

The cries came gladly from the two women as he bounded over the sill and extended his hand, first to the older woman, then to Phœbe.

"I just had to stop in here for a minute! Then I must run up the hill to mother. This place looks too good to pass by. How are you? You're both looking fine."

"Ach, we're well," Aunt Maria had to answer, Phœbe remaining speechless. "But why, David! You got two legs and no crutches! I thought you lost a leg."

"I did," he said, smiling, "but Uncle Sam gave me another one."

"Why, abody'd hardly know it. Ain't, Phœbe, he just limps a little? Now I bet your mom'll be glad to see you—to have you back again, I mean."

"Yes. I can't wait to get up the hill. I must go now. I'll be down later, Phœbe," he added.

"All right," she said quietly.

"Ach, Phœbe," Aunt Maria exclaimed after he left, "did you hear me? I almost give it away that his mom can see. Abody can be awful dumb still! But won't he be glad when he knows that she ain't blind! She can see him again. Ach, Phœbe, it's lots of nice people in the world, for all. It makes abody feel good to know them two are havin' a happy time."

"I'm so glad for both I could sing."

"Go on," said the woman; "I'm glad too, and I believe I could help you to holler."

As David climbed the hill by the woodland he thought musingly, "Strikes me Phœbe didn't seem extra glad to see me. Perhaps she was just surprised, perhaps my being crippled changed her. Oh, Phœbe, I want you more than ever! I wonder—is it some nerve to ask you to marry a cripple?"

However, all disquieting thoughts were forgotten as he reached the summit of the hill and saw his boyhood home.

He whistled his old greeting whistle. At the sound of it Mother Bab ran to the door.

"It's David come home!" she cried, her renewed eyes turned to the road, her hands outstretched.

"I'm back, mommie!" he called before his running feet could take him to her. But as he held her again to his heart there were no words adequate for the greeting. Their joy was great enough to be inarticulate for a while.

"But, Davie," the mother said after a long silence, "you come running! You have no crutches!"

"Why, mommie!" There was questioning wonder in his voice. "How do you know? You couldn't see! You are blind!"

"Oh, Davie, not any more! I can see!"

"You can see?" He put a hand at each side of the white-capped head and looked into her eyes. They were not the dull, half-staring eyes of blindness but eyes lighted by loving recognition.

Again words failed him as he swept her into his arms. But he could not long be silent. "Tell me," he cried. "I must know! What miracle—who—how—who did it? When?"

"Oh, Davie, you're not changed a bit! Same old question box! But I'll tell you all about it."

Throughout the story Mother Bab told ran the name of Phœbe. "Phœbe planned it all, Phœbe made the arrangements with the doctor, Phœbe took me down to Philadelphia, Phœbe was there when I found I could see"—it was Phœbe, Phœbe, till the man felt his heart singing the name.

"Isn't she going on with her music lessons?" he asked. "I was afraid she'd be in the city when I got back."

"She's given them up. It ain't like her to begin a thing and get tired of it so soon. All at once after we came back from Philadelphia she said she had enough of music, she was tired of it, and was going to stay at home and be useful. I'm glad she's not going off again, for it gets lonesome without her. You stopped to see her on the way up?"

"Yes, just a minute. I'm going down again later. She hardly said two words to me."

"You took her by surprise, I guess. Give her a chance and she'll ask you a hundred questions."

But when he paid the promised visit to Phœbe he was again disappointed by her lack of the old comradely friendliness. She shared his joy at Mother Bab's restored sight but when he began to thank her for her part in it she disclaimed all credit and asked questions to lead him from the subject of the operation. The girl seemed interested in all he said yet there was a restraint in her manner. For the first time in his life David was baffled by her attitude. As he climbed the hill again he thought, "Now, what's the matter with Phœbe? Was she or wasn't she glad to see me? I couldn't tell her I love her when she acts like that! And I'm a cripple, and she's beautiful—— Oh, my mind's in a muddle! But one thing's clear—I want Phœbe Metz for my wife."

CHAPTER XXXVII
"A LOVE THAT LIFE COULD NEVER TIRE"

The next morning Phares Eby called David, "Wait, I want to see you. I—David," the preacher began gravely, "perhaps I shouldn't tell you, but I really think I ought. Do you know all Phœbe did for your mother while you were gone?"

"Why, yes. Mother told me. Phœbe was lovely to her. She's been great! Writing her letters and doing ever so many kind things for her."

"I know—but—I guess you don't know all she did. That story about a great doctor operating for charity didn't quite please me. I thought as long as it was in the family I'd pay him for what he did. So I wrote to him and his secretary wrote back that the bill had been paid by a check signed by Phœbe Metz—the bill had been five hundred dollars. I guess that explains her giving up the music lessons. What a girl she is to make such a sacrifice! She don't know that I know, but I felt I ought to tell you."

"Five hundred dollars! Phœbe did that for us—she paid it? Oh, Phares, I'm glad you told me! I'm going to find her right away and thank her! You're a brick for telling me!"

The preacher smiled as David turned and ran down the hill, but preachers are only human—he felt a pang of pain as he went back to his work in the field while David went to find Phœbe.

David forgot for the time that he was crippled as he ran limping over the road. Dressed in his working clothes, his head bare to the October sunlight, he hurried to the gray farmhouse.

"Phœbe here?" he asked Aunt Maria.

"What's wrong? Anything the matter at your house?" she asked.

"No. Nothing's wrong. Where's Phœbe?"

"Ach, over at the quarry again for weeds or something like she brings home all the time."

"All right." He turned to the gate. "I'll find her."

He half ran up the sheltered road to the old stone quarry.

"Phœbe," he cried when he caught sight of her as she stooped to gather goldenrod that fringed the woods.

"Why, David, what's the matter?" she asked as she stood erect and faced him.

"You angel!" he cried, taking her hands in his and spilling the goldenrod over the ground. "You angel!" he said again, and the full gratitude of his heart shone from his eyes. "You bought Mother Bab's sight! You gave up the music lessons that she might see!"

"How d'you know?" she challenged.

"Oh, I know!" He told her briefly. "That's all true, isn't it?"

"Yes," she admitted. "I can't lie out of it now, I guess. Though I've lied like a trooper about it already. But you needn't get excited about it. Mother Bab's earned more than that from me!"

"Oh, Phœbe!" The man could hardly refrain from taking her in his arms. "You're an angel! To sacrifice all that for us—it's the most unselfish thing I've ever heard of! You gave her sight so she could see me. I came right down to bless you and to thank you."

Other words sought utterance but he fought them back. Phœbe must have read his heart, for she looked up suddenly and asked, "And you came all the way down here just to say thank you! There's nothing else——"

Then, half-ashamed and startled at her forwardness, her gaze dropped.

But the words had worked their magic. "There is something else!" David cried, exulting. "I can't wait any longer to tell you! I love you!"

He held out his arms and as she smiled into his face his arms enfolded her and he knew that she loved him. But he wanted to hear the sweet words from her lips. "Is it so?" he asked. "You do care for me, you'll marry me?"

"Oh, Davie, did you think I could live the rest of my life without you? Did you think I could love you any less because you're crippled?"

He flushed. "It seemed like working on your sympathy to ask you."

"And if you hadn't asked me, Davie," she began.

"Yes, go on. If I hadn't asked you——"

"I should have asked you!"

They both laughed at that, but a moment later were serious as he said, "Just the same, Phœbe, it seems presumptuous for a maimed man to ask a girl like you to marry him. You are beautiful

182

and you have a wonderful voice—and you've done such wonderful things for Mother Bab and me. You have sacrificed so much——"

"Stop, David!" she cried, her voice ominously tearful. "David, don't hurt me like that! Do you love me?"

"I do." His words had all the solemnity of a marriage vow.

"You know I love you?"

"I do."

"Then, David, can't you see that we love each other not only in prosperity but in misfortunes as well?"

"What a big heart you have, dear, what a woman's heart! I have two wonderful women in my life, Mother Bab and you."

Phœbe felt the delicacy and magnitude of the tribute. "I'm happy, Davie," she said softly. "I feel so safe with you—no doubts, no fears."

"Just love," he added.

"Just love," she repeated.

"Then, Phœbe"—how she loved the name from his lips—"you'll marry me?" He said it as though he could not quite believe his good fortune. "Then you will marry me?"

"Yes, if you want."

"If I want! Oh, Phœbe, Phœbe, I have always wanted it!"